1

ISBN-13: 978-1-948909-068

THIRTY-THREE & 1/3 PUBLISHING

Printed in the USA

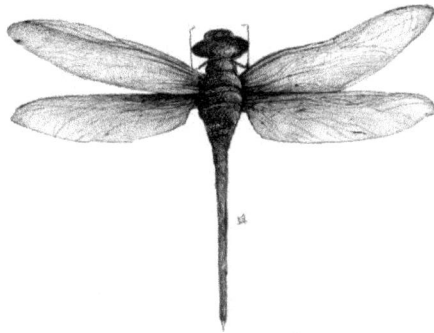

for Mosé Luciano & Giovanna Strazzera

We are the children, the grandchildren and the great-grandchildren of Southern Italian emigrants. Our families literally risked everything in coming to America. Amazingly, they survived; not only did they survive, but they prospered.

"I have been impressed with the urgency of doing. Knowing is not enough; we must apply. Being willing is not enough; we must do."

Leonardo da Vinci
1452-1519

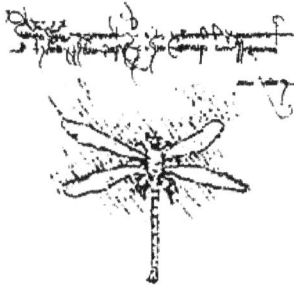

Italian Dual Citizenship: by the Right of Blood

Comprehensive step-by-step instructions to guide you

through the entire process of obtaining Italian Dual Citizenship.

Alessandra Luciano

INDEX.

1. Preface   15

2. Introduction   19

3. European Union Visa Rule   23

4. Criteria   27

5. Benefits   31

6. Process   35

7. Qualifications   41

8. Italian Citizenship Categories   45

    a) Mother   49
    b) Mother-Grandfather   53
    c) Mother-Grandfather-Great Grandfather   59
    d) Mother- Grandmother   61
    e) Mother-Grandmother-Great Grandfather   65
    f) Father   69
    g) Father Grandfather   73
    h) Father-Grandfather-Great Grandfather   77
    i) Father-Grandmother   81
    j) Father-Grandmother-Great Grandfather   85

9. Italian Genealogy Research   89

10. Naturalization Documents   105

11. Italian Certificates   121

12. Scheduling Appointments   131

13. US Certificates   133

14. New York City Documents   137

15. Document Errors and Entitlement Issues   145

16. Apostilles   151

17. Italian Translations   159

18. Applcation Review   163

19. Completing your Application   167

20. Appointment Day   171

21. What Happens Next   177

22. Your Italian Birth Certificate   183

23. A.I.R.E. Registration   187

24. Certificate of Italian Citizenship   191

25. Your Italian Passport   195

26. Your Italian Marriage Certificate   201

27. Italian Citizenship by Marriage or Civil Union (Same-Sex Marriage) & Law. 132 Italian Language Requirement for Spouses   205

28. Italian Clubs   213

29.	Learning Italian	217
30.	Life in Italy	223
31.	Italian Consulates	233
32.	Family Tree	255
33.	Italian Citizenship Law	269
34.	The European Union	313
35.	Regions, Provinces & Town References	333
36.	Sample Forms	337
	Sample Form Index	339
	NARA Request	340
	County Clerk Request	341
	G1041 Index Search Request USCIS	342
	G1041 Instructions	343
	G1041A Records Request USCIS	344
	G1041A Instructions	345
	BC 600 Census Request	346
	1910 Census	351
	1920 Census	352
	1930 Census	353
	Sample Affidavit	354
	Application Form 1	355
	Application Form 2	356
	Application Form 3	357
	Application Form 4	358
	Spouse Application	359
	A.I.R.E Registration Form	361
	N-565 Naturalization Replacement Form	362
	G-639 FOIA Request	366
	Certificate of Clerk or No Appeal	371

Italian Vital Records Request   372

Comune Declaration   373

Correction to Vital Records Example   374

Affidavit to Request Marriage Records   375

Affidavit to Request Death Records   376

Apostille Cover Letter   377

USCIS Cover Letter – Non Existence   378

Sample Naturalization Documents   379

Arrival Record   386

Military Draft Card   387

Certificate of Non Existence   388

Sample Apostille   389

*(**NOTE: Most sample forms are available for download online. Be sure to check the Italian Consulate web site and Google the form title and number for most current version available. ***)*

CHAPTER 1
PREFACE.

CHAPTER 1 | PREFACE.

Inheritance of Italian citizenship is available through a concept called Jure Sanguinis or citizenship by descent.

This concept relates to a person's birthright or blood heritage to claim citizenship to Italy, based on the fact that they are descendants of an Italian citizen.

Some Italian American's only have to prove that they are related to one person in their lineage that is or was a citizen of Italy.

This guide is designed to help you discover and understand the process of obtaining Italian dual citizenship by descent and what is required to prepare a successful application step-by-step.

Through the right of blood it may be possible for you to be recognized as an Italian citizen and enjoy all of the benefits that Italy and the entire European Union has to offer while maintaining and cherishing the liberties of being an American.

The layout is intended to address specific topics and in doing so will offer you a greater understanding of the process and allow you, if qualified, to be successful in obtaining Italian dual citizenship by descent for you and your family members.

The focus of this publication is to walk you step-by-step through the process and address issues that you should look out for, ways to avoid stumbling blocks, and helpful hints to make your visit to the Italian Consulate a success.

Since each person will begin this process at a different place and understanding of the process please select the section of the index that applies to your situation and understanding of the process.

CHAPTER 2
INTRODUCTION.

CHAPTER 2 | INTRODUCTION.

To determine whether you qualify for jure sanguinis ("right of blood") Italian citizenship recognition, you will need to prove that an unbroken chain exists, starting from your Italian citizen-ancestor and passing parent to child, as many generations as required and without skipping generations, to you. Italian citizenship law is the basis for judging whether a chain is unbroken or not.

Italian citizenship law changed over time. This guide briefly explains, in chapter 31, the major Italian citizenship laws that could affect your jure sanguinis application. This guide is not an exhaustive exploration of Italian citizenship law, but it should provide useful information for ruling in (or ruling out) jure sanguinis eligibility in most cases.

Please note that the opinions and interpretations listed here are those most commonly employed by the Ministry of Foreign Affairs and its consular network.

To use this guide you can start from your Italian ancestor and review the laws from 1861 to 1992 to determine whether your chain is unbroken. Or, you can start with your own situation and work backwards from 1992.

To use this guide effectively you should know the exact dates of important "life events" for you and for all the ancestors in your possible chain(s). These dates include birth (and/or legal adoption), marriage, naturalization, and death. In other words, you may need to do some research to obtain official records verifying these important dates before you can make a clear determination whether you qualify.

This reference book is a guide and intended to provide you will the tools you need to become informed and hopefully eliminate some potential pit falls along the way.

CHAPTER 3
EU VISA RULE.

CHAPTER 3 | VISA RULE 2021

EUROPEAN UNION VISA REQUIREMENTS.

By 2021, the European Union will implement an electronic visa waiver program. The program will be called ETIAS, which stands for the European Travel Information and Authorisation System, and has been readily accepted by nearly every EU country.

Under the ETIAS program, when someone is a dual national of an EU country, as well as a non-EU country, the passenger should know that they do not need to apply for an ETIAS, as they can enter the Schengen Zone using the passport of the EU member country.

Completing the process of obtaining Italian citizenship will allow you, as a recognized Italian citizen to get your Italian passport, and ultimately become an EU member as well.

YOU HAVE OPTIONS.

- You can effectively use this book to guide you through the process on your own.
- You can hire a guide to counsel you in the process.
- You can hire an expert to complete your application package for you.
- Or even take an online class to learn about each step in the process.

FOR MORE INFORMATION.

http://www.myitaliandualcitizenship.com

CHAPTER 4
CRITERIA.

CHAPTER 4 | CRITERIA.

Italian Citizenship by Descent - Italian Citizenship Jure Sanguinis.

Italian citizenship is granted by birth through the paternal line (with no limit on the number of generations) or through the maternal line (for individuals born after January 1, 1948).

If you were born in the United States or any other country where citizenship is acquired by birth, and any one of the situations listed below pertains to you, you may be considered an Italian citizen. Criteria for Italian Citizenship by descent (for each category all conditions must be met.):

1) Your father was an Italian citizen at the time of your birth and you never renounced your right to Italian citizenship.

2) Your mother was an Italian citizen at the time of your birth, you were born after January 1st, 1948 and you never renounced your right to Italian citizenship.

3) Your father was born in the United States, your paternal grandfather was an Italian citizen at the time of your father's birth, neither you nor your father ever renounced your right to Italian citizenship.

4) Your mother was born in the United States, your maternal grandfather was an Italian citizen at the time of her birth, you were born after January 1, 1948 and neither you nor your mother ever renounced your right to Italian citizenship.

5) Your paternal or maternal grandfather was born in the United States, your paternal great grandfather was an Italian citizen at the time of his birth, neither you nor your father nor your grandfather ever renounced your right to Italian citizenship (please note: a grandmother born before 01/01/1948 can claim the Italian citizenship only from her father and can transfer it to descendants after 01/01/1948).

6) Your ancestor did not naturalize before July 1st of 1912. Ancestors naturalized before July 1st, 1912 cannot transmit citizenship (Law n. 555 of June 13, 1912).

***A woman born before 01/01/1948 can claim the Italian citizenship only from her father and can transfer it to descendants after 01/01/1948).

***"Italian citizen at the time of birth" means that he/she did not acquire any other citizenship through naturalization, before the descendant's birth.

If by an uninterrupted line of descent, you have been conveyed Italian citizenship from your ancestor jure sanguinis.

In order to have it recognized, you must collect the appropriate documents to prove your lineage back to Italy. This means the birth, marriage and death records of each person in your line of inheritence. Certain documents need an authentication (Apostille) and translation into Italian.

The specific documents will be listed in Chapter Six (6) under qualifications and Italian citizenship categories.

CHAPTER 5
BENEFITS.

CHAPTER 5 | BENEFITS.

Become Globally Integrated

As our society continues to become more globally integrated the value of Dual Citizenship and a second passport has become immeasurable. With Italian Dual Citizenship you can continue to enjoy the benefits of being an American citizen, while gaining all of the benefits and liberties the European Union has to offer it's citizens!

Italian Citizenship will enable you to live, work, retire, go to school, and travel freely in 28 European Union (EU) countries! For Italian-Americans, the acquisition of Italian Dual Citizenship is truly a gift, of unlimited potential for you, your children and grandchildren!

Just a hand full of the benefits associated with obtaining your Italian Dual Citizenship are reflected below:

⇒ Live, work, retire, go to school, and travel freely in 28 European Union (EU) countries.
⇒ Travel through the EU Schengen Zone without a Visa when you have an Italian passport.
⇒ Reconnect with your cultural background and strengthen the fabric of your heritage.
⇒ Travel safer abroad.
⇒ Pass on the lifelong gift of Italian Dual Citizenship to other members of your family.
⇒ Access financial investment rights available only to EU citizens.
⇒ Access medical benefits, including potentially free healthcare.
⇒ Access educational benefits, including potentially free higher education.
⇒ Leverage tax shelters and benefits.
⇒ Seek health care treatments that may not be available in the United States.

CHAPTER 6
THE PROCESS.

CHAPTER 6 | THE PROCESS.

In this chapter you will be given the step-by-step punch list of what you must accomplish. This will be followed by subsequent chapters detailing the individual steps. You can walk through the entire process yourself or hire a service to do it for you.

If you would like a service or need counseling along the way consider:

> http://www.myitaliandualcitizenship.com

Assembling your package for Italian citizenship takes an immense dedication to detail and time. So you can be assured that the individuals you meet along the way are dedicated beyond financial gain. They are qualified professionals who are available to guide you step-by-step through the entire process. But you can, with time and dedication, complete the steps on your own.

Your Punch List for Success is included within this chapter so that you can photo copy it and use it as a reference. This will be a helpful tool if you proceed on your own or hire an agency to assist you.

Phases for Document Acquisition

You should approach the acquisition of your documents in three phases as outlined below to make sure you are able to proceed without incurring a great deal of expense on something that may or may not materialize along the way due to an inability to acquire specific documents. A reputable service will approach the acquisition in this manner if they are looking out for your best interest.

⇒ **Phase 1:** Obtain your ancestor's Italian Vital Records and his or her Naturalization documents (or statements of no record).

⇒ **Phase 2:** Obtain all US or non-Italian Vital Records.

⇒ **Phase 3:** Obtain all authentications (Apostilles) and translate your non-Italian documents into Italian (not all documents require translation. See your category for a specific list of documents that must be translated in Chapter 6 (of this reference).

Recommended Service Organizations

Throughout this book recommendations will be made that you do a step yourself or you can hire a service to assist you with step by step services, online classes, counseling and even complete package services.

My Italian Dual Citizenship: http://www.myitaliandualcitizenship.com

Punch List for Success

| 1| Determine if you are qualified | Move Ahead |

| 2 | Italian genealogy research if applicable |Move Ahead |

| 3 | Naturalization Certificate | Certificates of No Record | Move Ahead |

| 4 | Italian Certificates | Italian Birth Certificate I Italian Marriage Certificate I Italian Death Certificate| Move Ahead|

| 5 | US Certificates | Move Ahead |

| 6 | Apostilles | Move Ahead |

| 7 | Italian Translations | Move Ahead |

| 8 | Review| Application | Appointment | Italian Consulate | Italian Dual Citizenship | Move Ahead |

| 9 | A.I.R.E Registration | Certificate of Citizenship | Italian Birth Certificate | Italian Passport | Move Ahead |

| 10 | Spouse Application | Certificate of Citizenship | Italian Birth Certificate| Italian Marriage Certificate | Italian Dual Citizenship |

CHAPTER 7
QUALIFICATIONS.

CHAPTER 7 | QUALIFICATIONS.

Italian citizenship is granted by birth through the paternal line, <u>with no limit on the number of generations</u>, or through the maternal line for individuals born after January 1, 1948. If you were born in the United States or any other country where citizenship is acquired by birth, and any one of the situations listed below pertains to you, you may be considered an Italian citizen.

Criteria for Italian Citizenship by descent (for each category all conditions must be met):

1) Your father was an Italian citizen at the time of your birth and you never renounced your right to Italian citizenship.

2) Your mother was an Italian citizen at the time of your birth, you were born after January 1st, 1948 and you never renounced your right to Italian citizenship.

3) Your father was born in the United States, your paternal grandfather was an Italian citizen at the time of your father's birth, neither you nor your father ever renounced your right to Italian citizenship.

4) Your mother was born in the United States, your maternal grandfather was an Italian citizen at the time of her birth, you were born after January 1, 1948 and neither you nor your mother ever renounced your right to Italian citizenship.

5) Your paternal or maternal grandfather was born in the United States, your paternal great grandfather was an Italian citizen at the time of his birth, neither you nor your father nor your grandfather ever renounced your right to Italian citizenship (please note: a grandmother born before 01/01/1948 can claim the Italian citizenship only from her father and can transfer it to descendants after 01/01/1948).

6) Your ancestor did not naturalize before July 1st of 1912. Ancestors naturalized before July 1st, 1912 cannot transmit citizenship (Law n. 555 of June 13, 1912).

***A woman born before 01/01/1948 can claim the Italian citizenship only from her father and can transfer it to her descendants after 01/01/1948).

So Are You Qualified?

If you are still wondering if you are qualified at this point a good place to start is your ancestor's documents.   Here are places your ancestor's citizenship is revealed through documents.

1. Your ancestor's naturalization documents tell a specific date that he or she became a US citizen. That date, the date they took the oath, must have been after the date of birth of the first generation in the US.
2. His or her marriage certificate will often tell citizenship status. While not proof for the consulate, this will give you an idea if you are on the right track.
3. Alien Ship Manifests. When your ancestor arrived in the US did he or she arrive as an Alien? The citizenship status is listed on a ship manifest.
4. US Census reports will tell a person's citizenship status.
5. US Military draft cards also reveal a person's citizenship status.
6. Alien Registration cards file by your ancestor indicates they were not US citizens.
7. Passport applications are also searchable online.
8. Birth Certificates, Marriage and Death records can reveal information necessary to assist you in determining the status of your ancestor's citizenship.

Remember, the key is they must have been an Italian citizen, at the time of birth of the next generation.

CHAPTER 8
ITALIAN DUAL
CITIZENSHIP
CATEGORIES.

CHAPTER 8 | CATEGORIES FOR ITALIAN DUAL CITIZENSHIP BY DESCENT.

To see if you are qualified and for complete information on your Italian citizenship category - select your path of inheritance from the index below:

⇒ Mother
⇒ Mother-Grandfather
⇒ Mother-Grandfather-Great Grandfather
⇒ Mother-Grandfather-Great Grandfather-Great Great Grandfather
⇒ Mother- Grandmother
⇒ Mother-Grandmother-Great –Grandfather
⇒ Mother-Grandmother-Great Grandfather-Great Great Grandfather
⇒ Father
⇒ Father-Grandfather
⇒ Father-Grandfather-Great Grandfather
⇒ Father-Grandfather-Great Grandfather–Great Great Grandfather
⇒ Father-Grandmother
⇒ Father-Grandmother-Great Grandfather
⇒ Father-Grandmother-Great Grandfather-Great Great Grandfather

Example:

If you are inheriting the citizenship from your mother (born in US) , through your grandfather (born in US) to your great grandfather (born in Italy) your Italian citizenship category would be:

MOTHER-GRANDFATHER–GREAT GRANDFATHER.

(**NOTE: Be sure to check the web site of the Italian Consulate of your jurisdiction to confirm the following documents are required. SOME consulate's require LESS documents than outlined in this chapter).

MOTHER.

Your mother was an Italian citizen at the time of your birth, you were born after January 1st, 1948 and you never renounced your right to Italian citizenship. If citizenship is acquired by birth in your country and you meet all these conditions, you qualify for Italian citizenship jure sanguinis.

The following documents will be required to your Italian citizenship application package:

- o   Your mother's birth certificate from Italy
- o   Your father's birth certificate
- o   Your parents' marriage certificate (If married outside of Italy, you will need an apostille and a translation into Italian.)
- o   Your parents' divorce decree/certificate, if applicable (with apostille and translation
- o   Your mother's certificate of naturalization OR statement of "No Record" OR Alien Registration Card – Green Card
- o   Your birth certificate (with apostille and translatio)
- o   Your mother's death certificate, if applicable (with apostille and translation)
- o   Your father's death certificate, if applicable
- o   Your marriage certificate, if applicable (with apostille and translation)
- o   Your divorce decree/certificate, if applicable (with apostille and translation)
- o   Your spouse's birth certificate, if applicable
- o   Birth certificates for all your children under the age of eighteen, if applicable (with apostille and translation)

Special Rules that may impact your eligibility:

A woman born before 01/01/1948 can claim the Italian citizenship only from her father and can transfer it to her descendants after 01/01/1948).

Italian citizen at the time of "birth" means that he/she did not acquire any other citizenship through naturalization, before the descendant's birth.

Ancestors naturalized before July 1st, 1912 cannot transmit citizenship (Law n. 555 of June 13, 1912).

If your grandmother became a naturalized citizen before your mother's birth, you are not entitled to Italian citizenship jure sanguinis unless you fit into another category.

You will want to make sure that:

- All of your Certificates will be new "Certified Copies" a.k.a. "Long Form" or "Full Form" (not "certification" or "abstract").
- Your Non-Italian Birth / Marriage / Death records related to the "Italian side" will bear an apostille (according to Hague Convention of Dec. 5, 1961) except for the Certificate of Naturalization and/or similar documentation.
- All of your Certificates in other languages than Italian, will be translated into Italian. The only document which will not be translated and does not need an "Apostille" is the U.S. Certificate of Naturalization or any statement releasing information on the naturalization status of the interested party.

Foreign Documents and Discrepancies:

Your documents issued in Countries other than the U.S.A. or Italy must comply with the local regulations on the legalization of documents, they must be translated into Italian and the translation certified by the Italian Consulate/Embassy in the Country where the document was issued. To find out how a document should be legalized in its Country of origin you must obtain the information from the website of the competent Italian Consulate/Embassy. A list of all Italian Consulate/Embassies abroad is available at www.esteri.it ("Farnesina" – "Rappresentanze Diplomatiche" – "Ambasciate e Consolati" –

Country)

Check all documents word for word to make sure that there are no discrepancies or changes in the names, last names, dates and places of birth. If there are major discrepancies in last names, dates, ages, and places of birth these variations or errors must be corrected with an official "affidavit to amend a record" to be requested from the Vital Statistics Office that issued the document or with another appropriate official document.

MOTHER-GRANDFATHER.

Your maternal grandfather was born in your native country, your maternal great grandfather was an Italian citizen at the time of his birth, you were born after January 1st, 1948, and neither you nor your mother nor your grandfather ever renounced your right to Italian citizenship. If citizenship is acquired by birth in your country and you meet all these conditions, you qualify for Italian citizenship jure sanguinis.

The following documents will be required to your Italian citizenship application package:

- o Your maternal great grandfather's birth certificate from Italy
- o Your maternal great grandmother's birth certificate
- o Your great grandparents' marriage certificate (If married outside of Italy, you will need an apostille and a translation into Italian.)
- o Your maternal great grandfather's certificate of naturalization OR statements of "No Record"
- o Your maternal grandfather's birth certificate (with apostille and translation)
- o Your maternal grandmother's birth certificate
- o Your grandparents' marriage certificate (with apostille and translation)
- o Your mother's birth certificate (with apostille and translation)
- o Your father's birth certificate
- o Your parents' marriage certificate (with apostille and translation)
- o Your birth certificate (with apostille and translation)
- o Your marriage certificate, if applicable (with apostille and translation)
- o Your spouse's birth certificate, if applicable
- o Birth certificates for all your children under the age of eighteen, if applicable (with apostille and translation)
- o Any applicable divorce decrees/certificates (with apostille and translation)
- o Death certificates for anyone listed above (with apostille and translation, if for your mother, grandfather or great grandfather)

Special Rules that may impact your eligibility:

A woman born before 01/01/1948 can claim the Italian citizenship only from her father and can transfer it to descendants after 01/01/1948).

Italian citizen at the time of birth" means that he/she did not acquire any other citizenship through naturalization, before the descendant's birth.

Ancestors naturalized before July 1st, 1912 cannot transmit citizenship (Law n. 555 of June 13, 1912).

If your grandmother became a naturalized citizen before your mother's birth, you are not entitled to Italian citizenship jure sanguinis unless you fit into another category.

You will want to make sure that:

o All of your Certificates will be new "Certified Copies" a.k.a. "Long Form" or "Full Form" (not "certification" or "abstract").
o Your Non-Italian Birth / Marriage / Death records related to the "Italian side" will bear an apostille (according to Hague Convention of Dec. 5, 1961) except for the Certificate of Naturalization and/or similar documentation.
o All of your Certificates in other languages than Italian, will be translated into Italian. The only document which will not be translated and does not need an "Apostille" is the U.S. Certificate of Naturalization or any statement releasing information on the naturalization status of the interested party.

Foreign Documents and Discrepancies:

Your documents issued in Countries other than the U.S.A. or Italy must comply with the local regulations on the legalization of documents, they must be translated into Italian and the translation certified by the Italian Consulate/Embassy in the Country where the document was issued. To find out how a document should be legalized in its Country of origin you must obtain the

information from the website of the competent Italian Consulate/Embassy. A list of all Italian Consulate/Embassies abroad is available at www.esteri.it ("Farnesina" – "Rappresentanze Diplomatiche" – "Ambasciate e Consolati" – Country).

Check all documents word for word to make sure that there are no discrepancies or changes in the names, last names, dates and places of birth. If there are major discrepancies in last names, dates, ages, and places of birth these variations or errors must be corrected with an official "affidavit to amend a record" to be requested from the Vital Statistics Office that issued the document or with another appropriate official document.

MOTHER-GRANDFATHER-GREAT GRANDFATHER.

Your maternal grandfather was born in your native country, your maternal great grandfather was an Italian citizen at the time of his birth, you were born after January 1st, 1948, and neither you nor your mother nor your grandfather ever renounced your right to Italian citizenship. If citizenship is acquired by birth in your country and you meet all these conditions, you qualify for Italian citizenship jure sanguinis.

The following documents will be required to your Italian citizenship application package:

- Your maternal great grandfather's birth certificate from Italy
- Your maternal great grandmother's birth certificate
- Your great grandparents' marriage certificate (If married outside of Italy, you will need an apostille and a translation into Italian.)
- Your maternal great grandfather's certificate of naturalization OR statements of "No Record"
- Your maternal grandfather's birth certificate (with apostille and translation)
- Your maternal grandmother's birth certificate
- Your grandparents' marriage certificate (with apostille and translation)
- Your mother's birth certificate (with apostille and translation)
- Your father's birth certificate
- Your parents' marriage certificate (with apostille and translation)
- Your birth certificate (with apostille and translation)
- Your marriage certificate, if applicable (with apostille and translation)
- Your spouse's birth certificate, if applicable
- Birth certificates for all your children under the age of eighteen, if applicable (with apostille and translation)
- Any applicable divorce decrees/certificates (with apostille and translation)
- Death certificates for anyone listed above (with apostille and translation,

if for your mother, grandfather or great grandfather)

Special Rules that may impact your eligibility:

A woman born before 01/01/1948 can claim the Italian citizenship only from her father and can transfer it to descendants after 01/01/1948).

Italian citizen at the time of birth" means that he/she did not acquire any other citizenship through naturalization, before the descendant's birth.

Ancestors naturalized before July 1st, 1912 cannot transmit citizenship (Law n. 555 of June 13, 1912)

If your grandmother became a naturalized citizen before your mother's birth, you are not entitled to Italian citizenship jure sanguinis unless you fit into another category.

You will want to make sure that:

- o All of your Certificates will be new "Certified Copies" a.k.a. "Long Form" or "Full Form" (not "certification" or "abstract").
- o Your Non-Italian Birth / Marriage / Death records related to the "Italian side" will bear an apostille (according to Hague Convention of Dec. 5, 1961) except for the Certificate of Naturalization and/or similar documentation.
- o All of your Certificates in other languages than Italian, will be translated be into Italian. The only document which will not be translated and does not need an "Apostille" is the U.S. Certificate of Naturalization or any the statement releasing information on the naturalization status of the interested party.

Foreign Documents and Discrepancies:

Your documents issued in Countries other than the U.S.A. or Italy must comply with the local regulations on the legalization of documents, they must be translated into Italian and the translation certified by the Italian

Consulate/Embassy in the Country where the document was issued. To find out how a document should be legalized in its Country of origin you must obtain the information from the website of the competent Italian Consulate/Embassy. A list of all Italian Consulate/Embassies abroad is available at www.esteri.it ("Farnesina" – "Rappresentanze Diplomatiche" – "Ambasciate e Consolati" – Country).

Check all documents word for word to make sure that there are no discrepancies or changes in the names, last names, dates and places of birth. If there are major discrepancies in last names, dates, ages, and places of birth these variations or errors must be corrected with an official "affidavit to amend a record" to be requested from the Vital Statistics Office that issued the document or with another appropriate official document.

60

MOTHER-GRANDMOTHER.

Your mother was born in your native country after January 1st, 1948, your maternal grandmother was an Italian citizen at the time of her birth, and neither you nor your mother ever renounced your right to Italian citizenship. If citizenship is acquired by birth in your country and you meet all these conditions, you qualify for Italian citizenship jure sanguinis.

The following documents will be required to your Italian citizenship application package:

- o Your maternal grandmother's birth certificate from Italy
- o Your maternal grandfather's birth certificate
- o Your grandparents' marriage certificate (If married outside of Italy, you will need an apostille and a translation into Italian.)
- o Your maternal grandmother's certificate of naturalization OR statements of "No Record"
- o Your mother's birth certificate (with apostille and translation)
- o Your father's birth certificate
- o Your parents' marriage certificate (with apostille and translation)
- o Your birth certificate (with apostille and translation)
- o Your marriage certificate, if applicable (with apostille and translation)
- o Your spouse's birth certificate, if applicable
- o Birth certificates for all your children under the age of eighteen, if applicable (with apostille and translation)
- o Any applicable divorce decrees/certificates (with apostille and translation)
- o Death certificates for anyone listed above (with apostille and translation, if for your mother or grandmother)

Special Rules that may impact your eligibility:

A woman born before 01/01/1948 can claim the Italian citizenship only from her father and can transfer it to descendants after 01/01/1948).

Italian citizen at the time of birth" means that he/she did not acquire any other citizenship through naturalization, before the descendant's birth.

Ancestors naturalized before July 1st, 1912 cannot transmit citizenship (Law n. 555 of June 13, 1912).

If your grandmother became a naturalized citizen before your mother's birth, you are not entitled to Italian citizenship jure sanguinis unless you fit into another category.

You will want to make sure that:

- o All of your Certificates will be new "Certified Copies" a.k.a. "Long Form" or "Full Form" (not "certification" or "abstract").
- o Your Non-Italian Birth / Marriage / Death records related to the "Italian side" will bear an apostille (according to Hague Convention of Dec. 5, 1961) except for the Certificate of Naturalization and/or similar documentation.
- o All of your Certificates in other languages than Italian, will be translated into Italian. The only document which will not be translated and does not need an "Apostille" is the U.S. Certificate of Naturalization or any statement releasing information on the naturalization status of the interested party.

Foreign Documents and Discrepancies:

Your documents issued in Countries other than the U.S.A. or Italy must comply with the local regulations on the legalization of documents, they must be translated into Italian and the translation certified by the Italian Consulate/Embassy in the Country where the document was issued. To find out how a document should be legalized in its Country of origin you must obtain the information from the website of the competent Italian Consulate/Embassy. A list of all Italian Consulate/Embassies abroad is available at www.esteri.it ("Farnesina" – "Rappresentanze Diplomatiche" – "Ambasciate e Consolati" – Country).

Check all documents word for word to make sure that there are no discrepancies or changes in the names, last names, dates and places of birth. If there are major discrepancies in last names, dates, ages, and places of birth these variations or errors must be corrected with an official "affidavit to amend a record" to be requested from the Vital Statistics Office that issued the document or with another appropriate official document.

MOTHER-GRANDMOTHER-GREAT GRANDFATHER.

Your maternal grandfather was born in your native country, your maternal great grandfather was an Italian citizen at the time of his birth, you were born after January 1st, 1948, and neither you nor your mother nor your grandfather ever renounced your right to Italian citizenship. If citizenship is acquired by birth in your country and you meet all these conditions, you qualify for Italian citizenship jure sanguinis.

The following documents will be required to your Italian citizenship application package:

- o   Your maternal great grandfather's birth certificate from Italy
- o   Your maternal great grandmother's birth certificate
- o   Your great grandparents' marriage certificate (If married outside of Italy, you will need an apostille and a translation into Italian.)
- o   Your maternal great grandfather's certificate of naturalization OR statements of "No Record"
- o   Your maternal grandfather's birth certificate (with apostille and translation)
- o   Your maternal grandmother's birth certificate
- o   Your grandparents' marriage certificate (with apostille and translation)
- o   Your mother's birth certificate (with apostille and translation)
- o   Your father's birth certificate
- o   Your parents' marriage certificate (with apostille and translation)
- o   Your birth certificate (with apostille and translation)
- o   Your marriage certificate, if applicable (with apostille and translation)
- o   Your spouse's birth certificate, if applicable
- o   Birth certificates for all your children under the age of eighteen, if applicable (with apostille and translation)
- o   Any applicable divorce decrees/certificates (with apostille and translation)
- o   Death certificates for anyone listed above (with apostille and translation,

if for your mother, grandfather or great grandfather)

Special Rules that may impact your eligibility:

A woman born before 01/01/1948 can claim the Italian citizenship only from her father and can transfer it to descendants after 01/01/1948.

Italian citizen at the time of birth" means that he/she did not acquire any other citizenship through naturalization, before the descendant's birth.

Ancestors naturalized before July 1st, 1912 cannot transmit citizenship (Law n. 555 of June 13, 1912).

If your grandmother became a naturalized citizen before your mother's birth, you are not entitled to Italian citizenship jure sanguinis unless you fit into another category.

You will want to make sure that:

- o All of your Certificates will be new "Certified Copies" a.k.a. "Long Form" or "Full Form" (not "certification" or "abstract").
- o Your Non-Italian Birth / Marriage / Death records related to the "Italian side" will bear an apostille (according to Hague Convention of Dec. 5, 1961) except for the Certificate of Naturalization and/or similar documentation.
- o All of your Certificates in other languages than Italian, will be translated into Italian. The only document which will not be translated and does not need an "Apostille" is the U.S. Certificate of Naturalization or any statement releasing information on the naturalization status of the interested party.

Foreign Documents and Discrepancies:

Your documents issued in Countries other than the U.S.A. or Italy must comply with the local regulations on the legalization of documents, they must be translated into Italian and the translation certified by the Italian

Consulate/Embassy in the Country where the document was issued. To find out how a document should be legalized in its Country of origin you must obtain the information from the website of the competent Italian Consulate/Embassy. A list of all Italian Consulate/Embassies abroad is available at www.esteri.it ("Farnesina" – "Rappresentanze Diplomatiche" – "Ambasciate e Consolati" – Country).SEP

Check all documents word for word to make sure that there are no discrepancies or changes in the names, last names, dates and places of birth. If there are major discrepancies in last names, dates, ages, and places of birth these variations or errors must be corrected with an official "affidavit to amend a record" to be requested from the Vital Statistics Office that issued the document or with another appropriate official document.

FATHER.

Your father was an Italian citizen at the time of your birth and you never renounced your right to Italian citizenship. If citizenship is acquired by birth in your country and you meet all these conditions, you qualify for Italian citizenship jure sanguinis.

The following documents will be required to your Italian citizenship application package:

- Your father's birth certificate from Italy
- Your mother's birth certificate
- Your parents' marriage certificate (If they were married in your native country, you will need an apostille and a translation into Italian.)
- Your parents' divorce decree/certificate, if applicable (with apostille and translation)
- Your father's certificate of naturalization OR statement of "No Record" OR Alien Registration Card – Green Card
- Your birth certificate (with apostille and translation)
- Your father's death certificate, if applicable (with apostille and translation)
- Your mother's death certificate, if applicable
- Your marriage certificate, if applicable (with apostille and translation)
- Your divorce decree/certificate, if applicable (with apostille and translation)
- Your spouse's birth certificate, if applicable
- Birth certificates for all your children under the age of eighteen, if applicable (with apostille and translation)

Special Rules that may impact your eligibility:

A woman born before 01/01/1948 can claim the Italian citizenship only from her father and can transfer it to descendants after 01/01/1948).

Italian citizen at the time of birth" means that he/she did not acquire any other citizenship through naturalization, before the descendant's birth.

Ancestors naturalized before July 1st, 1912 cannot transmit citizenship (Law n. 555 of June 13, 1912).

If your grandmother became a naturalized citizen before your mother's birth, you are not entitled to Italian citizenship jure sanguinis unless you fit into another category.

You will want to make sure that:

- o All of your Certificates will be new "Certified Copies" a.k.a. "Long Form" or "Full Form" (not "certification" or "abstract").
- o Your Non-Italian Birth / Marriage / Death records related to the "Italian side" will bear an apostille (according to Hague Convention of Dec. 5, 1961) except for the Certificate of Naturalization and/or similar documentation.
- o All of your Certificates in other languages than Italian, will be translated into Italian. The only document which will not be translated and does not need an "Apostille" is the U.S. Certificate of Naturalization or any statement releasing information on the naturalization status of the interested party.

Foreign Documents and Discrepancies:

Your documents issued in Countries other than the U.S.A. or Italy must comply with the local regulations on the legalization of documents, they must be translated into Italian and the translation certified by the Italian Consulate/Embassy in the Country where the document was issued. To find out how a document should be legalized in its Country of origin you must obtain the information from the website of the competent Italian Consulate/Embassy. A list of all Italian Consulate/Embassies abroad is available at www.esteri.it ("Farnesina" – "Rappresentanze Diplomatiche" – "Ambasciate e Consolati" – Country).

Check all documents word for word to make sure that there are no discrepancies or changes in the names, last names, dates and places of birth. If there are major discrepancies in last names, dates, ages, and places of birth these variations or errors must be corrected with an official "affidavit to amend a record" to be requested from the Vital Statistics Office that issued the document or with another appropriate official document.

FATHER-GRANDFATHER.

Your father was born in your native country, your paternal grandfather was an Italian citizen at the time of his birth, and neither you nor your father ever renounced your right to Italian citizenship. If citizenship is acquired by birth in your country and you meet all these conditions, you qualify for Italian citizenship jure sanguinis.

The following documents will be required to your Italian citizenship application package:

- o Your paternal grandfather's birth certificate from Italy
- o Your paternal grandmother's birth certificate
- o Your grandparents' marriage certificate (If married outside of Italy, you will need an apostille and a translation into Italian.)
- o Your paternal grandfather's certificate of naturalization OR statement of "No Records" .
- o Your father's birth certificate (with apostille and translation)
- o Your mother's birth certificate
- o Your parents' marriage certificate (with apostille and translation)
- o Your birth certificate (with apostille and translation)
- o Your marriage certificate, if applicable (with apostille and translation)
- o Your spouse's birth certificate, if applicable
- o Birth certificates for all your children under the age of eighteen, if applicable (with apostille and translation)
- o Any applicable divorce decrees/certificates (with apostille and translation)
- o Death certificates for anyone listed above (with apostille and translation, if for your father or grandfather)

Special Rules that may impact your eligibility:

A woman born before 01/01/1948 can claim the Italian citizenship only from her father and can transfer it to descendants after 01/01/1948).

Italian citizen at the time of birth" means that he/she did not acquire any other citizenship through naturalization, before the descendant's birth.

Ancestors naturalized before July 1st, 1912 cannot transmit citizenship (Law n. 555 of June 13, 1912.

If your grandmother became a naturalized citizen before your mother's birth, you are not entitled to Italian citizenship jure sanguinis unless you fit into another category.

You will want to make sure that:

- o All of your Certificates will be new "Certified Copies" a.k.a. "Long Form" or "Full Form" (not "certification" or "abstract").
- o Your Non-Italian Birth / Marriage / Death records related to the "Italian side" will bear an apostille (according to Hague Convention of Dec. 5, 1961) except for the Certificate of Naturalization and/or similar documentation.
- o All of your Certificates in other languages than Italian, will be translated into Italian. The only document which will not be translated and does not need an "Apostille" is the U.S. Certificate of Naturalization or any statement releasing information on the naturalization status of the interested party.

Foreign Documents and Discrepancies:

Your documents issued in Countries other than the U.S.A. or Italy must comply with the local regulations on the legalization of documents, they must be translated into Italian and the translation certified by the Italian Consulate/Embassy in the Country where the document was issued. To find out how a document should be legalized in its Country of origin you must obtain the information from the website of the competent Italian Consulate/Embassy. A list of all Italian Consulate/Embassies abroad is available at www.esteri.it ("Farnesina" – "Rappresentanze Diplomatiche" – "Ambasciate e Consolati" – Country).

Check all documents word for word to make sure that there are no discrepancies or changes in the names, last names, dates and places of birth. If there are major discrepancies in last names, dates, ages, and places of birth these variations or errors must be corrected with an official "affidavit to amend a record" to be requested from the Vital Statistics Office that issued the document or with another appropriate official document.

FATHER-GRANDFATHER-GREAT GRANDFATHER.

Your paternal grandfather was born in your native country, your paternal great grandfather was an Italian citizen at the time of his birth, and neither you nor your father nor your grandfather ever renounced your right to Italian citizenship. If citizenship is acquired by birth in your country and you meet all these conditions, you qualify for Italian citizenship jure sanguinis.

The following documents will be required to your Italian citizenship application package:

- Your paternal great grandfather's birth certificate from Italy
- Your paternal great grandmother's birth certificate
- Your great grandparents' marriage certificate (If married outside of Italy, you will need an apostille and a translation into Italian.)
- Your paternal great grandfather's certificate of naturalization OR statements of "No Record"
- Your paternal grandfather's birth certificate (with apostille and translation)
- Your paternal grandmother's birth certificate
- Your grandparents' marriage certificate (with apostille and translation)
- Your father's birth certificate (with apostille and translation)
- Your mother's birth certificate
- Your parents' marriage certificate (with apostille and translation)
- Your birth certificate (with apostille and translation)
- Your marriage certificate, if applicable (with apostille and translation)
- Your spouse's birth certificate, if applicable
- Birth certificates for all your children under the age of eighteen, if applicable (with apostille and translation)
- Any applicable divorce decrees/certificates (with apostille and translation)
- Death certificates for anyone listed above (with apostille and translation, if for your father, grandfather or great grandfather)

Special Rules that may impact your eligibility:

A woman born before 01/01/1948 can claim the Italian citizenship only from her father and can transfer it to descendants after 01/01/1948).

Italian citizen at the time of birth" means that he/she did not acquire any other citizenship through naturalization, before the descendant's birth.

Ancestors naturalized before July 1st, 1912 cannot transmit citizenship (Law n. 555 of June 13, 1912).

If your grandmother became a naturalized citizen before your mother's birth, you are not entitled to Italian citizenship jure sanguinis unless you fit into another category.

You will want to make sure that:

- o All of your Certificates will be new "Certified Copies" a.k.a. "Long Form" or "Full Form" (not "certification" or "abstract").
- o Your Non-Italian Birth / Marriage / Death records related to the "Italian side" will bear an apostille (according to Hague Convention of Dec. 5, 1961) except for the Certificate of Naturalization and/or similar documentation.
- o All of your Certificates in other languages than Italian, will be translated into Italian. The only document which will not be translated and does not need an "Apostille" is the U.S. Certificate of Naturalization or any statement releasing information on the naturalization status of the interested party.

Foreign Documents and Discrepancies:

Your documents issued in Countries other than the U.S.A. or Italy must comply with the local regulations on the legalization of documents, they must be translated into Italian and the translation certified by the Italian Consulate/Embassy in the Country where the document was issued. To find out how a document should be legalized in its Country of origin you must obtain the

information from the website of the competent Italian Consulate/Embassy. A list of all Italian Consulate/Embassies abroad is available at www.esteri.it ("Farnesina" – "Rappresentanze Diplomatiche" – "Ambasciate e Consolati" – Country).

Check all documents word for word to make sure that there are no discrepancies or changes in the names, last names, dates and places of birth. If there are major discrepancies in last names, dates, ages, and places of birth these variations or errors must be corrected with an official "affidavit to amend a record" to be requested from the Vital Statistics Office that issued the document or with another appropriate official document.

FATHER-GRANDMOTHER.

Your father was born in your native country after January 1st, 1948, your paternal grandmother was an Italian citizen at the time of his birth, and neither you nor your father ever renounced your right to Italian citizenship. If citizenship is acquired by birth in your country and you meet all these conditions, you qualify for Italian citizenship jure sanguinis.

The following documents will be required to your Italian citizenship application package:

- o Your paternal grandmother's birth certificate from Italy
- o Your paternal grandfather's birth certificate
- o Your grandparents' marriage certificate (If married outside of Italy, you will need an apostille and a translation into Italian.)
- o Your paternal grandmother's certificate of naturalization OR statements of "No Record"
- o Your father's birth certificate (with apostille and translation)
- o Your mother's birth certificate
- o Your parents' marriage certificate (with apostille and translation)
- o Your birth certificate (with apostille and translation)
- o Your marriage certificate, if applicable (with apostille and translation)
- o Your spouse's birth certificate, if applicable
- o Birth certificates for all your children under the age of eighteen, if applicable (with apostille and translation)
- o Any applicable divorce decrees/certificates (with apostille and translation)
- o Death certificates for anyone listed above (with apostille and translation, if for your father or grandmother)

Special Rules that may impact your eligibility:

A woman born before 01/01/1948 can claim the Italian citizenship only from her father and can transfer it to descendants after 01/01/1948).

Italian citizen at the time of birth" means that he/she did not acquire any other citizenship through naturalization, before the descendant's birth.

Ancestors naturalized before July 1st, 1912 cannot transmit citizenship (Law n. 555 of June 13, 1912).

If your grandmother became a naturalized citizen before your mother's birth, you are not entitled to Italian citizenship jure sanguinis unless you fit into another category.

You will want to make sure that:

- All of your Certificates will be new "Certified Copies" a.k.a. "Long Form" or "Full Form" (not "certification" or "abstract").
- Your Non-Italian Birth / Marriage / Death records related to the "Italian side" will bear an apostille (according to Hague Convention of Dec. 5, 1961) except for the Certificate of Naturalization and/or similar documentation.
- All of your Certificates in other languages than Italian, will be translated into Italian. The only document which will not be translated and does not need an "Apostille" is the U.S. Certificate of Naturalization or any statement releasing information on the naturalization status of the interested party.

Foreign Documents and Discrepancies:

Your documents issued in Countries other than the U.S.A. or Italy must comply with the local regulations on the legalization of documents, they must be translated into Italian and the translation certified by the Italian Consulate/Embassy in the Country where the document was issued. To find out how a document should be legalized in its Country of origin you must obtain the information from the website of the competent Italian Consulate/Embassy. A list of all Italian Consulate/Embassies abroad is available at www.esteri.it ("Farnesina" – "Rappresentanze Diplomatiche" – "Ambasciate e Consolati" – Country)

Check all documents word for word to make sure that there are no discrepancies or changes in the names, last names, dates and places of birth. If there are major discrepancies in last names, dates, ages, and places of birth these variations or errors must be corrected with an official "affidavit to amend a record" to be requested from the Vital Statistics Office that issued the document or with another appropriate official document.

FATHER-GRANDMOTHER-GREAT GRANDFATHER.

Your paternal grandmother was born in your native country, your paternal great grandfather was an Italian citizen at the time of her birth, your father was born after January 1st, 1948, and neither you nor your father nor your grandmother ever renounced your right to Italian citizenship. If citizenship is acquired by birth in your country and you meet all these conditions, you qualify for Italian citizenship jure sanguinis.

The following documents will be required to your Italian citizenship application package:

- Your paternal great grandfather's birth certificate from Italy
- Your paternal great grandmother's birth certificate
- Your great grandparents' marriage certificate (If married outside of Italy, you will need an apostille and a translation into Italian.)
- Your paternal great grandfather's certificate of naturalization OR statements of "No Record"
- Your paternal grandmother's birth certificate (with apostille and translation)
- Your paternal grandfather's birth certificate
- Your grandparents' marriage certificate (with apostille and translation)
- Your father's birth certificate (with apostille and translation)
- Your mother's birth certificate
- Your parents' marriage certificate (with apostille and translation)
- Your birth certificate (with apostille and translation)
- Your marriage certificate, if applicable (with apostille and translation)
- Your spouse's birth certificate, if applicable
- Birth certificates for all your children under the age of eighteen, if applicable (with apostille and translation)
- Any applicable divorce decrees/certificates (with apostille and translation)
- Death certificates for anyone listed above (with apostille and translation, if for your father, grandmother or great grandfather)

Special Rules that may impact your eligibility:

A woman born before 01/01/1948 can claim the Italian citizenship only from her father and can transfer it to descendants after 01/01/1948).

Italian citizen at the time of birth" means that he/she did not acquire any other citizenship through naturalization, before the descendant's birth.

Ancestors naturalized before July 1st, 1912 cannot transmit citizenship (Law n. 555 of June 13, 1912).

If your grandmother became a naturalized citizen before your mother's birth, you are not entitled to Italian citizenship jure sanguinis unless you fit into another category.

You will want to make sure that:

- All of your Certificates will be new "Certified Copies" a.k.a. "Long Form" or "Full Form" (not "certification" or "abstract").
- Your Non-Italian Birth / Marriage / Death records related to the "Italian side" will bear an apostille (according to Hague Convention of Dec. 5, 1961) except for the Certificate of Naturalization and/or similar documentation.
- All of your Certificates in other languages than Italian, will be translated into Italian. The only document which will not be translated and does not need an "Apostille" is the U.S. Certificate of Naturalization or any statement releasing information on the naturalization status of the interested party.

Foreign Documents and Discrepancies:

Your documents issued in Countries other than the U.S.A. or Italy must comply with the local regulations on the legalization of documents, they must be translated into Italian and the translation certified by the Italian Consulate/Embassy in the Country where the document was issued. To find out how a document should be legalized in its Country of origin you must obtain the

information from the website of the competent Italian Consulate/Embassy. A list of all Italian Consulate/Embassies abroad is available at www.esteri.it ("Farnesina" – "Rappresentanze Diplomatiche" – "Ambasciate e Consolati" – Country).

Check all documents word for word to make sure that there are no discrepancies or changes in the names, last names, dates and places of birth. If there are major discrepancies in last names, dates, ages, and places of birth these variations or errors must be corrected with an official "affidavit to amend a record" to be requested from the Vital Statistics Office that issued the document or with another appropriate official document.

CHAPTER 9
ITALIAN GENEALOGY
RESEARCH.

CHAPTER 9 | ITALIAN GENEALOGY RESEARCH.

To be successful you must know some basic family information for those in your line of inheritence.

You must know the names of your parents, grandparents and great grandparents (if applicable).

Additionally the dates and places of their births, marriages, and deaths (if applicable). If there is a name change or a divorce you will also need to know the date and place of those events.

If you do not have that information available it is recommended that you consider several online recourses or you can visit your local LDS library. There is a great deal of information that has been filmed and is available for your use to track down the information.

If you do not have the time or have exhausted what is available to you locally you can consult a professional service to assist you. You will need to commission a research project from a professional genealogist.

The fee can range from $50 - $100 US per hour. You should anticipate at least 5 – 10 hours to locate the town in which your ancestor hails.

Italian and US genealogy research may be necessary to locate your ancestors vital records and assist you in preparing your complete application package of documentation for the Italian Consulate.

Do It Yourself

If hiring a professional to locate the information for you does not fit into your budget you can always do it yourself! If that is your plan then you should carefully read the following to better prepare yourself and potentially save you a great deal of time headed off in the wrong direction.

Italian Research Overview

It is important to understand the history, culture, and language of your Italian ancestors in order to discover the trail of records they may have left behind. Most Italian research can be performed using records at the Family History Library in Salt Lake City, but understanding the people you are researching can make finding and

analyzing those genealogical resources easier, whether they are microfilmed records or documents located in the parishes and archives of Italy.

Place of Origin

It is important to begin your Italian research (whether at home or abroad) with a place of origin. Understanding when and why your Italian ancestor left Italy may help to shed light on his or her town of origin. The years 1880 to 1920 were record years for Italian immigration to the United States. A vast majority of these immigrants came from southern Italy, or an area commonly referred to as the mezzogiorno. They came for many different reasons, but most were seeking a better life in a new world.

For some Italian-Americans, their ancestors' points of immigration to the United States are recent enough that they know the town, province, and region their family came from. But for some researchers, the task is not that easy. Many immigrants identified themselves by their town (comune) and province (provinicia) before they identified themselves with the nation-state of Italy. Some immigrants may even have named their frazione (fraction or hamlet) if they were from a larger city such as Rome, Naples, or Palermo. Immigrants remained loyal to the local body rather than the national body because Italy was not fully unified until 1871. It is, therefore, not uncommon to hear Italians referring to themselves as Genoese, Neapolitan, Sicilians, Tuscans, Venetians, and so forth.

Clues to the origin of your Italian ancestors may be found in your own home. Ask if your relatives have any information that documented the lives of your immigrant ancestors.

Letters from family members in Italy, and a passport, all of which helped me locate the exact place of origin for another ancestor. Besides the sources already mentioned, home sources can include birth, marriage, and death certificates, family Bibles, journals, obituaries, passenger lists, photos, naturalization papers, military service records, and many other records.

Beginning Your Research

Once the place of origin has been established, it is important to look at historical and modern gazetteers, maps, and atlases to understand the civil, court,

ecclesiastical, or military jurisdiction to which your ancestor belonged. These jurisdictions provide clues to where certain records may be located.

It is important to know both the town and province of origin, as there may be several towns with the same name, each located in a different province.

One of the most useful tools for correctly identifying the place of origin is the Nuovo Dizionario dei comuni e frazioni di comuni, a gazetteer of communities and hamlets in Italy. This gazetteer provides very valuable information, such as military and court jurisdictions. It is available on film or in book form at the Family History Library in Salt Lake City, Utah. Local LDS locations can order it for you to view at your local LDS.

For information on Catholic ecclesiastical jurisdictions, use the Annuario delle Diocesi d'Italia. This church directory gives an alphabetical listing of towns and names of Catholic parishes in each town, as well as the diocese to which the town belongs.

Other maps and historical atlases may be found in public or university libraries. Consult the "LDS Research Outline" for more ideas on geographical research tools. The outline is available at familysearch.org.

Local History

To learn more about how and where your ancestors lived, read general histories of Italy from your local or university libraries. You may be able to find specific books about regions of Italy or even towns in Italy through interlibrary loan. Or there may be a Web site for your ancestral town. You can search online for the town you believe your Ancestor to be from. There might be useful information about the town's history. You may be lucky to even find English translations on this particular site, remember that a majority of the pertinent Web sites will be in Italian.

Language

The Italian language, as it is spoken and written today, was not known or understood among the general population of Italy until the late 1800s and early 1900s. Most Italians spoke the dialects of their regions and towns. Even today, it is not uncommon to speak a specific dialect at home, and to learn modern Italian in the schools, hear it on radio and television, and use it in business transactions.

It is important to consider the diversity of language when searching for records in Italy. The two predominant languages are Latin and Italian. Most church records are written in Latin, and most civil records are written in Italian. Also, depending on the area, records may have influences of French, German, Spanish, and a variety of other languages. Understanding the history of the area can be very beneficial to understanding the records.

Naming Patterns

The given and surname patterns of your Italian ancestors may help distinguish them from other individuals with the same name. In Italy, a couple's first son was traditionally named after the paternal grandfather. The second son was named after the maternal grandfather, the first daughter was named after the paternal grandmother, and the second daughter was named after the maternal grandmother. If a couple had more than four children, they may have chosen names of aunts, uncles, cousins, or close friends for the succeeding children.

If a child died in infancy, a couple may have named their next baby the same name to preserve the naming patterns.

Also, the history of a surname can yield important ancestral clues. Italian surnames can be derived from geographical areas, animal names, occupations, nicknames, kinship names, or a variety of other things. Two helpful books for determining the origin of a surname are Joseph Fucilla's Our Italian Surnames (GPC, 1996) and Andrea Malossini's Cognomi Italiani (aVallordi, 1997).

Some surnames are found only in specific regions or towns of Italy. Web sites such as Ancestry.com have made the Italy White Pages available online. While these databases list persons currently living in Italy, they are a valuable way of determining the location of particular surnames. Another good web site to check is www.gens.labo.net. This site shows the distribution of surnames on a map by region.

Geography

For the most part, families in Italy traditionally remained in the same geographic area. The peninsula shape of the country, along with the Apennine and Alps mountain ranges, which cover a large portion of the land, create a unique geographic environment. While there are several coastal cities in Italy that allowed for a mobile community, a majority of the inhabitants of the land remained fairly immobile. Towns were often built on the tops of mountains as a defense against opposing forces. Therefore, many communities were isolated from neighboring towns, which helps to explain the different foods, clothing styles, and dialects found throughout Italy.

More Detail on Researching Italian Records for those who are DIY

Once you've established a firm background in U.S. records, located the exact place of origin, and studied the history, culture, and language of the area, it's time to search the actual records. Some of the most common records used in tracing Italian family histories are civil registration records and church records. These are the best record sets to use when beginning your research in Italian records; however, your research should not be limited solely to these two record groups.

The Family History Library in Salt Lake City has microfilmed many of the Italian civil registration records, some church records, and various other records. Check the Family History Library Catalog to determine if records for your ancestral commune, province, and region are available on microfilm.

Archived Civil records dating from the pre-unification of Italy are located in the provincial or state archive. For state archives, the Italian cultural ministry has a Web site at www.archivi.beniculturali.it. The Web site provides hours of operation, location, and other important information for each state archive in Italy. It also provides a copy of the general guide to Italian archives, which lists record types and year spans covered by those records. This general guide is by no means a comprehensive guide to each state archive; other published and unpublished guides may be used to find out what information is contained in the communal, or state archive of your ancestor. Some state, communal, and church archives publish a guide for their individual archives, giving much more detail about the actual holdings. Other less equipped archives only have a copy of their guides on hand at the archive. I have been successful in finding several guides to Italian archives in U.S. libraries. For a small fee, you can access these guides at your local public or university library through interlibrary loan. Records seventy-five years or older are considered public records and are generally kept in the state/provincial archive.

Civil Registration Records (1804—66)

Civil registration records (birth, marriage, and death) are divided into two main sections, in relation to the leadership dates of Napoleon Bonaparte. When Napoleon annexed large portions of Italy, he began the process of keeping civil records. Therefore, the Napoleonic records date between 1804 and 1815. The earliest civil records in Italy begin anywhere from 1804, in Piedmont, to 1806, in Veneto and Lombardia, but may not be found in Sardinia or in areas where Napoleon did not rule. These records are kept in each Italian state archive, which is usually located in the major city of the province.

When Napoleon lost power in 1815, most areas under his control stopped keeping civil registers. However, in other areas such as Veneto, Trento-Alto-Adige, and parts of Lombardia, parish priests kept a separate civil registration. Post-Napoleonic records date from 1809 to 1865.

In the area known as the Kingdom of the Two Sicilies, which extends from Naples and Campania down through Sicily, there is some variation in years, but generally the recordkeeping years are consistent. For Tuscany, Abruzzo, Naples, Campania, and farther southward, these records were generally kept from 1809—65. In Sicily, Napoleonic-like records span from 1820—65. Because there was no central government in Italy at this time, there was no one to monitor whether or not a civil register was kept and how thoroughly they were kept; however, if they are available for your particular town of interest, they can yield valuable information on ancestral births, marriages, and deaths.

Civil Registration Records (1866 to present)

Registration of civil records by the Italian government began between 1860 and 1871, when the country was united. In most areas, the records began in 1866 and extend to the present. These records are kept in the local registrar's office (anagrafe) of the town in which your ancestor lived. These records are generally not open to the public for perusal unless the records are over seventy-five years old. (Even then, a researcher must also have written permission from either a provincial authority or the mayor of the town to view the records.)

If a researcher supplies a name and exact date, he or she can request documents from the registrar's office. Officials are often busy and do not have time to fill requests for extensive research. When requesting a record, it is best to ask for either a photocopy of the original or an extract of the document. Most offices will send only a certificate copy, which does not provide as much detail as the photocopy or extract. There is usually a fee (which varies from town to town) required for this service.

Church Records

The Roman Catholic church is the predominate religion in Italy. While there are other religions such as Waldensian, Eastern or Greek Orthodox, etc., the majority of genealogical research takes place in the Catholic parish and diocese records. In 1563, reforms brought about by the Council of Trent required priests to keep records of baptisms, marriages, and deaths. This decree was reinforced by a Papal proclamation in 1595. Generally, church records begin during the mid- to late-1500s, but for cities such as Palermo, the records begin in the 1300s.

Each parish priest has the custodial rights for the records of his parish. Access to records is given under the discretion of the parish priest. Most church records are still located in the parish in which they were created, unless the church was destroyed by war. However, after the 1900s, duplicate church records were sent to the diocesan archives.

Besides baptism, marriage, and death records, you may also find records of confirmations and first communions, and church census records, known as stato delle anime (state of the souls). These records provide valuable information about your ancestors names and dates, and the places they lived. In some cases, they also provide the names of godparents and witnesses who were often close friends or relatives. Again, these records are usually written in Latin, but can also be found in modern Italian or the local dialect.

Researching Italian records can be very rewarding. Learning more about the history, culture, and language of your ancestors can help you find, analyze, and decipher the old records. More important, this knowledge can help bring your ancestors' stories to life.

Even More on Italian Names for those who are DIY

The Surname, also called the Family Name, is added to an original or baptismal name, inherited and held in common by members of a family. The Italian word "cognome" comes from the Latin "cum nomine", something that accompanies the name. In antiquity no surnames were used, then for the first time in ancient Rome the use of the tria nomina for the citizens was established. As an example, the three parts in "Marcus Tullius Cicero", consisted of "Marcus" - preanomen, or individual's name; "Tullius", the nomen identifying the gens or family, and the cognomen "Cicero" which was a kind of nickname to identify the individual still further.

This custom was lost in the Middle Ages, and individuals were known just with their baptismal name, as Gionata, Giuseppe, Simeone, until about the year 1000, when starting from Venice already a second name was added, to avoid confusion. The custom gradually spread from the nobility to all classes of people, and by the 15th century most surnames were formed. Finally in 1564 the Council of Trento ordered parish priests to record each individual with name and surname.

Origin of Surnames - When it was necessary to distinguish individuals with the same Christian name, most often the name of the father was added - Giovanni son of Berardo, which was shortened to Giovanni di Berardo or Giovanni Berardi. In the place of the father's name, especially if the father was not known by the community since the individual had come from another place, the toponymic could be used, as in Giovanni Calabrese or di Genova, or the job, as Mastro Giovanni.

His descendants then would often maintain this addition to the Christian name, giving origin to the present surnames. There is a great variety of surnames in Italy also because of the many dialects, the variations such as Grasso/Grassi (singular and plural), and the presence of derivatives consisting of a final suffix, "smaller" as in surnames ending in -ello, -etto, -ino; "bigger" (-one) or "bad" (-accio, - azzo). The following are the main classes of surnames:

Patronymics - The widest category, present almost in all cultures, identified a person by his connection with another person, usually his father, more rarely his mother: the father's name with "son" immediately after it in English, or "van", "von" "di" "de" in other European languages, example: Di Giovanni, Johnson; most of these Italian surnames end in -o (masculine name) or in -i derived from a Latin masculine genitive (example: Bernardi means "of Bernardo"). The same origin appears in the preposition "de" or "di" as in De Luca, D'Angelo, Di Francesco. In case of a double name it is possible that the second identified the grandfather, as in Colaianni meaning son of Nicola (Cola), grandson of Giovanni (Ianni).

Toponymics - To identify where a person or family lived or came from, example Montagna, Milani, Wood, York.

> **Local area:** the surname was associated to a place well known to the community, as for example Fontana, Della Valle, La Porta, Montagna (from the fountain, the valley, the door, mountain)

> **Geographical origin:** this was applied as a consequence of the migrations of people; the place had to be known to the community that applied the toponimic, therefore if the individual came from near villages, the name of the village was used; if he came from a more remote city, region or country, a more general name was used, like Milani, di Genova, Napolitano, Pugliese, Albanese.

Occupational names - The job, especially an artisan's job in a small village, was possibly held by only one person or family, so that the profession was added to the Christian name, example Fabbri, Ferrari, Carpenter, Smith. The activity was often also shown with a typical object or animal connected to the profession, as Farina or Forni for a baker, Zappa for a farmer, Tenaglia or Martelli for a carpenter or smith.

Nicknames - Some features of the personality or appearance, at times ironical, identified an individual and his descendants, example Piccoli, Short, Selvaggi,

Savage. The nickname was often associated to the color or form of the hair (some of the most common surnames have this origin) as in Rossi, Morelli, Ricci, size, like Corti, Grossi, Testa; more creatively, the (often ironical) nickname was made with a verb and an object indicating an action typical of the individual as in Pappalardo (that who eats lard).

Other surnames may have come from moral features, as Selvaggio or Allegretti. Names of animals could serve to the same purpose, so there were Mosca (someone small or annoying), Cavallo (someone big, noisy or with large front teeth), Gatto, Grillo, Lepore, Volpe. Finally a nickname may have come from some feature in the coatsofarm of the family, like De Argento, Mazzei, D'Arco.

Surnames of Foundlings - This kind of surnames was chosen by religious institutions or, after the establishment of Civil Records, by the civil officer; they vary according to places and traditions, so that we have Esposito in Campania, Proietti in central Italy, Trovato in Sicily, Casadio in Emilia Romagna; in the late 19th century the custom was introduced to give to foundlings surnames of non-residents, or surnames invented on the spot.

More on History and Culture and how it Impacts Research for those who DIY

This may seem repetitive, but if you are researching Italian records it can be very helpful to hear the information a few times or have it presented in a different way. Since we all learn differently this section is worth a second presentation.

Again, when researching your Italian ancestors, it is important to understand their history, culture and language in order to uncover the records they may have left behind. Understanding when and why your Italian ancestor left Italy, as well as their preferred foods, clothing styles and dialects, may help to shed light on their town of origin, a necessary starting point for researching Italian roots.

Where Did They Come From?

Typically, families in Italy traditionally remained in the same geographic area. The unique geography of the country left many communities isolated from neighboring towns, restricting mobility and discouraging migration. This can be a boon for Italian genealogists, but also makes it necessary to begin your Italian research with a place of origin. Clues to the origin of your Italian ancestors may be found in your own home, or those of other family members. Talk to your relatives to see if they know the town, province or region in Italy the family originally came from. Ask them if they have any documents from the family, including wills, naturalization records, passenger lists, birth records, marriage records, etc. Any of these may help you to pinpoint your family's town of origin in Italy.

Place Them on the Map

Before delving head-first into Italian records, you should first identify your ancestor's town or village on both historical and modern gazetteers, maps and atlases in order to determine the civil, court, ecclesiastical and/or military jurisdictions which applied to your ancestors. Knowing these jurisdictions can better help you determine where the records will be found. Some of the best sources include:

Nuovo Dizionario dei comuni e frazioni di comuni - This gazetteer of communities and hamlets in Italy provides important information on military and court jurisdictions. It is available on microfilm from the Family History Library, or through your local Family History Center.

Annuario delle Diocesi d'Italia - This church directory gives an alphabetical listing of towns and names of Catholic parishes in each town, as well as the diocese to which the town belongs, making it a valuable resource for determining Catholic ecclesiastical jurisdictions.

Church Registers - Registri Parrocchiali

The predominate religion in Italy is Roman Catholic, so the majority of genealogical research takes place in Catholic parish and diocese records. In 1563, reforms brought about by the Council of Trent required priests to keep records of baptisms (atti di battesimo), marriages (atti di matrimonio), and burials (atti di sepoltura), meaning that most church records in Italy date back to this time. For some cities, however, church records begin as early as the 1300s. Italian church records usually include baptisms, marriages, deaths, confirmations and first communions, as well as possibly church census records. They are usually written in Latin, though some may be found in Italian.

Most church records are still located in the parish in which they were created, unless the church was destroyed by war, and access is determined by the parish priest. Duplicate copies of church records after 1900 are also available in the diocesan archives.

Certificate of Family Status or Genealogy | Certificato dello Stato di Famiglia

If your ancestors left Italy after about 1880 and you know the name of the town in which they lived, you can write to the local Ufficio Anagrafe (Registry Office) and request a cerificato di stato di famiglia. This certificate, unique to Italy, records information on the entire family, rather than just an individual. It usually contains the name, relationship, and date and place of birth for each family member, often including family members who moved away or died. Some towns began keeping this record as early as 1869, but it wasn't in widespread use until after 1911.

Census Records Censimenti

The first Italian census was taken in 1871, with new censuses taken each successive decade. The censuses taken from 1871-1901 are inconsistent from region to region, and usually only name the head of household, his/her occupation, and the number of people living in the household. Census records from 1911 on, however, list names, ages, occupations, birthplaces and relationships to the head of household for each resident. Census records from 1911 to 1991 are usually found in each comune's anagrafe (register office), and in the state archive of each province. Availability differs from comune to comune, and all census records may not be yet open to the public.

Military and Conscription Records | Ufficio Matricola e Centro Documentale

Beginning about 1869 and continuing to the present day, all male Italian citizens are required to register at the age of eighteen. These conscription records typically include name, birth date, address at time of registration, parents, next of kin, and physical description of the registrant, as well as an explanation of their military status - whether they ever served, deserted, were exempted, etc. These records are in the custody of the local Military District (Distretto Militare). Records from 1870-1920 can be obtained from the State Archives.

Italian Military Draft Obligation

The Italian Army, Navy, Air Force and Gendarmerie collectively form the Italian armed forces, under the command of the Supreme Defence Council, presided over by the President of the Italian Republic. Although registration is required actual military service has been voluntary.

Decree n. 226 of 23 August 2004 (G.U. n. 204 of 23/8/2004), called for, as of January 2005, the early suspension of obligatory military service and the establishment of professional military service.

Italian citizens who intend to repatriate in order to perform voluntary military service are not eligible for the benefits stated in decree 433/66, which governs repatriation procedures at the expense of the Treasury for the sole purpose of obligatory military service.

CHAPTER 10
NATURALIZATION
DOCUMENTS.

CHAPTER 10) NATURALIZATION DOCUMENTS.

The application to be recognized as an Italian citizen will not be accepted unless the applicant is in a position to prove that their Italian ancestor, who was born in Italy, did <u>not</u> become naturalized before the birth of the first generation that was born in USA.

Remember, it is okay if your Ancestor *did naturalize.* He or she must have done it *after* the birth of the next generation. It is not the date he filed his intention **it is the date he or she took the oath.**

To prove your qualifications you must obtain:

1) <u>the Certificate of Naturalization.</u>

If it is **not available** you must provide the following:

2) <u>Official statement</u> (in original, not photocopy, and with the Office Seal) from the United States Citizenship and Immigration Services (USCIS) (www.uscis.gov) in Washington D.C. (425 I Street North West, 2nd Floor, ULLICO Bldg, Washington, DC 20536) AND FROM THE Court County in which he resided, stating the number of the Certificate of Naturalization and the date of his naturalization. The statement must show your Italian ancestor's full name (and any other names he/she went by on any official documents), place of birth and date of birth, date of the naturalization, certificate number; if he never became a US citizen, you have to show his Italian passport and Alien Registration Card.
3)
4) For more information visit: http://www.uscis.gov/portal/site/uscis

5) Or Record from the USCIS Genealogy Program. Follow the procedures on the Genealogy web site www.uscis.gov/genealogy .

6) <u>If the Research shows NO RECORD:</u> you are requested to double check with the National Archives (www.archives.gov) requesting a full search under his name and nicknames, possible dates of birth

which he may have declared in the course of his life. If the record is found, you will obtain from the National Archives a certified copy of his "petition for naturalization" and "oath of allegiance" (Please note: this Office may at any time request that you present documentation from the National Archives – in case of discrepancies – to confirm the identity reported on the certificate of Naturalization).

IF YOUR ITALIAN ANCESTOR WENT TO A COUNTRY OTHER THAN THE U.S.A. YOU MUST PRESENT THE NATURALIZATION RECORD ISSUED BY THAT COUNTRY.

For more information see the website of the competent Italian Consulate/Embassy. A list of all Italian Consulate/Embassies abroad is available at: www.esteri.it ("Farnesina" - "Rappresentanze Diplomatiche" - "Ambasciate e Consolati" – Country).

Understanding The Naturalization Process

Since September 27, 1906, the U.S. Citizenship & Immigration Services (USCIS, formerly INS) in Washington D.C. has maintained copies of naturalization records. Prior to 1906 the records might be found in an individual county's Court of Common Pleas, Quarter Sessions, or other county courts, the State Supreme Court, and the U.S. Circuit and District Courts. County records were usually maintained by the Prothonotary of the County Court. The National Archives and State Archives have copies of some naturalization records.

Where to find Naturalization Records

Again, like all steps in this process, you can hire a service or complete the task yourself.

Prior to 1906, any "court of record" (municipal, county, state, or Federal) could grant U.S. citizenship. As a general rule, the National Archives (NARA) does not have naturalization records created in State or local courts.

However, a few indexes and records have been donated to the National Archives from counties, states and local courts and are available as National Archives microfilm publications. See the list of this county and state microfilm available.

For pre-1906 naturalizations:

Contact the State Archives for the state where the naturalization occurred to request a search of state, county, and local courts records.

Contact the NARA regional facility that serves the state where naturalization occurred to request a search of Federal court records

After 1906, the courts forwarded copies of naturalizations to USCIS (INS).

Naturalizations from Federal Courts are held in the NARA's regional facilities for the Federal courts for their area.

The National Archives in Washington, D.C. holds naturalization records for Federal Courts in Washington, D.C.

USCIS Washington DC.

Prior to September 27, 1906, there was no US Naturalization Service, therefore the USCIS has no naturalization records dated before September 1906. To locate pre-1906 naturalization records, or any naturalization records filed with courts, start your research at the National Archives.

Naturalization Records

Naturalization is the process by which an alien becomes an American citizen. It is a voluntary act; naturalization is not required. Of the foreign-born persons listed on the 1890 through 1930 censuses, 25 percent had not become naturalized or filed their "first papers."

This information is adapted from Claire Prechtel-Kluskens, "The Location of Naturalization Records," The Record, Vol. 3, No. 2, pp. 21-22 (Nov. 1996).

The Courts

From the first naturalization law passed by Congress in 1790 through much of the 20th century, an alien could become naturalized in any court of record. Thus, most people went to the court most convenient to them, usually a county court.

The names and types of courts vary from State to State. The names and types of courts have also varied during different periods of history--but may include the county supreme, circuit, district, equity, chancery, probate, or common pleas court. Most researchers will find that their ancestors became naturalized in one of these courts. A few State supreme courts also naturalized aliens, such as the supreme courts of Indiana, Idaho, Iowa, Maine, New Jersey, and South Dakota. Aliens who lived in large cities sometimes became naturalized in a Federal court, such as a U.S. district court or U.S. circuit court.

General Rule: The Two-Step Process

Congress passed the first law regulating naturalization in 1790 (1 Stat. 103). As a general rule, naturalization was a two-step process that took a minimum of 5 years. After residing in the United States for 2 years, an alien could file a "declaration of intent" (so-called "first papers") to become a citizen. After 3 additional years, the alien could "petition for naturalization." After the petition was granted, a certificate of citizenship was issued to the alien. These two steps did not have to take place in the same court. As a general rule, the "declaration of intent" generally contains more genealogically useful information than the "petition." The "declaration" may include the alien's month and year (or possibly the exact date) of immigration into the United States.

Exceptions to the General Rule

Having stated this "two-step, 5-year" general rule, it is necessary to note several exceptions.

The first major exception was that "derivative" citizenship was granted to wives and minor children of naturalized men. From 1790 to 1922, wives of naturalized men automatically became citizens. This also meant that an alien woman who married a U.S. citizen automatically became a citizen. (Conversely, an American woman who married an alien lost her U.S. citizenship, even if she never left the United States.) From 1790 to 1940, children under the age of 21 automatically became naturalized citizens upon the naturalization of their father. Unfortunately, however, names and biographical information about wives and children are rarely included in declarations or petitions filed before September 1906. For more information about women in naturalization records, see Marian

L. Smith, "Women and Naturalization, ca. 1802-1940," Prologue: Quarterly of the National Archives, Vol. 30, No. 2 (Summer 1998): 146-153.

The second major exception to the general rule was that, from 1824 to 1906, minor aliens who had lived in the United States 5 years before their 23rd birthday could file both their declarations and petitions at the same time.

The third major exception to the general rule was the special consideration given to veterans. An 1862 law allowed honorably discharged Army veterans of any war to petition for naturalization--without previously having filed a declaration of intent--after only 1 year of residence in the United States. An 1894 law extended the same no-previous-declaration privilege to honorably discharged 5-year veterans of the Navy or Marine Corps. Over 192,000 aliens were naturalized between May 9, 1918, and June 30, 1919, under an act of May 9, 1918, that allowed aliens serving in the U.S. armed forces during "the present war" to file a petition for naturalization without making a declaration of intent or proving 5 years' residence. Laws enacted in 1919, 1926, 1940, and 1952 continued various preferential treatment provisions for veterans.

The Records

It is impossible to provide hard-and-fast rules about the content or even the existence of naturalization records. The 1905 Report to the President of the Commission on Naturalization remarked:

The methods of making and keeping the naturalization records in both the Federal and State courts are as various as the procedure in such cases. Thus the declaration of intention in some courts consists merely of the bare statement of the intention and the name and allegiance of the alien, while in other courts it also includes a history of the alien.... In a majority of courts alien applicants are not required to make the declaration of intention required by law ... and in other courts he is. Previous to 1903 a majority of courts did not require petitions or affidavits; other courts did. Some courts keep a naturalization record separate from the other records; other courts include the naturalization record in the regular minutes of the court. Some records contain full histories of the aliens, but a majority of the records show only the name, nationality, oath of allegiance, and date of admission.

In 1903 a Justice Department investigator made even more condemnatory comments:

I find the naturalization records in many cases in a chaotic condition, many lost and destroyed, and some sold for old paper. Most of the records consist of merely the name and nativity of the alien with no means of identifying other aliens with the same name....In numerous cases I find aliens naturalized under initials instead of Christian names, surnames misspelled or changed entirely, and names of witnesses inserted in place of the alien naturalized. The examination of the records discloses the remarkable fact that never, since the first enactment of the naturalization laws, has any record been made in any court of the names of minor children who, under the operation of the statutes, were made citizens by the naturalization of their parents.

The Location of these Records

County Court Records

Naturalization records from county courts may still be at the county court, in a county or a States archive, or at a regional archives serving several counties within a State. Some of these records or indexes have been published, such as the Index of Naturalizations, Ashtabula County, Ohio, 1875-1906, published by the Ashtabula County Genealogical Society.

Do not be surprised if county court employees tell you that their naturalization records are at "the National Archives" or that their court never conducted naturalizations. Most current court employees are probably not genealogists and may not be familiar with the court's older records. It is up to the researcher to determine the location of older court records.

County Court Records in the National Archives

As a general rule, the National Archives do not have naturalization records created in State or local courts. However, some county court naturalization records have been donated to the National Archives and are available as National Archives microfilm publications:

NATIONAL ARCHIVE LOCATIONS

National Archives in Washington, DC

700 Pennsylvania Avenue, NW,

Washington, DC 20408

National Archives at Anchorage, AK (Pacific Alaska Region)

654 West Third Avenue,

Anchorage, AK 99501-2145

National Archives at Atlanta, GA (Southeast Region)

4712 Southpark Blvd.,

Ellenwood, GA 30294

National Archives at Atlanta, GA (Southeast Region)

5780 Jonesboro Road,

Morrow, GA 30260

National Archives at Boston, MA (Northeast Region)

Frederick C. Murphy Federal Center

380 Trapelo Road

Waltham, Massachusetts 02452-6399

National Archives at Chicago, IL (Great Lakes Region)

7358 South Pulaski Road,

Chicago, IL 60629-5898

National Archives at College Park, MD

8601 Adelphi Road,

College Park, MD 20740-6001

National Archives at Dayton, OH (Great Lakes Region)

3150 Springboro Road

Moraine, OH, 45439

National Archives at Dayton-Miamisburg, OH (Great Lakes Region)

8801 Kingsridge Drive

Dayton, OH 45458

National Archives at Denver, CO (Rocky Mountain Region)

Denver Federal Center

17101 Huron Street

Broomfield, CO 80023-8909

National Archives at Fort Worth, TX (Southwest Region)

2600 West 7th Street, Suite 162

Fort Worth, TX, 76107

National Archives at Fort Worth, TX (Southwest Region)

1400 John Burgess Drive

Fort Worth, Texas 76140

National Archives at Kansas City, MO (Central Plains Region)

400 West Pershing Road

Kansas City, MO 64108-4306

National Archives at Laguna Niguel, CA (Pacific Region)

24000 Avila Rd., Suite 3513

Laguna Niguel, CA 92677

National Archives at Lee's Summit, MO (Central Plains Region)

200 Space Center Drive

Lee's Summit, MO 64064-1182

National Archives at Lenexa, KS (Central Plains Region)

17501 West 98th Street

Lenexa, KS 66219

National Archives at New York City, NY (Northeast Region)

Alexander Hamilton US Customs House

1 Bowiling Green

New York, NY 10004

National Archives at Northeast Philadelphia, PA (Mid Atlantic Region)

14700 Townsend Rd.

Philadelphia, PA 19154-1096

National Archives at Pittsfield, MA (Northeast Region)

Silvio O. Conte National Records Center

10 Conte Drive

Pittsfield, Massachusetts 01201-8230

National Archives at Riverside, CA (Pacific Region)

23123 Cajalco Road

Perris, CA 92570

National Archives at San Francisco, CA (Pacific Region)

1000 Commodore Dr.

San Bruno, CA 94066-2350

National Archives at Seattle, WA (Pacific Alaska Region)

6125 Sand Point Way, NE.

Seattle, WA 98115-7999

National Archives at St. Louis, MO

1 Archives Drive

St. Louis, MO 63138

National Personnel Records Center (Civilian Records)

111 Winnebago Street

St. Louis, MO 63118-4199

National Personnel Records Center (Military Records)

1 Archives Drive

Spanish Lake, MO 63138

Washington National Records Center

4205 Suitland Road

Suitland, MD 20746

PUNCH LIST TO OBTAIN ANCESTOR'S

CERTIFICATE OF NATURALIZATION OR CERTIFIED NO RECORD

1) WRITE LETTER TO NARA

2) WRITE LETTER TO COUNTY CLERK

   A) CHECK ON INTERNET FOR COUNTY NAME
   B) LOOK ON COUNTY WEB SITE TO DETERMINE WHERE THE RECORDS ARE HELD (RANGE OF DATES YOU ARE SEEKING)

      i. IF RECORDS HAVE BEEN ARCHIVED THE COUNTY WILL INFORM YOU OF THAT. ASK FOR THE NAME , ADDRESS, CONTACT INFORMATION FOR THE STATE ARCHIVE AND LOCATE THEM ON THE INERNET OR CALL THEM FOR THE MAILING ADDRESS.
      ii. SEND LETTER TO STATE ARCHIVES

   C) CALL THE COUNTY FOR EXACT ADDRESS

3) FILL OUT FORM FOR USCIS (uscis.gov) –G1041 – INDEX & GET RESULTS BACK

   A) FILL OUT FORM FOR USCIS – G1041A – TO OBTAIN DOCUMENT
   B) SEND LETTER TO DHS USCIS, WASHINGTON DC TO GET CERTIFICATION OF NO RECORD

4) REQUEST CERTIFIED COPY OF US CENSUS – BC 600 (census.gov)

   A) INCLUDE COPY OF PHOTO ID & DEATH CERTIFICATE IF REQUIRED
   B) OBTAIN EXTENDED FORM SHOWING ALL FAMILY MEMBERS

120

CHAPTER 11
ITALIAN CERTIFICATES.

CHAPTER 11 | ITALIAN VITAL RECORDS.

Under Italian law, records of births, marriages, and deaths are maintained by the Registrar of Vital Statistics (Ufficio dello Stato civile) in the City Office (Comune or Municipio) of the place where the event occurred. There is no central, regional, or provincial office established which keeps such records.

When applying for one of these certificates, the applicant must supply all relevant information. The office of the registrar cannot undertake extensive research of its files to locate a record which is not properly identified, and will not translate requests in a foreign language. A request written in the Italian usually produces faster results. The municipalities may or may not respond to your written request.

A small fee is charged for the issuance of a certificate, varying from place to place, but on the average does not exceed 5 euro and you should include a prepaid return mailing envelope with your request. A form is provided at the end of this chapter for your use.

To request:

BIRTH CERTIFICATE (Certificato di Nascita), provide full name of person at birth, place and date of birth, name of parents; specify that the document should include the name of the parents.

MARRIAGE CERTIFICATE (Certificato di Matrimonio), provide full names at birth of both parties, their birthdates, place and date of marriage.

DEATH CERTIFICATE (Certificato di Morte), provide full name at birth of deceased, date and place of birth if available, place and date of death.

NOTE: Italian registrars are not required by law to assist in genealogical research work.

In most places, records dating back as far as the mid-19th century are available but unless complete and correct information is provided, no search can be undertaken.

If you are engaged in family tree reconstruction and do not have the essential information bearing on your ancestors, you may wish to retain the aid of professional researchers.

When to hire a service to obtain your Italian Vital Records

As I mentioned above the municipality is not required by law to assist you. And often applicants will write to the Italian comune in English expecting a reply. This does not often occur. Further, they will attempt to use a machine translator from some online website to no avail. *These computer or online translators are not accurate and should never be used in this process.*

Depending on your timeline and experience ordering the document on your own should generate a response in about 90 days. Keep in mind records are not computerized and a human will flip page by page in a dusty register book to locate the record you are requesting and then the certificate will be typed / written for you. It is not like in the United States. There is no central data base.

If your timeline demands it or you have waited three months without a reply I recommend you hire a service to assist you. You will be charged a fee ranging from 75 – 150 euro. If you think this is a lot to pay for a single document you are mistaken. Your Italian citizenship hinges upon you being able to link your lineage to your Italian Ancestor. I highly recommend a service for this step in the process.

They routinely furnish official Italian family records of your ancestors and family members directly from the Registrar of Vital Statistics (Ufficio della Stato Civile) in the City office (Comune o Municipio) in Italy. They provide official certified documents that meet the requirements for Italian Dual Citizenship.

Roma and Milano

In an attempt to combat fraud the Cities of Roma and Milano have recently added additional requirements for documents. These new requirements require that they go to the Municipal Building and submit your request. they must then wait a month and then return to pick up the certificate. Additionally they will have to prepare a special letter called a Delega; signed by you giving them permission to acquire the document for you. This letter must be accompanied by your photo ID.

The Process

A benefit to hiring an Agency is that they will forward the information to the appropriate office and then call where the records are kept, speak in Italian to the records clerk and send a formal request by letter along with their other requirements. They follow up with additional inquiries spaced one week apart until they receive your document/s or a certified letter stating that there is no record for the name and dates submitted.

If the service is reputable, they will not start the process if they see that there is no chance to get the certificate because the information is obviously incorrect. For example, the name of a commune that does not exist or other information they know is incorrect.

Do your research before ordering the document. Get the names and city spellings correct. Remember Italian names typically are not John or Patrick. Look up the Italian version of your ancestor's assumed Americanized name.

FAC-SIMILE RICHIESTA ATTI DI STATO CIVILE DI CITTADINI ITALIANI A COMUNI ITALIANI

La richiesta deve essere inviata **direttamente** dall'interessato al proprio Comune, il cui indirizzo può essere reperito sul web www.comuni.it e dovrà essere riportato sulla busta.

*The request must be **directly** sent from the person concerned to the own Italian "Comune" City Hall, whose direction can be find in the*

Al Sindaco del Comune di

....

....

Il sottoscritto/a chiede cortesemente, uso _____, l'invio del/i seguente certificato/i:

☐ integrale con eventuali annotazioni (*complete with notes if needed*)

☐ modello internazionale plurilingue (*multilingual International form*)

Dell'atto di stato civile *(of the following certificate)*:

☐ Estratto per riassunto atto di NASCITA (*Birth Certificate*)

☐ Estratto per riassunto atto di MATRIMONIO (*Marriage Certificate*)

☐ MORTE (*Death Certificate*)

Relativi alla seguente persona: (*Pertinent to the following person*)

Cognome (*Last name*):   Nome (*First name*):

_____

Nome da nubile (*Maiden name*):

_____

Nato/a a (*Birth place*):

_____

il (*Birth date*): (day/month/year) _____/_____/_____

Indirizzo per l'invio del certificato (*Direction to send and return the certificate*):

Cognome richiedente (*Applicant's last name*):

_____

Nome richiedente (*Applicant's name*):

_____

Via (*Full address*):

_____

Città (*City*): _____

Zip _____

Stato (*State*):_____

Tel. (*Phone no.*)_____

FAX:_____

E-mail:_____

Osservazioni (*Other comments*):

Data (*Date*):_____   Firma (*Applicant's*

signature):_____

ALLEGARE FOTOCOPIA DEL DOCUMENTO D'IDENTITÀ' ED UNA BUSTA VUOTA DI RISPOSTA CON L'INDIRIZZO DEL RICHIEDENTE (AVVERTENZA: I COMUNI POSSONO ESIGERE L'INTEGRAZIONE DELLE RELATIVE SPESE POSTALI O IL PAGAMENTO DEI CERTIFICATI EMESSI)

Il Consolato Generale non si rende responsabile delle mancate risposte

ENCLOSE THE I.D. COPY AND THE SELF-ADDRESSED STAMPED RETURN ENVELOPE.

(IMPORTANT: THE ITALIAN "COMUNI" (City halls) CAN DEMAND A SUPPLEMENT POSTAL FEES OR THE ISSUED CERTIFICATE'S PAYMENT)

The General Consulate is not responsible for unanswered requests.

CHAPTER 12
SCHEDULING
APPOINTMENTS.

CHAPTER 12) APPOINTMENTS.

The minute you decide to move forward in pursuit of your Italian citizenship through ancestry it is recommended you schedule your appointment. Most Italian consulates will be booked one to even three years out just to schedule the appointment. So make the appointment and then collect your documents.

You can anticipate that it will take you six (6) months (if you are diligent in your efforts) to nine (9) months (some agency's can be slow to reply) to collect all of the required documentation. This of course can occur more quickly if you use a service to assist you in the acquisition of the documents.

To schedule an appointment use the PRENOTA Online registration system. This system is free of charge. You will need to create an account to schedule an appointment. They also offer a step – by – step guide on the consulate web site if you have questions regarding the system itself.

Do not accept an earlier appointment than that. You do not want to go to your consulate appointment ill prepared. You want everything in order BEFORE that appointment.

Keep in mind there is enormous interest in obtaining Italian citizenship and, with about 4 million people of Italian ancestry in the New York Consulate's jurisdiction, many applications are processed every year. However, this may also mean that your appointment for citizenship jure sanguinis may be given in about one years time. Citizenship by marriage, on the other hand, is on a faster track, and appointments are given within a much shorter time. This is because some documents have a limited validity (criminal records are valid only for a few months) and must be presented to the Consulate before they expire. In any event, it is particularly important that you read carefully the information on the consulate's website, so that your application can be processed faster after your appointment.

To summarize, look on your Italian consulate of your jurisdiction web site to confirm how they want you to schedule the appointment. Look under Consular Services and for the Prenota Online reservation system.

*****SEE CHAPTER 29**** to determine your consulate of jurisdiction nearest your residence and the web site and contact information.

CHAPTER 13
COLLECTING US
CERTIFICATES.

CHAPTER 13 | US CERTIFICATES.

You will need to obtain the birth, marriage and death records for each person in your line of inheritence.

When requesting the records make sure you obtain LONG FORM (FULL FORM) certified and EXEMPLIFIED copies of the documents.

Have them issued from state offices if possible and make sure the Marriages have a HAND SIGNATURE (live signature).

State Registrar or VitalChek.

You can do this on line through many state registrars or using a third party called Vitalchek.

When making your requests, include a prepaid return envelope to make sure your documents are quickly returned to you.

Include a photo copy of your state issued ID. Be sure it is enlarged and clear enough for it to be read.

If paying by credit card typically the documents can only be shipped to the billing address on the credit card.

If you do not want to write to them directly it may be more convenient for you to obtain the birth, marriage and death records for your family members using an online service.   VitalChek has been approved by many of the state vital records offices.

VitalChek.

VitalChek is your official source for government-issued vital records. With secure online ordering, partnerships throughout the country, and quick turnaround.

www.vitalchek.com

CHAPTER 14
NEW YORK
DOCUMENTS.

CHAPTER 14 | NEW YORK CITY DOCUMENTS.

For vital records in the five boroughs of NYC contact the New York City Dept. of Health.

The Office of Vital Records (http://www.nyc.gov/html/doh/html/vr/vr.shtml) issues, corrects, and amends certified copies of birth and death certificates. They only have your birth certificate if you were born in one of the five boroughs of New York City: Brooklyn, the Bronx, Manhattan, Queens, or Staten Island. Where your family lived then or now is not important, just where you were born. Similarly, they only have death certificates for people who died in the five boroughs.

Birth certificates issued prior to 1910 and death certificates issued prior to 1949 are not available through the Office of Vital Records. For these documents, please contact the Municipal Archives by calling 311 (or 212-639-9675 outside New York City) or visiting the agency's website. You also can visit the Municipal Archives in Manhattan at 31 Chambers Street, Room 103.

To apply for a certificate online, you must use a credit card, debit card, or electronic check in your name. Your order will be processed by the Office of Vital Records within 24 hours. Please allow an additional 10 business days for vault copies of NYC birth certificates and letters of exemplification.

Your purchase will appear on your credit or debit card statement as a charge from VitalChek. It also may appear as "VCN" or "NYC Vital Records." The NYC Department of Health and Mental Hygiene reviews and verifies all information submitted online to prevent sending a birth certificate to the wrong person. In some cases, additional information may be required to complete this process so please ensure that all relevant contact information is entered correctly.

A credit card, debit card, or electronic check may be used only to order birth certificates for you and your children, provided you are named on the birth certificates. To request a birth certificate for any other person, including any child where your name does not appear on the birth certificate, you must submit an order in-person or by mail

If you legally changed your name (other than for marriage) and have not notified the Office of Vital Records, you must submit your application by mail. Please submit the application along with the original name change order, a copy of your valid photo identification including signature, and the appropriate payment.

NEW YORK CITY VITAL RECORDS AT THE MUNICIPAL ARCHIVES

The Municipal Archives has records of births reported in the five Boroughs of New York City (Manhattan, Brooklyn, Bronx, Queens and Staten Island), prior to 1910; deaths reported prior to 1949, and marriages reported prior to 1930.

Please note that New York State Vital Records outside the five boroughs of New York City are maintained by NYS Department of Health.

There are two ways you may obtain a copy of a vital record. You may use one of our convenient forms to receive your search result by mail.

Alternatively, you may visit the Municipal Archives to use our self-service microfilm facility to research the genealogy collections. You can access all indexes and certificates on microfilm and receive certified copies of certificates.

ORDER A COPY BY MAIL:

VITAL RECORD	YEARS	AGENCY IN CHARGE
Birth Certificate	prior to 1910	Department of Records
	1910 - present	Department of Health
Death Certificate	prior to 1949	Department of Records
	1949 - present	Department of Health
Marriage Certificate	prior to 1930	Department of Records
	1930 - present	Office of the City Clerk

NEW YORK CITY MARRIAGE RECORDS

You can obtain a Marriage Record by appearing at the appropriate City Clerk office in person or mailing in a completed application (in PDF). **BE SURE TO ASK FOR A LIVE HAND SIGANTURE ON THE CERTIFIED COPY.**

You may also use City Clerk Online to fill out an application which you can print and bring to one the City Clerk's offices in person or mail in. We have records relating to all Marriage Licenses issued by our offices from 1930 to the present. If you obtained your Marriage License from a town or city clerk outside of the five boroughs of New York City, please contact the New York State Department of Health in Albany.

Fees

All fees listed are by credit card or money order payable to the City Clerk. (Confirm current pricing on their website).

Locations for In-Person Requests

You may obtain a Marriage Record from 1996 to present in person at any of the office locations.

You may obtain a Marriage Record from 1930 to 1995 at their Record Room Division located at our Manhattan Office.

Marriage Records Request by Mail

To obtain a Marriage Record by mail, please call the main office at 212-669-8090 to request a form or download the Marriage Record mail request form here. All requests must be accompanied with a copy of valid identification as stated on the form.

Marriage Records Older than 50 Years

A Marriage Record older than 50 years from today's date is considered a historic record and is available to the general public.

You may request a Marriage Record that is older than 50 years either by mail as described above or by visiting our Record Room Division in our Manhattan office with the appropriate fee.

Marriage Records Less than 50 Years Old

If you wish to request a Marriage Record created within 50 years from today's date, you must meet one of the following criteria:

- You are either the bride or groom, or
- You have written, notarized authorization from either the bride or groom, or
- You wish to purchase a Marriage Record for another person to be mailed directly to that other person's address based on your sworn statement (the record will not be given to you), or
- You are an attorney and you require the record as evidence in a legal proceeding, or
- The bride and groom are deceased and you can present their original death certificates, or
- You have a judicial or other proper purpose.

Procedure for the Bride or Groom

- You will need proper identification and the appropriate fee.
- You will be asked to fill out an application where you will provide all of the information you have about your wedding and the location of our office where you first obtained the license.

Procedure for Persons with Written Authorization from the Bride or Groom

- You may give any person you like written authorization to obtain your Marriage Record.
- You must provide the person an original consent letter that you signed and is notarized. Download a sample consent letter.
- Your representative will not be able to use a photocopy or fax copy of the original letter.
- Your representative must be named in the letter and the name must be exactly the same as the name on your representative's proper identification.
- Your representative must provide the appropriate fee by money order only.

Procedure for an Attorney

- If you are an attorney, you may obtain a confidential Marriage Record if you require the Marriage Record as evidence in a legal proceeding.
- If you are making the request in person, you must present either a valid New York State Secure Pass or a business card and matching proper identification.
- You must provide the appropriate fee by attorney's check or money order payable to the City Clerk.
- You may send a messenger or representative on your behalf if you give them an original signed letter from you on your letterhead where you name the messenger or representative and where you make this statement: "the Marriage Record is required as evidence in a legal proceeding."
- The messenger or representative must present proper identification and the appropriate fee by money order only.

Procedure when Bride and Groom are Deceased

- When both the bride and groom in a marriage are deceased, their Marriage Record may be obtained by anyone presenting both parties' original Death Certificates along with proper identification and the appropriate fee by money order only.

Procedure for a Judicial or other Proper Purpose

- If you have a judicial or other proper purpose you may obtain a confidential Marriage Record if you have the correct documentation.
- One example of a judicial or other proper purpose is a Marriage Record needed by a party to claim benefits. The original letter from the agency requesting the Marriage Record would be considered correct documentation.

Proper Identification

If you do have proper identification, you may give written authorization to another person with proper identification to obtain your record.

CHAPTER 15
DOCUMENT ERRORS
& ENTITLEMENTS.

CHAPTER 15 | DOCUMENT ERRORS, CORRECTIONS & ENTITLEMENTS.

Entitlements. Entitlements. Entitlements. Some US vital record offices may require applicants to provide a letter from the Consulate stating a reason for the request of certificates relevant to the applicants' ancestors.

You can ask the consulate for the letter. Unfortunately, they will in most cases not write a letter to authorize any American Government Office to issue such records.

Some consulates suggest you copy the text from their web site and show the officials the requirement in an attempt to acquire the document.

There may be cases that you must have a parents or grandparent's signature and photo ID to get a record or show death certificates first to prove you are entitled.

Other states may offer, when asked, that you provide an individuals death certificate before you are allowed to request their documents if your name is not listed on the document.

Even others will demand a court order to release the records. In the last chapter of this book you will find many sample forms that may be of use to you if you are having trouble getting certain documents. New York for example allows one to complete an affidavit to release certain documents. Each state will be different and you must look at entitlements for each state, on the vital records website.

You can file a court order asking the court of jurisdiction to force the state to release the record. You can use an attorney for this or do it your self. It is not as difficult as it may seem.

The clerk of the court can inform you of the specific requirements, you will pay a very minimal filing fee and appear to explain to the judge that acquisition of the document is essential and a requirement for your Italian dual citizenship.

Incorrect certificates.

It is your responsibility to make sure that all documents contain the correct information with regard to names, last names, dates and places of birth, and that such information matches in all submitted papers.

Incorrect certificates may delay processing of your application or affect your eligibility for Italian citizenship. If there are too significant differences in the certificates, please provide an official statement from a Court Judge or a Vital Statistic Officer asserting the true and correct information.

It is recommended that you check all documents word for word to make sure that there are no discrepancies or changes in the names, last names, dates and places of birth.

If there are major discrepancies in last names, dates, ages, and places of birth these variations or errors must be corrected with an official "affidavit to amend a record" to be requested from the Vital Statistics Office that issued the document or with another appropriate official document.

What is your Surname…really.

Your family name may not be what you are used to. Your family name is in fact the name that appears on your ancestor's original Italian birth certificate.

For example Grandpa was named Giovanni Labrizzi. You use the family name of Labrie because the name was Americanized along the way. **Your actual name is Labrizzi not Labrie unless there was a formal name change.**

Do not argue or defend the assumed name. It is not yours. You are trying to be an Italian. So all records *__are supposed to match__* the Italian records. **They are correct and everything after their issuance is considered a mistake or in error if different.**

The consulate can force you to amend the records. This is *__very__* subjective since each consulate interprets the errors or minor name changes differently. Consult their individual web sites before changing all of your documents. Some consulate clearly accept minor discrepancies others will demand they be addressed.

This can be done by contacting the local register who issued the record. The fee again is minimal and worth taking the time.

Some individuals will proceed with an Affidavit addressing the MINOR discrepancy. (Antonio assumed the name Anthony for example). <u>It is however, up to the individual consulates if they will accept an affidavit.</u>

Since each person's documents will be different consider the number of discrepancies and if the fixes are simple.

Another option is to get a court order stating that this person is in fact that person and that he assumed an Americanized version of the name.

Samples are included under the form section of this book for your use.

Remember.

If you go to the consulate and they do not accept the documents you **ARE NOT** refused OR denied your Italian citizenship.

They are simply saying, go back and FIX THIS or GET THIS. They will give you on the average of 90 days to generate the revised information without you having to reschedule another appointment.

CHAPTER 16
APOSTILLES.

CHAPTER 16 | APOSTILLES.

Since October 15, 1981, the United States has been part of the 1961 Hague Convention abolishing the Requirement of Legalization for Foreign Public Documents (Only).

The Convention provides for the simplified certification of public (including notarized) documents to be used in countries that have joined the convention. Documents destined for use in participating countries and their territories should be certified by one of the officials in the jurisdiction in which the document has been executed. Said official must have been designated as competent to issue certifications by "Apostille" (usually in the office of the State Secretary of State of his/her counterpart) as provided for by the 1961 Hague Convention.

With this certification by the Hague Convention Apostille, the document is entitled to recognition in the country of intended use, and no certification by the U.S. Department of State, Authentications Office or legalization by the embassy or consulate is required.

For more information on countries participating in the 1961 Hague Convention (abolishing the requirement of legalization for foreign public documents -- Article 12) please visit: www.hcch.net.

To obtain an authentication, which is called an Apostille, for your US documents you will want to visit the web site of the Secretary of State where the document was issued for the procedure for that state. Example: You would contact the Secretary of the State of Michigan for a birth certificate that was issued in the state of Michigan.

The following index is a listing of the secretaries. You may contact their offices to find out specific details for your documents and the required formats and fees required for your individual documents.

ALABAMA (R) (CEO)
Hon. Beth Chapman
Secretary of State -E P.O.
Box 5616 Montgomery,
AL 36103 (334) 242-7200
Fax (334) 242-4993
Beth.chapman@sos.alab
ama.gov

ALASKA (R) (CEO)
Hon. Mead Treadwell
Lieutenant Governor -E
P.O. Box 110015 Juneau,
AK 99811 (907) 465-3520
Fax (907) 465-5400
lt.governor@alaska.gov

AMERICAN SAMOA (D)
Hon. Ipulasi A. Sunia
Lieutenant Governor -E
Office of the Governor
Pago Pago, AS 96799
(684) 633-4116
(684) 633-2269
administrator@asg-
gov.net

ARIZONA (R) (CEO)
Hon. Ken Bennett
Secretary of State - E
Capitol Executive Tower
7th Floor
1700 West Washington
St. Phoenix, AZ 85007
(602) 542-4285 Fax ((602)
542-1575
sosadmin@azsos.gov

ARKANSAS (R) (CEO)
Hon. Mark Martin
Secretary of State -E 256
State Capitol Building
Little Rock, AR 72201
(501) 682-1010 Fax (501)
682-3510
sos@sos.arkansas.gov

CALIFORNIA (D) (CEO)
Hon. Debra Bowen
Secretary of State –E
1500 11th Street
Sacramento, CA 95814
(916) 653-7244
Fax (916) 653-4795
secretarybowen@sos.ca.
gov

COLORADO (R) (CEO)
Hon. Scott Gessler
Secretary of State-E 1700
Broadway, Suite 250
Denver, CO 80290 (303)
894-2200 Fax (303) 869-
4860
secretary@sos.state.co.u
s

CONNECTICUT (D) (CEO)
Hon. Denise Merrill
Secretary of State -E
State Capitol, Room 104
Hartford, CT 06105 (860)
509-6200
Fax (860) 509-6209
denise.merrill@ct.gov
DELAWARE (D)
Hon. Jeffrey Bullock

Secretary of State -A
Townsend Building 401
Federal St, Ste. 3 Dover,
DE 19901 (302) 739-4111
Fax (302) 739-3811
Monique.hampton@stat
e.de.us

DISTRICT OF COLUMBIA
(D)
Hon. Cynthia Brock-Smith
Secretary of the District -
A 1350 Pennsylvania
Ave., NW Suite 419
Washington, DC 20004
(202) 727-6306 Fax (202)
727-3582
secretary@dc.gov

FLORIDA (R) (CEO)
Hon. Kurt Browning
Secretary of State -A 500
S. Bronough, Suite 100
Tallahassee, FL 32399
(850) 245-6500 Fax: (850)
245-6125
secretaryofstate@dos.sta
te.fl.us

GEORGIA (R) (CEO)
Hon. Brian Kemp
Secretary of State -E 214
State Capitol Atlanta, GA
30334 (404) 656-2881
Fax (404) 656-0513
sos@sos.ga.gov

GUAM (R)
KANSAS (R) (CEO)
Hon. Kris Kobach
Secretary of State –E
Memorial Hall – 1st Fl.
120 SW 10th Avenue
Topeka, KS 66612 (785)
296-4575
Fax (785) 368-8033
sos@sos.ks.gov

KENTUCKY (D) (CEO)
Hon. Elaine Walker
Secretary of State -E 700
Capital Ave., Suite 152
Frankfort, KY 40601 (502)
564-3490 Fax (502) 564-
5687
sos.secretary@ky.gov

LOUISIANA (R) (CEO)
Hon. Tom Schedler
Secretary of State –E P.O.
Box 94125 Baton Rouge,
LA 70804 (225) 342-4479
Fax (225) 342-5577
admin@sos.louisiana.gov

MAINE (R) (CEO)
Hon. Charles Summers
Secretary of State -LEG
148 State House Station
Augusta, ME 04333 (207)
626-8400
Fax (207) 287-8598
sos.office@maine.gov

MARYLAND (D)
Hon. John McDonough
Secretary of State -A 16
Francis Street Annapolis,
MD 21401 (410) 974-
5521
Fax (410) 974-5527
swiedemer@sos.state.m
d.us

MASSACHUSETTS (D)
(CEO) Hon. William
Galvin Secretary of
Cmwlth -E State House,
Room 337 Boston, MA
02133 (617) 727-9180
Fax (617) 742-4722
cis@sec.state.ma.us

MICHIGAN (R) (CEO)
Hon. Ruth Johnson
Secretary of State -E 430
W. Allegan Street
Lansing, MI 48918 (517)
373-2510
Fax (517) 373-0727
secretary@michigan.gov

MINNESOTA (D) (CEO)
Hon. Mark Ritchie
Secretary of State -E 180
State Office Building 100
Rev. Dr. Martin Luther
King Jr. Blvd. St. Paul, MN
55155 (651) 201-1328
Fax (651) 215-0682
secretary.state@state.m
n.us

MISSISSIPPI (R) (CEO)
Hon. C. Delbert
Hosemann, Jr. Secretary
of State-E P.O. Box 136
Jackson, MS 39205 (601)
359-1350
Fax (601) 359-6700
delbert.hosemann@sos.
ms.gov

MISSOURI (D) (CEO)
Hon. Robin Carnahan
Secretary of State -E
State Capitol, Room 208
Jefferson City, MO 65101
(573)751-4936
Fax (573)552-3082
SOSMain@sos.mo.gov

MONTANA (D) (CEO)
Hon. Linda McCulloch
Secretary of State -E P.O.
Box 202801 Helena, MT
59620 (406) 444-2034
Fax (406) 444-4249
sos@mt.gov
Hon. Ray Tenorio
Lieutenant Governor -E
P.O. Box 2950 Hagatna,
GU 96932 (671) 475-9380
x9 Fax (671) 472-2007
webmaster@guamletgov
ernor.net

HAWAII (D)
Hon. Brian Schatz
Lieutenant Governor -E
State Capitol, Fifth Floor
Honolulu, HI 96813 (808)

586-0255 Fax (808) 586-0231 ltgov@hawaii.gov

IDAHO (R) (CEO)
Hon. Ben Ysursa
Secretary of State –E P.O. Box 83720 Boise, ID 83720 (208) 334-2300 Fax (208) 334-2282 secstate@sos.idaho.gov

ILLINOIS (D)
Hon. Jesse White
Secretary of State -E 213 State Capitol Springfield, IL 62756 (217) 782-2201 Fax (217) 785-0358 jessewhite@ilsos.net

INDIANA (R) (CEO)
Hon. Charlie White
Secretary of State -E 201 State House Indianapolis, IN 46204 (317) 232-6532 Fax (317) 233-3283 sos@sos.in.gov

IOWA (R) (CEO)
Hon. Matt Schultz
Secretary of State -E State Capitol, Room 105 1007 E. Grand Ave. Des Moines, IA 50319 (515) 281-8993 Fax (515) 242-5952 sos@sos.state.ia.us

NEBRASKA (R) (CEO)
Hon. John Gale Secretary of State-E P.O. Box 94608 Lincoln, NE 68509 (402) 471-2554
Fax (402) 471-3237 secretaryofstate@nebraska.gov

NEVADA (D) (CEO)
Hon. Ross Miller
Secretary of State-E 101 North Carson Street, Suite 3 Carson City, NV 89701 (775) 684-5708 Fax (775) 684-5724 sosmail@sos.nv.gov

NEW HAMPSHIRE(D)(CEO)
Hon. William Gardner
Secretary of State-LEG State House Room 204 Concord, NH 03301 (603) 271-3242
Fax (603) 271-6316 kladd@sos.state.nh.us

NEW JERSEY (R) (CEO)
Hon. Kim Guadagno
Lieutenant Governor -E P.O. Box 300 Trenton, NJ 08625 (609) 777-2581 Fax (609) 777-1764 lt.governor@gov.state.nj.us

NEW MEXICO (R) (CEO)
Hon. Dianna Duran
Secretary of State -E 325 Don Gaspar, Suite 300 Capitol Annex Santa Fe, NM 87503 (505) 827-3600 Fax (505) 827-3634 diannaj.duran@state.nm.us

NEW YORK (I)
Hon. Ruth Noemí Colón
Acting Secretary of State -A One Commerce Plaza 99 Washington Ave, Ste.1100 Albany, NY 12231 (518) 486-9844 Fax (518) 474-4765 malli@dos.state.ny.us

NORTH CAROLINA (D)
Hon. Elaine Marshall
Secretary of State -E P.O. Box 29622 Raleigh, NC 27626 (919) 807-2005 Fax (919) 807-2010 emarshal@sosnc.com

NORTH DAKOTA (R) (CEO)
Hon. Alvin (Al) A. Jaeger
Secretary of State -E 600 East Boulevard Dept 108 Bismarck, ND 58505 (701) 328-2900 Fax (701) 328-2992 sos@nd.gov

OHIO (R) (CEO)
Hon. Jon Husted
Secretary of State -E 180
E. Broad Street
Columbus, OH 43215
(614) 466-2655
Fax (614) 644-0649
jhusted@sos.state.oh.us

OKLAHOMA (R)
Hon. Glenn Coffee
Secretary of State -A
2300 N. Lincoln Blvd.
Suite 101
Oklahoma City, OK 73105
(405) 521-3912 Fax (405)
521-3771
michelle.waddell@sos.ok
.gov

OREGON (D) (CEO)
Hon. Kate Brown
Secretary of State -E 136
State Capitol Salem, OR
97301 (503) 986-1523
Fax (503) 986-1616
oregon.sos@sos.or.us

PENNSYLVANIA (R) (CEO)
Hon. Carol Aichele Acting
Secretary of the Cmwlth-
A 302 North Office
Building Harrisburg, PA
17120 (717) 787-8727
Fax (717) 787-1734 ST-
PRESS@state.pa.us

PUERTO RICO (NPP)
Hon. Kenneth McClintock
Secretary of State -A
Department of State Box
9023271
San Juan, PR 00902 (787)
722-4010 Fax (787) 722-
2684
kenneth.mcclintock@yah
oo.com

RHODE ISLAND (D) (CEO)
Hon. A. Ralph Mollis
Secretary of State –E 82
Smith Street 217 State
House Providence, RI
02903 (401) 222-1035
Fax (401) 222-1356
armollis@sos.ri.gov

SOUTH CAROLINA (R)
Hon. Mark Hammond
Secretary of State-E P.O.
Box 11350 Columbia, SC
29211 (803) 734-2170
Fax (803) 734-1661
rdaggerhart@sos.sc.gov

SOUTH DAKOTA (R) (CEO)
Hon. Jason Gant
Secretary of State-E 500
E. Capitol Ave., Ste. 204
Pierre, SD 57501 (605)
773-3537 Fax (605) 773-
6580 sdsos@state.sd.us

TENNESSEE (R)
Hon. Tre Hargett
Secretary of State-LEG
First Floor, State Capitol
Nashville, TN 37243 (615)
741-2819 Fax (615) 741-
5962 tre.hargett@tn.gov

TEXAS (R) (CEO)
Hon. Esperanza "Hope"
Andrade Secretary of
State-A P.O. Box 12887
Austin, TX 78711 (512)
463-5770 Fax (512) 475-
2761
secretary@sos.state.tx.us

U.S. VIRGIN ISLANDS (D)
Hon. Gregory Francis
Lieutenant Governor -E
18 Kongens Gade St.
Thomas, VI 00801 (340)
774-2991
Fax (340) 774-6953
sonia.boyce@lgo-vi.gov

UTAH (R) (CEO)
Hon. Greg Bell Lieutenant
Governor -E Utah State
Capitol, Ste. 220 Salt Lake
City, UT 84114 (801) 538-
1041 Fax (801) 538-1133
gbell@utah.gov

VERMONT (D) (CEO)
Hon. Jim Condos
Secretary of State -E 26
Terrace Street
Montpelier, VT 05609
(802) 828-2148 Fax (802)
828-2496
jim.condos@sec.state.vt.
us

VIRGINIA (R)
Hon. Janet Polarek
Secretary of Cmwlth-A
P.O. Box 2454 Richmond,
VA 23218 (804) 786-2441
Fax (804) 371-0017
Socmail@governor.virgini
a.gov

WASHINGTON (R) (CEO)
Hon. Sam Reed Secretary
of State -E P.O. Box
40220 Olympia, WA
98504 (360) 902-4151
Fax (360) 586-5629

sam.reed@sos.wa.gov

WEST VIRGINIA (D) (CEO)
Hon. Natalie Tennant
Secretary of State -E
Building 1, Suite-157K
1900 Kanawha Blvd., E.
Charleston, WV 25305
(304) 558-6000
Fax (304) 558-0900
wvsos@wvsos.com

WISCONSIN (D)
Hon. Douglas La Follette
Secretary of State –E P.O.
Box 7848 Madison, WI
53707 (608) 266-8888
Fax (608) 266-3159
doug.lafollette@sos.state
.wi.us

WYOMING (R) (CEO)
Hon. Max Maxfield
Secretary of State -E
State Capitol Building 200

West 24th Cheyenne, WY
82002 (307) 777-7378
Fax (307) 777-6217
Secofstate@state.wy.us
CONTACT NASS:
Leslie Reynolds Executive
Director
reynolds@sso.org
Kay Stimson
Communications
Director/ Special Projects
Manager nass@sso.org
Stacy Fisher Executive
Assistant/ Events
Coordinator
sfisher@sso.org
John Milhofer Policy
Analyst
jmilhofer@sso.org
444 N. Capitol Street, NW
Suite 401 Washington,
D.C. 20001 (202) 624-
3525 (202)624-3527 fax
www.nass.org

CHAPTER 17
ITALIAN
TRANSLATIONS.

CHAPTER 17 | ITALIAN TRANSLATIONS.

All non-Italian documents related to your Italian line must be translated into Italian with the exception of you ancestor's naturalization documents.

Check the categories section and determine which specific documents and compare the list with the Italian consulate of your jurisdiction.

Quality & Accuracy

There are many services that offer professional Italian translation service and specialize in Italian translations of US Vital records for Italian Dual Citizenship.

What ever you do, DO NOT, use a machine or internet program to translate your documents. Do not sit with a dictionary assuming you can properly translate your documents. They will in most cases be rejected causing significant delays in the processing of your application.

Use only professional, human translators for all required document translations.

All US certificates being used for Italian Dual Citizenship must be in "certified copy" a.k.a. "long form" or "full form" (not "certification" or "abstract"). Said forms can be obtained at the Vital Statistics Office of the State in which the birth/marriage/death took place.

Certificates reporting only the "County" of birth can not be accepted. You must request the Vital Statistics Authority to state the city of birth. The document must contain a legible signature from the county clerk as well a have a raised seal in order to be authenticated.

Get Professional Italian Translations – www.myitaliandualcitizenship.com

CHAPTER 18
APPLICATION REVIEW.

CHAPTER 18 | APPLICAITON REVIEW.

Once you have procured your Italian and US documents along with your ancestor's naturalization documents you should methodically review them for each person in your line. There are services that can do this for you if you would like.

For example compare your Grandfather's Birth with his marriage and death certificates (if applicable).

Consider if everything matches. Look at his name, date of birth, place of birth, parent's names.

Take note of all items that do not match. These are your possible areas of concern that you may wish to address ahead of time.

EXAMPLE.

GRANDFATHER			
Document	Birth Certificate	Marriage Certificate	Death Certificate
Name	Antonino Rossi	Anthony Rossi	Tony Ross
Date of Birth	April 4, 1890	April 2, 1890	April 2, 1890

In this situation it is always better to be fully prepared and know what is coming. By knowing what possible errors will be noticed you will be able to prepare your documents accordingly with one of several options.

1. Do nothing and wait for the consulate to tell you to fix them.

2. Prepare an affidavit ahead of time and get it translated with an Apostille.

3. Have the individual documents amended to match the original spelling on the Italian birth certificate and date of birth on the Italian document.

4. Get a court order saying that they are in fact the same person and the documents are in error.

Remember, it will be the final decision of the Italian consulate if they accept these options and your discretion as to which route you elect to take. If you elect to do any of them and you are told later to amend the documents by the consulate, you are NOT denied your Italian citizenship. You are simply being asked to correct them and come back later when you are done. Typically they will give you about 90 days to return with the corrected items without you having to reschedule another appointment.

CHAPTER 19
YOUR
APPLICATION.

CHAPTER 19 | YOUR APPLICATION.

Each consulate will use their own individual forms for your application. Typically they will be forms 1, 2, 3, and 4 as well as a brief cover letter.

Examples of these forms are in the forms section of this book. However, you should download current forms from the Consulate's web site of your jurisdiction, since individual consulates may use similar but not exact forms.

Points to remember when completing your application be sure to list a mailing address, email address and telephone number where they can reach you. Contact information must be updated and remain current throughout the process. If you move or transfer be sure to put in a change of address. You will be waiting in many cases, for a letter stating your citizenship is recognized so you don't want to miss it!

The next point is when completing the form is think European!

The dates are in DD/MM/YYYY format. Date first, then month, then the year.

Print clearly taking the information directly from the documents you have procured.

Who fills out what form:

Form 1 – Each applicant for citizenship by descent, over the age of 18, completes the form. Sign this form in front of a notary public OR wait and sign it at the consulate.

Form 2 - Each applicant for citizenship by descent, over the age of 18, completes the form. Sign this form in front of a notary public OR wait and sign it at the consulate.

Form 3 - Each Living Ascendant in your line of inheritence for citizenship by descent, over the age of 18, completes the form. Sign this form in front of a notary public OR wait and sign it at the consulate.

Form 4 – Each applicant for citizenship by descent, over the age of 18, must complete this form for each Deceased Ascendant in your line of inheritence. Sign this form in front of a notary public OR wait and sign it at the consulate.

EXAMPLE COMUNE DECLARATION

YOUR FULL NAME (MAIDEN)

YOUR STREET ADDRESS

YOUR CITY, STATE ZIP CODE

YOUR TELEPHONE NUMBER

YOUR EMAIL ADDRESS

Date: _____

Dear Sir or Madam,

Please accept this completed packet of documents and affidavits. All have been properly notarized, translated and affixed with Apostilles.

I would like to register my civil status documents in the comune of my Italian ancestor:

Comune Di _____

Thank you for your prompt attention to my application.

Sincerely,

_____

SIGNED BY YOU

CHAPTER 20
APPOINTMENT DAY.

CHAPTER 20 | APPOINTMENT DAY.

By now you should be fully prepared for your appointment. Many times individuals will wonder what will happen at the Italian consulate.

Most times, despite some negative press, *the appointments go very smoothly if the individual followed the instructions, and did not try to beat the process, or take short cuts.*

You are trying to have your Italian citizenship recognized. There are not any real short cuts. Nor did our ancestor's find any when they sailed toward a new land with little money and unable to speak the language.

Payment.

As of July 8th, 2014, all applicants are subject to the payment of €300 (subject to change) consular fee (Law n. 66 April 24th, 2014 and modifications Law n. 89 June 23rd, 2014 at. 5-bid, comma.) Payment must be made in dollars at most consulates. Some consulates will ask for a wire to be sent in advance. And yet others only accept cash and others only accept money orders. To determine how you should remit payment and the exhange rate be sure to **check your consulate website** to determine the exact amnout you must pay before or at your appointment. Each applicant must pay a fee to submit their application.

How to dress.

As your mother may have told you, first impressions do matter.

Dress like an Italian. You are Italian after all. To do so is to show respect for the process, the consulate, yourself and your ancestors.

Don't go in wearing a jogging suit, tennis shoes, bed head and slurping on a big 2-liter of diet coke! ;-)

I recommend business casual or better, or for more clarification, your Sunday best. Is it a requirement, not at all. It is merely a recommendation.

The Appointment.

At some consulates you will stand in very long lines waiting to get into the building, then stand even longer before being seen at the window. Once you reach the window you will pass the documents through the glass opening and be reviewed right where you stand.

Other consulates will be plush, with a beautiful waiting room, where you will be greeted kindly, then escorted back to a conference room or to the intake professional's desk.

At that point there is little you can do but graciously answer any questions and provide the documentation they are asking for.

One should keep in mind that the consulate employees work for the Italian ministry not for you, unlike the US interpretation of civil service. These workers serve the ministry <u>not the people</u>; more specifically they do not serve Italian – American. When you consider the very different work philosophy of the average Italian worker.

I recommend that you remain calm, no matter the findings, and graciously bite your tongue to insure a smooth process along the way.

Remember the level of bureaucracy is immense and you are signing up to be Italian. As a good Italian you must learn to '*work to live not live to work*'.

Likewise, the process will unfold at it's own tempo, not yours, and you can do <u>nothing</u> but allow it to do so. It must breath and unfold in it's own time. The sooner you accept that the smoother the process will become.

<u>You will not ever speed the process up by having an entitlistic attitude or a demanding nature.</u>

At this point you know you are qualified so it is a matter of time and money. How much time will it take, how many hoops will you jump through and how much will it cost in documents, Apostilles, translations and potential amendments. So roll your sleeves up and get your mind around the fact that this will unfold in it's own time.

If there is an issue, kindly offer an explanation if you have one, for example, "Yes, he Americanized his first name from Antonio to Anthony...I have provided an affidavit with Apostille and translation here.", while handing them the affidavit.

Despite some individual interpretations, the person you will meet with is a professional. They are highly educated and typically will even have obtained a PhD. They are not some minimum wage employee tasked to accept paperwork. They are highly respected professionals who are in a position to greatly assist you. How you interact with them will impact the process.

I recommend that you foster a positive professional relationship and ask very little if anything of them in return. They are bombarded with applications and hear every excuse and American justification that can be dreamed up. Remember, there are no short cuts so it is better not to look like you are trying to get over or beat the system.

If you are sent away.

If you are qualified, no worries. If you are sent away it is simply the consulate saying, 'fix this or get me that".

You are in no way denied your Italian citizenship and they will give you about 90 days to return the missing information to them. They should also provide you with a short list of the deficiencies that you will need to address.

Highly Recommended.

- ❖ Review the consulate website in advance for requirements.

- ❖ Make sure you have remitted or bring the payment with you as directed on the Italian Consulate web site that has jurisdiction over your residence.

- ❖ Take a small pen and paper with you to take notes.

❖ Ask what the standard turn around time is.

❖ Ask for the person's business card and/or contact information.

❖ Ask where to send back any additional information via UPS, Fed Ex or USPS Express so you do not have to make an additional trip to the consulate.

What do you need to know.

Nothing. Only your family information that you have before you in your packet. There are no tests, you do not need to speak Italian, you don't need to know any Italian history. You need to know what documents are required and have them authenticated with an Apostille and proper Italian translation. That is it.

There are several sections in the book you may find interesting that I recommend you review but this is NOT a requirement.

You will NOT be tested. You will not be tested on anything. Nothing at all.

Spouse applications.

There are different rules and requriements for a spouse application, which include but are not limited to background checks and a language requirement as of December of 2018.

CHAPTER 21
WHAT
HAPPENS NEXT.

CHAPTER 21 | WHAT HAPPENS NEXT.

Depending on how you leave the consulate, you will be done, waiting on the letter saying you are recognized or you will be returning the requirements for them to review a second time. At a certain point they will confirm they have all they need and you will begin the waiting process. At your interview you should have asked about the turn around time for the particular consulate of your jurisdiction.

It seems to average between six months to even two years depending on the consulate's volume.

The intake professional at the Italian consulate should have provided you with their business card of contact information. DO NOT bombard them with weekly or even monthly emailing asking for an update. They will not respond and find it very annoying. And keep in mind, you don't want to do anything to slow down the process. The consulates are highly overwhelmed with an increasing number of applications.

A relatively new program has been implemented which may be helpful for you. It is a call center service to receive information on the applications for citizenship.

It's overall effectiveness has yet to be determined but it is worth mentioning.

THE CALL CENTER

A service to receive information on the applications for citizenship

The Department for Civil Liberties and Immigration has organized a call center that makes it possible to:

• Provide information on the procedures to obtain the Italian citizenship
• Provide applicants with information on the progress of the applications; for this option the identification code of the file is needed.

Information on the progress of cases will be given to applicants who will have to supply the following data:

- Code of the file
- Name and surname
- Date and place of birth, place of residence
- Prefecture – Utg where the application was submitted

The service is available as follows:

Monday - Friday
9-14:00
14.30-18.30

By dialing :

011-39-06– 48042101
011-39-06– 48042102
011-39-06– 48042103
011-39-06– 48042104

All Applicants

Due to the huge workload and number of e-mail messages, Italian consulates generally do not answer questions of a general nature that are already covered on the website and by the telephone service.

Consider as an example, that just one consulate, with 15,000 registered Italians and 1.3 million Americans of Italian origin within the Consulate's jurisdiction, employees are asked to either assist the public during opening hours or to handle paperwork. There is a dedicated time for answering questions over the phone, which is Monday-Friday between 2.00 and 4.00. If the line rings free, that means the operators are on another line answering other calls. They urge you to consult their website where you will find answers to most of your questions.

Please avoid requests of general information already available on this website or through the telephone service.

Don't call us

As shocking as it may be that is the gist of it at some of the consulates with an exceptional work load. Due to the enormous interest and number of applications, the time period required for obtaining Italian citizenship has increased in the last few years. The consulates usually only contact applicants when information or documents are needed. If you are an applicant and have not been contacted since the completion of your application, your application is being processed.

If they need to contact you in order to request more data or to announce that your request has been successfully finalized, they will invariably do so.

Please understand also that you will have to wait for your turn not only for your application to be processed, but to be contacted by the office when many applicants need to be contacted in the same period.

As surprising as it may be, most consulates will ask that you NOT contact them for an update on the status of your application.

Further, that if any relevant fact concerning your application should become evident, you will be notified as soon as your turn comes.

However, do inform them in writing if your contact details (address, telephone etc.) have changed.

Upon completion of the file, the consulate will send confirmation in writing that your Italian citizenship has been recognized. This can take any where from six months to two years depending on your consulate and the comune (town) in Italy where your documents are registered.

***Ask when you are at your appointment how you will be notified the process is completed and what the average turn around time is. ***

CHAPTER 22
YOUR ITALIAN
BIRTH CERTIFICATE.

CHAPTER 22 | YOUR ITALIAN BIRTH CERTIFICATE.

The reason that, as a part of this process, you are required to submit all your documents proving your lineage is to simply, set the matter right.

When your ancestor left Italy he or she was supposed to report to the Italian government any changes in his or her civil status (birth's, marriage, deaths, name changes, naturalizations). It most cases your ancestor had no idea this was required, generally had no intention of ever returning to Italy and the Italian government was never updated.

Now, that you have submitted all of the documents and selected your Ancestor's birth city to register your documents, each event will be recorded in that little town just as if it occurred there and all the records will become up to date.

Once the consulate informs you that your citizenship has been successfully recognized you will then be required to obtain a certified copy of your ITALIAN birth certificate from the town where the documents were registered in Italy.

So, lets say you were born in Baltimore you will need the following information to request it on your own, as shown in the section for Italian vital records or to order it though a service. Once you have the document you will be able to obtain your Italian passport.

To order the document online visit: myitaliandualcitizenship.com

Information to order your Italian Birth Certicate.

FULL NAME AT BIRTH: JOHN JAMES VENDETTI

DATE OF BIRTH: 16 APRIL 1959

NAME OF MOTHER (MAIDEN): HARRIET MARIE JOHNSON

NAME OF FATHER: VINCENZO VENDETTI

BORN IN: BALTIMORE, MARYLAND, USA (OR WHEREVER)

REGISTERED IN: NAME OF COMUNE (CITY/TOWN), PROVIENCE, ITALY

MONTH/YEAR YOUR ITALIAN CITIZENSHIP WAS RECOGNIZED: JAN 2009

CHAPTER 23
A.I.R.E
REGAISTRATION.

CHAPTER 23 | A.I.R.E. REGISTRATION.

Now that your Italian citizenship is recognized you are effectively an Italian citizen. You must comply with Italian law. If your residence is OUTSIDE OF ITALY you are considered an alien living abroad by the Italian government.

Law no. 470/1988 states that all Italian citizens who intend to live abroad for a minimum of 12 months must register in **A.I.R.E. (Registry of Italian Nationals residing abroad)** within 90 days of arriving in their country of destination. Even those who emigrated before this law went into effect must register.

Application for registration with the A.I.R.E. can be made (by an individual Italian citizen and family members) through the Italian Consulate in the country of residence. A.I.R.E. registration is necessary for all registry-related procedures and in order to obtain any and all documents and certificates issued by the Consulate as well as requests for passport renewal or issuance.

Registration permits the exercise of all the rights and duties of a citizen depending on each individual situation. An Italian citizen registered in the A.I.R.E. will be deleted from the ASL (Local Health Insurance System in Italy).

To register in A.I.R.E., proceed as follows:

Fill out and complete the A.I.R.E. application form ;

Sign and date the form in the appropriate space;

Attach a photocopy of the following documents:

FOR DUAL CITIZENS:

Italian passport or proof of Italian citizenship;

Copy of the US passport ;

Verification of address in our jurisdiction (as above).

The above documentation must be included for each Italian family member requesting A.I.R.E. registration. Applications, which are illegible, not signed, partially complete or lacking the required documentation will not be accepted and will be returned to the sender.

Upon determining eligibility to register in the A.I.R.E., the consulate will forward the application directly to the appropriate town in Italy (last town of established residence or where your birth certificate has been sent for registration).

The applicant will be removed from the Resident Population Registry (A.P.R.) and entered in the Registry of Italian Nationals Residing Abroad (A.I.R.E.). Registration with AIRE can, therefore, be done in the absence of any direct initiative on the part of the citizen concerned, who will, however, be notified of the fact by means of an administrative act of the municipality.

UPDATE A.I.R.E. INFORMATION

The Italian citizen is obliged to notify his/her municipality of origin of any and all changes in civil status (birth, marital status, divorce, death, change of name), citizenship and address.

Transfer to another Consulate jurisdiction

If you are moving to another Consulate, you have to communicate via mail or e-mail which Consular jurisdiction you are transferring to. We inform that it is necessary to establish contact promptly with the competent Consulate or Embassy in order to know the procedure of registration and communicate the change of Consular jurisdiction to the Italian municipality.

Change of address inside the Consular jurisdiction

Notifying the Consulate of changes regarding address is necessary to receive immediate communication of electoral convocations.

You have to communicate via mail or e-mail:
- Personal data (First and last name, place and date of birth);
- E-mail and telephone number;
- Complete new and old address;
- Which family member the address change is for.

In case some of the family members will not move with you, let them know their address.

CHAPTER 24
CERTIFICATE OF
ITALIAN CITIZENSHIP.

CHAPTER 24 | CERTIFICATE OF ITALIAN CITIZENSHIP.

After your Italian citizenship has been recognized you can request a certificate of Italian citizenship from the Italian consulate of your jurisdiction. Obtaining this at the time your citizenship is recognized is not automatic.

Although it is rewarding to look at the document, I have yet to find a reason to present the certificate to any official authority in Italy or any other government agency abroad. I do recommend asking for it along the way. It is a very nice family heirloom and a great graduation gift! Something like a gift certificate to the European Union for that nearly high school graduate in your family!

If you would like to obtain this the fee is minimal. Typically the consulate will charge a fee of approximately $10 USD and can be requested from the Italian consulate of your jurisdiction.

You should mail a money order along with a prepaid self addressed envelope. Your cover letter should indicated you would like to obtain your "certificate of Italian citizenship". You can confirm the fees with the local consulate.

CHAPTER 25
YOUR ITALIAN PASSPORT.

CHAPTER 25 | ITALIAN PASSPORTS.

Once your Italian citizenship has been recognized, you are registered in A.I.R.E. and you have obtained your Italian birth certificate you can apply for your Italian passport.

The form is very straightforward and a sample form is included in the form sections of this book. You should confirm the requirements with the Italian consulate of your jurisdiction and anticipate presenting yourself to the consulate for it's issuance.

BIOMETRIC PASSPORTS.

You must schedule an appointment to apply for your Italian passport. Citizens must appear in person at the consulate in order for the Consulate to issue biometric passports with fingerprints. Therefore it will be no longer possible to apply by mail or at honorary offices.

People who hold an Italian passport that was issued or renewed by a Questura in Italy or by another Italian consulate abroad may send the preliminary documentation by mail so that this office may request the necessary authorization.
When the consulate receives authorization, they will then notify the applicant that he/she may appear in person for fingerprinting and issuance of the passport.

This procedure could also be followed by people not registered in AIRE.

Fingerprinting is not required for children under 12 years of age.

HOW TO OBTAIN YOUR ITALIAN PASSPORT

Passports issued on or after February 4, 2003 are valid for ten years (rather than five as they were before) and shall not be renewed upon expiry.

As of November 25, 2009, it is mandatory for children under 18 years of age to have their own individual passports as they may no longer be listed on their parents' passport.

The listing of those children who appear on their parents' passports before the new law took effect will remain in effect until the passport's expiration date.

The temporary validity will depend on the child's age: 3 years for children from zero to three years of age; 5 years for children from three to eighteen years old.

The adult Italian citizen, who requests a passport for the first time, must submit the application and documentation required in person to the offices of the Consulate.
Those who are already in possession of an Italian passport, may appear in person or send an application and documentation by mail.

COST OF ISSUANCE OF PASSPORTS

The cost for the issuance of passports is updated every quarter (3 months) and is based on the Euro/Dollar exchange rate.

Payment may be made by cash or money order only.

Money orders must be made out to "Italian Consulate General of Italy".

The consulates do not accept personal checks, or credit card.

The cost of issuance of passports is approximately $125, included the annual fee. (Check the consulate website for current fees).

The fees applied by the Consulate are the fees existing on the date of issue, not the date of submission of the application .

In case of quarterly increase of the cost of the issuance the Consulate will request the payment of the difference in costs unless the cost has decreased in which case the applicant will receive the change back.

ANNUAL FEE

The annual fee is about $55 (check the consulate website for current fees).

Italian citizens who reside in the United States, must pay the government tax on their passport after the first year of issuance, only if they are traveling to or from Italy.

The payment of the tax is not required if one is traveling from the United States to any country other than Italy.

INCOMPLETE APPLICATIONS WILL BE RETURNED TO APPLICANTS

Documentation required for the issuance of a new passport:

1) Passport application form filled out and signed by applicant
2) Expired Italian passport + photocopy;
3) 2 passport size photographs (1 ½ "x1 ½ "white background, one signed by the applicant on the edge);
4) Valid Residency Permit (US Permanent Resident Card/US Visa/ Visa Waiver/ US certificate of Naturalization) + photocopy (copy only if mailed);
5) Money order or cash for the amount indicated above
6) Consent form of spouse or other parent in case applicant has minor children (under 18), with:
    - photocopy of other parents ID/passport;
    - photocopy of children's birth certificate indicating both parents last names.

Please note: if the other parent is not Italian citizen or a citizen of the European Union, the signature must be authenticated by a consular officer (at the time of submission of the application), or by a Vice Consul, or by a Notary Public.

PASSPORTS FOR PARENTS OF MINORS

An Italian citizen, parent of a minor, in order to obtain his/her own passport, with the paperwork requested, must submit the consent of the other parent and a copy of the birth certificate of the minor.

If the other parent refuses to sign the act of consent for issuance of the passport, it is necessary for the applicant to go in person to the Passport Office with a signed letter explaining the motives for which the other parent refuses to come sign the act of consent. This letter must give the complete address and telephone numbers of the non-consenting parent.

If the motives for dissent are found to be unjustified, the Consul General can authorize the Office by special decree to issue the minor's parent's passport.

PASSPORTS FOR MINORS

The application must be signed by both parents or by one of them with the written and signed consent of the other.

If the minor was born abroad it is necessary to provide the authorized Consulate with his/her birth certificate, duly legalized (see instruction in Vital records registration).

If one of the parents refuses to sign the act of consent for issuance of the passport to the minor child or for listing the minor child on his/her passport, it is necessary for the applicant parent to go in person to the Passport Office with a signed letter explaining the motives for which the other parent refuses to come sign the act of consent. This letter must give the complete address and telephone numbers of the non-consenting parent.

If the motives for dissent are found to be unjustified, the Consul General can authorize the Office by special decree to issue the minor's passport.

THEFT OR LOSS OF PASSPORT: ISSUANCE OF A NEW PASSPORT

To obtain a new passport, the citizen must file the claim of theft or loss of passport at the local police authority.

THEFT OR LOSS OF PASSPORT: ISSUANCE OF A TRAVEL DOCUMENT

An Italian citizen in an emergency situation - e.g. a tourist in transit who must leave unexpectedly or who loses or is robbed of his/her passport - and has no time to apply for NULLA OSTA (clearance) for the issuance of a new passport from the Police Commissary or Consulate that issued the lost document, the Consulate General issues a document called a "Travel Document", which is valid only for re-entry in Italy. In order to obtain this document, it is necessary to file the claim of theft or loss of passport at the local police authority.

CHAPTER 26
YOUR ITALIAN MARRIAGE CERTIFICATE.

CHAPTER 26 | YOUR ITALIAN MARRIAGE CERTIFICATE.

After your Italian citizenship has been recognized you will need to have your marriage registered just as your birth was registered in Italy. This will occur when you apply for your Italian citizenship by descent. After you are informed your birth is registered you can also order a certified copy of your Italian marriage certificate. You will need this for your spouse to have Italian citizenship through marriage.

The reason that, as a part of this process, you are required to submit all your documents proving your lineage is to simply, set the matter right.

When your ancestor left Italy he or she was supposed to report to the Italian government any changes in his or her civil status (birth's, marriage, deaths, name changes, naturalizations). It most cases your ancestor had no idea this was required, generally had no intention of ever returning to Italy and the Italian government was never updated.

Now, that you have submitted all of the documents and selected your Ancestor's birth city to register your documents, each event will be recorded in that little town just as if it occurred there and all the records will become up to date.

Once the consulate informs you that your citizenship has been successfully recognized you will then be required to obtain a certified copy of your ITALIAN birth certificate from the town where the documents were registered in Italy.

So, lets say you were born in Baltimore you will need the following information to request it on your own, as shown in the section for Italian vital records or to order it though a service. Once you have the document you will be able to obtain your Italian passport.

To order an Italian Marriage Record online visit: myitaliandualcitizenship.com

SAMPLE INFORMATION REQUIRED TO OBTAIN

YOUR MARRIAGE CERTIFICATE FROM ITALY

FULL NAME OF GROOM AT BIRTH: JOHN JAMES VENDETTI

GROOM'S DATE OF BIRTH: 16 APRIL 1959

NAME OF GROOMS' MOTHER (MAIDEN): HARRIET MARIE JOHNSON

NAME OF GROOM'S FATHER: VINCENZO VENDETTI

GROOM BORN IN: BALTIMORE, MARYLAND, USA (OR WHEREVER)

DATE OF MARRIAGE: 19 JUNE 1999

PLACE OF MARRIAGE: NEW YORK CITY, NEW YORK, USA

NAME OF BRIDE: SUSAN ANNE GREEN

NAME OF BRIDES' MOTHER (MAIDEN): ANNE MARIE SMITH

NAME OF BRIDE'S FATHER: STEVEN ARNOLD GREEN

BRIDE'S DATE OF BIRTH: 25 MAY 1961

BRIDES PLACE OF BIRTH: DETROIT, MICHIGAN, USA

MARRIAGE REGISTERED IN WHAT ITALIAN COMUNE (CITY):   LUCCA, LUCCA, ITALY

YEAR YOUR MARRIAGE WAS REGISTERED IN ITALY: 2009

CHAPTER 27
ITALIAN CITIZENSHIP BY MARRIAGE OR CIVIL UNION (SAME-SEX MARRIAGE).

CHAPTER 27 | SPOUSES BY MARRIAGE OR CIVIL UNION (SAME-SEX MARRIAGE).

After your Italian citizenship is recognized, you have registered in A.I.R.E., and obtained a copy of your Italian birth certificate and Italian marriage certificate you can apply for your spouse to acquire Italian citizenship by marriage.

If the marriage occurred prior to April 27, 1983, a foreign female who married an Italian male citizen has automatically acquired Italian citizenship.

If the marriage occurred after April 27, 1983, the foreign spouse (male or female) of an Italian citizen can apply for citizenship through the "Prefettura in Italy" if he or she has established residence in Italy for two years. If he or she resides abroad, the request should be submitted through the appropriate Consulate after three years of uninterrupted marriage. Your spouse must provide a lack of criminal record and lack of national security concerns

You should contact the citizenship office of the Consulate General of Italy of your jurisdiction for more information regarding the documents that are required.

Citizenship by Marriage to an Italian Citizen

(Law n. 91 of February 5 1992)

The foreign spouse of an Italian citizen may apply for Italian citizenship to the Prefettura after being married for 2 years, if they reside in Italy, and to the Italian Consulate after being married for 3 years if they reside abroad.

The above periods are reduced by half if the spouses have biological or adopted children.

Two basic requirements to be met prior to submitting the application are:

       - the marriage must have already been registered at the Town Hall in Italy;
       - the Italian spouse must be registered at the Consulate as an Italian Citizen Residing Abroad (A.I.R.E.).

The application must be accompanied by the following documents and the receipt of the payment of apparoximately €200.00 (confirm current rates and payment methods on the Italian consulate website).

Documents that must be provided by the applicant:

- valid passport of both spouses;
- proof of residency for the foreign spouse: if a US national, the foreign spouse is required to show proof of residency (driver's license, utility bill or bank statement); for all other nationalities, the foreign spouse is required to show proof of legal residence in the United States (Green Card, Visa or other);
- birth certificate of the applicant.

Birth certificates issued in countries other than the U.S.A. must comply with the local regulations on the legalization of documents. They must be translated into Italian and the translation certified by the Italian Consulate/Embassy in the country where the document was issued or by other competent office (such a local court).

For further information, please visit the Italian consular network at: www.esteri.it.

- For applicants born in the USA the birth certificate must be in Long Form legalized with Apostille;
- criminal records from the Police Authorities of applicant's (1) place of birth and (2) each US State/Country where he/she resided after the age of 14 (see instructions below);
- marriage certificate (estratto del certificato di matrimonio) issued by the Town Hall (Comune) in Italy where the marriage was registered.
- Please note that the estratto is valid for six months;

Documents provided by the Italian Consulate

- certificate of citizenship for the Italian spouse;
- stato di famiglia.

The applicant with incomplete documentation will be allowed to submit the missing documents within a period of time established by the Italian Consulate. If he/she fails to do so the application will not be approved.

The processing time is about 500 days, from the day in which complete documentation have been submitted.

Italian citizenship through marriage or civil union (same-sex-marriage) to an Italian citizen is regulated by Articles 5, 6, 7 and 8 of the law of Citizenship n. 91 of 1992.

Requirements

- Italian residents **married** to Italian citizens can apply after two years of legal residency. The term is reduced by half when children are born or legally adopted within the couple (please note that Italian consulates abroad do not process citizenship application of Italian residents).
- **Foreign nationals** (or stateless persons) that are resident outside Italy are eligible to apply three years after the date of marriage / civil union to an Italian Citizen. The term is reduced by half when children are born or legally adopted within the couple.
- If the marriage / civil union was celebrated outside Italy, an Italian Comune must have registered it prior to application.
- The Italian spouse must be registered in the Registry of Italians citizens Resident Abroad (A.I.R.E.);
- The marriage / Civil Union must be current at the time of application and must remain so untilcitizenship is granted. In case of divorce / dissolution / annulment of marriage, legal or de-facto separation of the couple or decease of the Italian spouse in the course of the process, the application will be closed and citizenship will not be granted;
- The applicant must have not been convicted by Italian authorities for crimes leading to a penalty of 3 years or more in prison;
- The applicant must have not been convicted by a foreign judiciary authority for non-political crimes leading to a penalty of 1 year or more in prison;

- The applicant must have not been convicted for those crimes against the State listed in Book 2, Title I, items, I,II and III of the Italia Penal code;
- The applicant must not pose a known threat to the security and safety of the Republic of Italy.
- The applicant must be proficient in the Italian language to the level B1 or higher of the EU Language Framework. A certificate of proficiency issued by an approved school must be provided. it is infact to be noted that as of December 4th 2018 (Law. 132 – Dec. 1st 2018) applicants must be accomplished in the Italian language to the level B1 (or higher) of the EU Common Language Framework. Only certifications issued by such institutions will be accepted for the purpose of their application.

How to obtain certificates of good conduct

Those who have resided in the U.S. must provide:

1) Certificate of good conduct issued by Federal Bureau of Investigation, CJIS Division – Attn. SCU-MOD/D2 – 1000 Custer Hallow Road, Clarksburg, West Virginia 26306 – Tel (304) 625-3878

2) Certificate of good conduct issued by the Central Police Office of each town of residence.

For all US States or foreign countries, you are required to get in contact directly with the Italian Consular Authority competent for that area.

Non-EU citizens who resided in Italy for at least six months will also have to submit Certificato Generale del Casellario Giudiziale and Certificato dei Carichi Pendenti issued by the Procura della Repubblica/Pretura and Tribunale of where they resided.

NOTE: All criminal records documents must be presented in original and require the Apostille except for the FBI document. All documents must be submitted with their Italian translation.

Criminal records are valid for three months, unless otherwise specified.

The petition, the above documents and their translations must be submitted in 4 copies (one original and 3 sets of photocopies). The petition must be signed and dated at the time of the appointment.

AL CONSOLATO GENERALE D'ITALIA

_____

ISTANZA DI RICONOSCIMENTO DELLA CITTADINANZA ITALIANA AI SENSI DELL'
ART. 10, II COMMA, DELLA LEGGE N. 555/1912

La sottoscritta _____,

nata a _____ il _____,

coniugata con_____,

nato a _____ il _____,

matrimonio contratto in _____

il _____,

CHIEDE

Il riconoscimento della cittadinanza italiana per matrimonio ai sensi dell' art. 10,
II common L. 555/1912. Dichiara al riguardo di non aver mai rinunciato alla
cittadinanza italiana davanti ad alcuna Autorita Italiana in Italia o
Rappresentanza Consolare all'estro.

Lugo e data _____

_____

firma

211

Processing Time for Spouse Applications

There is a great deal of debate regarding the processing time for spouse applications.

After the "Italian" applicant is recognized, the spouse can apply through marriage. They acquire the required documents, make their appointment at the consulate, are accepted by the consulate and then the wait begins.

Once the consulate has all of the spouse's completed application it is sent to the Itlaian Ministry where it has a shelf life of 500 days. The applications, at the time of this publication, will sit for a waiting period of 500 days before processing through the Ministry. This is a built in deterrent to eliminate the attempts to gain European Union citizenship for ill or inappropriate reasoning beyond the bonds of matrimony. People do still marry just for the sake of a passport to a certain country.

So be prepared that despite the speed in which a spouse application may be accepted it can reasonably take 1-1/2 – to two (2) full years before it will become finalized through the Italian Ministry. This is not a decision of any one individual at the local Italian Consulate. This is a matter of procedure beyond the scope of the intake personnel you will meet.

It is recommended that you inquire at the time of your appointment what the turn around time will be for the application as processing time at each consulate can vary.

You should therefore, plan accordingly.

CHAPTER 28
ITALIAN CULTURAL CLUBS.

CHAPTER 28 | ITALIAN CLUBS & MEMBERSHIPS.

The National Italian American Foundation (NIAF) is a 501 (c) (3) nonprofit, nonpartisan educational foundation that promotes Italian American culture and heritage. NIAF serves as a resource on the Italian American community and has educational and youth programs including scholarships, grants, heritage travel, and mentoring.

NIAF is also the voice for Italian Americans in Washington, DC and works closely with the Italian American Congressional Delegation and the White House. NIAF's mission includes advancing US – Italy business, political, and cultural relations and has a business council that promotes networking with corporate leaders.

The NIAF was founded in 1975 as a non-profit organization in Washington, DC. It is entirely non-partisan.

National Italian American Foundation (NIAF)
1860 19th Street NW Washington, DC 20009
Telephone: 202-387-0600

Website: www.niaf.org

OSIA is a national organization of men and women who represent the estimated 26 million Americans of Italian heritage, dedicated to promoting our culture, our traditions, our language, the legacy of our ancestors, and our contributions to the U.S. and the world.

They are sons and daughters, grandmothers and grandfathers. They are corporate executives and they are union members...young students and retirees...teachers and attorneys...doctors and firefighters...bakers and Wall Street brokers...and everything in between. They are philanthropists and they are model global citizens with purpose beyond ourselves. And they are proud and patriotic Americans of Italian heritage. They exemplify the very best of what it is to be Italian American.

OSIA National Headquarters
219 E St., NE
Washington, D.C. 20002
Phone:
1.800.552.OSIA
1.202.547.2900
Fax: 1.202.546.8168
Website: http://www.osia.org/

Italian-American Cultural Organizations

MIDC: http://www.myitaliandualcitizenship.com

CHAPTER 29
LEARNING ITALIAN.

CHAPTER 29 | LEARNING ITALIAN.

Home Based Learning Resources:

Fluenz

Telephone: 877-358-369

Website: http://www.fluenz.com/languages/italian/learn-italian/index.html

Rosetta Stone

135 W. Market St.

Harrisonburg, VA 22801

USA

Telephone: 1.800.767.3882

Website: http://www.rosettastone.com/learn-italian

Pimsleur

Website: http://www.pimsleur.com/learn-italian

Telephone: 1.800.831.5497

Note: These options are not adequate to meet the Italian language B1 EU framework for the citizenship by marriage requirement for spouses.

DVD Learning for Children and Family:

Little Pim Co.

104 W. 14th Street, 4th Floor

New York, NY 10011

Telephone: 877.742.2059

Fax: 212.675.1367

Website: http://www.littlepim.com/store/italian-language-for-kids/

Muzzy BBC

Early Advantage

P.O. Box 743

Fairfield, CT 06824-9853

Telephone: 888-248-0480

Fax: 800-301-9268.

Website: http://www.early-advantage.com/stories/Mootsie.aspx

Learn Italian in Florence
at ABC School
Center for Italian Language and Culture

Study Italian at the ABC School of Florence

http://www.abcschool.com/

The ABC School of Florence offers a wide range of Italian Language courses, amazing offers and interesting extra curricular activities.

Courses are held by qualified teachers who frequently attend courses covering the Direct Teaching Method.

We take care of our students so that classes are made up of a maximum of 8 students and lessons are 55 minutes per hour.

You will appreciate our student care and our familiar atmosphere.

Let your study tour be a wonderful experience. Choose the ABC School of Florence to learn or improve the Italian language and culture.

Find out about all the advantages that the ABC School of Florence offers to its students.

Surf through these pages and you will find out why students from all over the world choose us every year.

CHAPTER 30
LIFE IN ITALY.

CHAPTER 30 | LIFE IN ITALY.

Below is a comprehensive list of resources for finding volunteering, working and interning opportunities in Italy adapted from a posting provided by NIAF. Some information will eventually change domains or contacts.

Before you begin, here are some useful resources (current at time of publishing). A quick google search and you will find a vast amount of information on this subject. So get excited and look around. Italy is waiting!

Studying in Italy at http://www.initaly.com/travel/study.htm or contact the Italian Cultural Institute near you.

Acquiring a work permit (permesso di lavoro) at www.italyemb.org or the Italian Consulate General near you.

Living in Italy: Living, Studying and Working in Italy: Everything You Need to Know to Fulfill Your Dreams of Living Abroad by Travis Neighbor, Monica Larner. Henry Holt (Paper); ISBN: 0805051023

Books and References for Study, Work, and Travel Abroad
Live and Work in Italy by Victoria Pybus, Huw Francis Vacation-Work; ISBN: 1854582879

Living, Studying and Working in Italy: Everything You Need to Know to Fulfill Your Dreams of Living Abroad by Travis Neighbor, Monica Larner. Henry Holt (Paper); ISBN: 0805051023

Making it Abroad: the International Job Hunting Guide
by Howard Schuman. Publisher: Wiley, John & Sons, Incorporated

Volunteer: The Comprehensive Guide to Voluntary Service in the US and Abroad
Publisher: Council on International Educational Exchange

Internships (Peterson's Internships)
Petersons Guides; ISBN: 076890904X

Directory of American Firms Operating in Foreign Countries (3 Vol Set)
Uniworld Business Pubns; ISBN: 0836000439

Great Jobs for Foreign Language Majors (Vgm's Great Jobs Series)
by Julie Degalan, Stephen Lambert McGraw Hill - NTC; ISBN: 0658004530

Career Opportunities for Bilinguals and Multilinguals
Publisher: Scarecrow Press, Incorporated

Teaching English in Italy
by Martin Penner

Teaching English in Italy

To provide comprehensive options for those seeking to teach English in Italy as
well as those seeking teacher training in Italy or online (from anywhere). The site
includes high quality TEFL certificate choices, teaching practice, and other
opportunities for teaching experiences in Italy.
http://www.teachingenglishinitaly.com

How to Get a Job in Europe (4th Ed.) by Robert Sanborn, Cheryl Matherly. Surrey
Books; ISBN: 1572840277

The Global Resume and CV Guide
by Mary Anne Thompson. John Wiley & Sons; ISBN: 0471380768; (November
2000) Help with writing an international resume.

Directory of Jobs & Careers Abroad
by Elisabeth Roberts(Editor), Jonathan Packer. ISBN: 1854582356

Work Abroad : The Complete Guide to Finding a Job Overseas
by Clayton A. Hubbs(Editor), Susan Griffith,William Nolting. ISBN: 1886732094

International Jobs: Where They Are, How to Get Them By Eric Kocher, Nina Segal.
Perseus Pr; ISBN: 0738200395

Getting a Job in Europe: How to Find Short or Long Term Employment
Throughout Europe (Living and Working Abroad Series) By Mark Hempshell. How
To Books; ISBN: 1857035356

Work Worldwide: International Career Strategies for the Adventurous Job Seeker
By Nancy Mueller. Avalon Travel Publishing; ISBN: 1562614908

Living and Working Abroad
By David Hampshire. Survival Books; ISBN: 1901130851

The Back Door Guide to Short-Term Job Adventures: Internships, Extraordinary Experiences, Seasonal Jobs, Volunteering, Work Abroad By Michael Landes, Ten Speed Press; ISBN: 1580081479

Vacation Work's International Directory of Voluntary Work
By Louise Whetter, Victoria Pybus. Vacation-Work;
ISBN: 185458237

The Internship Bible,
By Mark Oldman, Samer Hamadeh.
Princeton Review; ISBN: 0375762396

Teaching English Overseas - A Job Guide for Americans and Canadians
By Jeff Mohamed. English International;
ISBN: 0967706203

International Jobs Directory: A Guide to over 1001 Employers
By Ronald L. Krannich, Caryl Rae Krannich. Impact Publications; ISBN: 1570230862; 3rd edition.

Internet Resources

http://www.planetedu.com
Job/volunteer/internship resource for international community
http://www.ciee.org The Council on International Educational Exchange
http://www.escapeartist.com/transitions_abroad/magazine.html Transitions Abroad – A print and Internet resource
http://www.intemployment.com/ International Employment Gazette Print and Internet resource for job opportunities abroad
http://www.stepstone.it Europe's online career and HR service
http://www.monster.it
Europe's online career and HR service

http://www.recruitaly.it Services provided for employers looking for graduates and jobseekers that want to work in Italy

http://www.cercalavoro.it/ Site for job searching in Italy

http://www.obiettivolavoro.it/ Site for job searching in Italy

http:// www.fao.org Food and Agriculture Organization

http://www.ifad.org International Fund for Agricultural Development

http://www.rtpnet.org Internships International, LLC

http://www.cci-exchange.com/ The Center for Cultural Exchange offers host family exchange for students and adults.

http://www.alliancesabroad.com This website talks about internship work, teach and volunteer programs for students and graduates in and outside USA

http://www.olc-international.com Susan Clarke: sclarke@olc-international.com: The program, which is available in Florence and Milan, includes an intensive language course and a stay with a host family (if desired) as well as a guaranteed internship with an Italian company following the required language course. The total duration of the program averages 3 months and the cost varies depending on the length of the course and accommodation.

http://www.globalexperiences.com Emily Merson: emily@globalexperiences.com. This is a program that offers internships for all levels of Italian and in a variety of sectors. Some of the internships include a language course prior to the work experience. The cost depends on whether an Italian course is included and on the individual positions.

http://www.GoAbroad.com A compilation of study (includes high school programs), intern, volunteer, language, and employment options.

http://www.internabroad.com   A comprehensive list of employment, internship, and study abroad options in numerous countries from a variety of sources.

Applicable for both Italians and Americans.

http://www.iesabroad.org/default.htm: University level exchange programs for Americans who want to study abroad. There is the possibility of internships for credit.

http://www.iie.org the International Institution of Education. This organization offers 250 programs worldwide ranging from study to internships. They sponsor many scholarships, perhaps the most famous of which is the Fulbright.

Italian Internet Resources

The following websites are Italian search engines. A lot of the time, these websites contain additional, locally based sites you otherwise might not find. Knowledge of the Italian language is a must in most cases. http://www.excite.it http://www.google.it http://www.libero.it http://www.virgilio.it http://www.yahoo.it

Organizations that find Internships/Volunteer Opportunities

Council for International Education Exchange. Assistance provided in visas, housing, job hunting, and orientation. Students only. Contact: Work Exchanges Dept. at CIEE, 205 East 42nd St., New York, NY 10017. http://www.ciee.org

The Catholic Network of Volunteer Services. Offers full-time volunteer service opportunities worldwide. Contact: CNVS, 1410 Q. St. NW, Washington, DC 20009. http://www.cnvs.org

InterExchange. Dedicated to promoting international understanding through the development and implementation of affordable intercultural and educational work/training opportunities. http://www.interexchange.org/ InterExchange, Inc.161 Sixth Avenue New York, NY 10013 Telephone (212) 924-0446 Fax (212) 924-0575 E-mail:info@interexchange.org

Companies that offer Internships and Hire Volunteers

American Youth Hostels

733 15th Street NW Suite 840 Washington, DC 20005 http://www.hiayh.org/home.shtml

The Experiment in International Living. Offers positions worldwide as summer group leaders and semester academic directors for groups of students abroad, as well as home stays and international living programs.

Contact:
USA World Learning/US Experiment
PO Box 676, Kipling Road Brattleboro VT 05302 phone: 1 802 257 7751

fax: 1 802 258 3248 toll free phone (within USA): 1 800 345 2929
email: info@worldlearning.org web: http://www.usexperiment.org/

The International Association for the Exchange of Students for Technical Experience (IAESTE) Provides on job training for engineering, architecture, math, computer and physical science students. Contact: http://www.iaeste.org/

Aiesec. Offers one to three month long internships to graduate and undergraduate students who want practical experience in business related fields if their schools have AIESEC chapters. http://www.aiesecus.org

The American Overseas School of Rome (AOSR) hires U.S. citizens with at least 2 years of teaching experience. Preference is given to candidates who possess a Master's degree or higher. Contact: Via Cassia 811, 00189 Rome, Italy.
Tel. +39 06.334381   Fax. +39 06.3326
Web site: http://www.aosr.org

The U.S. Embassy in Rome has a highly competitive internship program in Foreign Commercial Service. It is voluntary and uncompensated. Offered to university seniors that study business administration, economics, international trade, or related field. Must be bilingual (written, read, and spoken). Contact: Jennifer Legan, American Embassy Rome (FCS), PSC 59, APO AE 09624. Tel: 0039-6-4674-2184. Fax: 0039-6-4674-2113.
Web site: http://www.usembassy.it

The United Nations offers internships to citizens of member countries. Many of the agencies offering internships are located in Italy: Food and Agriculture Organization of the United Nations (FAO), Rome
http://www.fao.org/info/faq/5_en.htm Contact: Recruitment Support and Temporary

Assistance Group, Personnel Division, FAO, Viale delle Terme di Caracalla, 00100 Rome. International Fund for Agricultural Development, Rome
http://www.ifad.org/job/intern/index.htm E-mail: internships@ifad.org United

Nations Interregional Crime and Justice Research Institute (UNICRI), Rome
http://www.unicri.it/index.htm Contact: Internship Program at internship@unicri.it United Nations Staff College (UNSC), Turin
http://www.unssc.org

Contact: Human Resources United Nations Staff College Viale Maestri del Lavoro, 10 10127 Turin, Italy
Fax: (+39 011) 65 35 902 k.sarajyan@unssc.org

The Peggy Guggenheim collection museum in Venice, Italy
www.guggenheim-venice.it

European Communities Information Office
www.comeur.it

UNICEF—Italian Committee
www.unicef.it

B. Volunteering Civil Service International
Via Castelnov 21/B 50047 Cavenaghi 4, 20149, Milan

Volunteers for Peace International
1034 Tiffany Road Belmont, Vermont 05730 USA Tel: 802-259-2759 Fax: 802-259-2922 E-mail: vfp@vfp.org http://www.vfp.org

Earthwatch Institute
680 Mt. Auburn Street P.O. Box 403 Watertown, MA 02272 (800) 776-0188
http://www.earthwatch.org

Greenpeace
E-mail: info@greenpeace.it http://www.greenpeace.org

World Wildlife Fund Italia
Via Garigliano, 57-00198 Roma (06) 844971 Largest environmental organization in Italy comprised of 20 regional offices and groups and a network of 4,000 volunteers. E-mail: suggest@wwf.it http://www.wwf.it

Additional Resources

UniWorld Business Publications, INC. publishes a list of American businesses operating in foreign countries. This helpful resource can be purchased online or through the mail. http://www.uniworldbp.com

UniWorld Publications 175 92nd Street Suite 3G New York, NY 10025
Intern Abroad - http://www.internabroad.com/search.cfm Comprehensive search listing of internships abroad.

International Job Hotline
(Within US): (618) 453-2391

Contact Center Network
Contact:
Maintains directory of worldwide nonprofit organizations with links to more than 50 nonprofits in Italy. http://www.idealist.org

Temporary staffing in Italy:

http://www.adecco.it http://www.randstand.it http://www.creyfs.it
http://www.obiettivolavoro.it
http://www.creyfs.it http://www.inwork.it http://www.temporary.it
http://www.genind.it http://www.kellyservices.it http://www.lavoropiu.it
http://www.umana.it http://www.vedior.it http://www.worknet.it

Italian government agency:
http://www.welfare.gov.it/Lavoro/OccupazioneEMercatoDelLavoro/centri+impiego/defa ult.htm http://www.informagiovani.it

CHAPTER 31
ITALIAN CONSULATES.

CHAPTER 30 | ITALIAN CONSULATES.

What consulate has jurisdiction over your residence?

Italian Consulate General BOSTON
600 Atlantic Ave.
Boston, MA 02210
Tel.: (617) 722-9201/02/03
Fax: (617) 722-9407
Homepage: http://www.consboston.esteri.it
E-mail: archivio.boston@esteri.it
Jurisdiction: Maine, Massachusetts, New Hampshire, Rhode Island, Vermont.

BOSTON ADJUNCT CONSULAR OFFICES

PROVIDENCE (RI) – Honorary Vice Consulate
49 Weybosset St.
Providence, RI 02903
Tel.: (401) 454-1492
Fax: (401) 421-9080
E-mail: ViceConsulRI@web-Italia.com
Jurisdiction: Rhode Island

WORCHESTER (MA)- Consular Agency
6 Seward St.
Worchester, MA 01604
Tel.: (508) 756-3651
Email: mustica.salvatore@gmail.com
Jurisdiction: Massachusetts

===

Italian Consulate General CHICAGO
500 North Michigan Ave., Suite 1850
Chicago, IL 60611
Tel.: (312) 467-1550
Fax: (312) 467-1335
Homepage: http://www.conschicago.esteri.it
E-mail: italcons.chicago@esteri.it
Jurisdiction: Colorado, Illinois, Iowa, Kansas, Minnesota, Missouri, Nebraska, North Dakota, South Dakota, Wisconsin, Wyoming.
CHICAGO ADJUNCT CONSULAR OFFICES

KANSAS CITY (KS) - Honorary Vice Consulate
Bryan Cave, LLP
13220 Metcalf Avenue
Suite 320
Overland Park, KSD 66213
Tel: 816-374-3200
Fax: 816-855-3350
e-mail: gino.serra@bryancave.com

ST. LOUIS (MO) - Honorary Vice Consulate
One Metropolitan Square, 211 North Broadway, Suite 3000
St. Louis, MO 63102
Tel: 314-259-5931
Fax: 314-259-5985
e-mail: joseph.colagiovanni@snrdenton.com

MILWAUKEE (Wisconsin) - Consular Correspondent
e-mail: italconsmke@wi.rr.com
Tel: 414-469-8192

MINNEAPOLIS-ST. PAUL (MO) - Consular Correspondent
e-mail: pavoloni@usinternet.com
Tel: 651-699-8442

==

Italian Consulate DETROIT
Buhl Building
535 Griswold, Suite 1840
Detroit, MI 48226
Tel.: (313) 963-8560
Fax: (313) 963-8180
Homepage: http://www.consdetroit.esteri.it
E-mail: inform.detroit@esteri.it
Jurisdiction: Indiana, Kentucky, Michigan, Ohio, Tennessee

DETROIT ADJUNCT CONSULAR OFFICES

CLEVELAND (OH) - Honorary Vice Consulate
1422 Euclid Avenue
618 Hanna Building
Cleveland, Ohio, 44115
216-861-1585
216-861-6304 (fax)
e-mail: serena.scaiola@att.net
Jurisdiction: OHIO

INDIANAPOLIS (IN) - Honorary Vice Consulate
13585 Brentwood Lane,
Carmel, Indiana 46033
317-748.57.44
e-mail : viceconsolatoindianapolis@yahoo.com
Jurisdiction: INDIANA

NASHVILLE (TN) - Honorary Vice Consulate
113 Wynthrope Way
Franklin, Tennessee, 37067
615-725-1669
e-mail : micol_cons@hotmail.com
Jurisdiction: TENNESSEE

GRAND RAPIDS (MI) - Consular Correspondent
3333 Mahogany Court
Grand Rapids, MI 49525
Tel: 616-245-6100
Fax: 616-245-0948
e-mail: cvanin@alphaangencyinc.com

LANSING (MI) - Consular Correspondent
4736 Clydesdale
Lansing, Michigan, 48906
517-321-0356
517-699-1677 (fax)

LIVONIA (MI) – Consular Correspondent
35902 Schoolcraft Livonia, MI 48150-1217
Tel. 734-591-0736
Fax 734-591-0746
e-mail: teresa.nascimbeni@sbcglobal.net

PARMA (OH) - Consular Correspondent
11264 Glamer Dr.
Parma, Ohio, 44130
Tel.: 440-885-1917
e-mail: bpar925@cox.net

CANTON (OH) - Consular Correspondent
3104 Miles, N.W.
Canton, Ohio, 44718
Tel.: 330-478-8388
Fax: 330-478-1888 (fax)

COLUMBUS (OH) - Consular Correspondent
P.O. Box 703
Canal Winchester, Ohio, 43110-0703
Tel.: 614-397-9455 e-mail: mliedolo@aol.com

YOUNGSTOWN (OH) - Consular Correspondent
5894 Sampson Drive
Girard, Ohio, 44420
Tel.: 330-759-3786
e-mail: vcdevito@yahoo.com

DYER (IN) - Consular Correspondent
2309 Boulder Rd.
Dyer, Indiana, 46311-1902
Tel.: 708-614-6400
Tel.: 219-322-2772
Fax: 219-322-6996
e-mail: b.dalsanto@yahoo.com

INDIANAPOLIS (IN) - Consular Correspondent
935 Tamarack Circle S.
Indianapolis, IN 46260
Tel.: 317 709 6821
e-mail: pgr@pgrolandlaw.com

===

Italian Consulate General PHILADELPHIA
150 S. Independence Mall West
Suite 1026
Philadelphia, PA 19106-3410
Tel.: (215) 592-7329
Fax: (215) 592-9808
Homepage: http://www.consfiladelfia.esteri.it
E-mail ufficio relazioni con il pubblico: urp.filadelfia@esteri.it
E-mail cittadinanza: cittadinanza.filadelfia@esteri.it
Giurisdizione: The Consulate General of Italy in Philadelphia provides services to residents in the following States: Pennsylvania, Delaware, North Carolina, West Virginia, New Jersey (only the following counties: Atlantic, Burlington, Camden, Cape May, Cumberland, Gloucester, Ocean and Salem. The remaining counties

are under the jurisdiciton of the Consulate General in New York for visas and for all other matters under the jurisdiction of the Consulate in Newark), ** Maryland (except for the counties of Montgomery and Prince George which fall under the jurisdiction of the consular section of the Italian Embassy in Washington, DC) and Virginia (except for the counties of Arlington and Fairfax which are also under the consular section of the Italian Embassy in Washington, DC).

PHILADELPHIA ADJUNCT CONSULAR OFFICES

BALTIMORE (MD) – Honorary Consulate General
Equitable Building, Suite 940
10 North Calvert St.
Baltimore, MD 21202-1820
Tel.: (410) 727-6550
Fax: (410) 727-6563
E-mail: Info@ItalConBalto.org
Jurisdiction: Maryland (except Montgomery and Prince Georges counties)

CHARLOTTE (NC) – Honorary Consulate
1704 East Boulevard
Charlotte, NC 28203
Tel. 704 – 373 – 1505
Fax 704 – 373 – 2603
e-mail: console@carpano.us
e-mail: ccarpano@uncc.edu
Jurisdiction: Nord Carolina

NORFOLK (VA) - Honorary Consulate
300 East Main St., Suite 1180
Norfolk, VA 23510
Tel.: (757) 622-4898
Fax: (757) 622-0562
E-mail: itcon@live.com
Jurisdiction: Virginia (except Arlington and Fairfax counties)

PITTSBURGH (PA) - Honorary Consulate
Fisher Hall Suite 728
600 Forbes Ave.
Pittsburgh, PA 15282
Tel.: (412) 765-0273
Fax: (412) 765-0582
E-mail: italyconsulpgh@gmail.com
Jurisdiction: The 18 western Pennsylvania counties.

PHILADELPHIA area - Consular Correspondent
7459 Brockton Road
Philadelphia, PA 19151
Tel.: (215) 477-8419
Fax: (215) 477-8419
e.mail: cifoni@aol.com

AMBLER (PA) - Consular Correspondent
81 East Butler Avenue
Ambler, PA 19002
Tel.: (215) 643-1336
Fax: (215) 643-1316
Cell: (215) 264-2074
e.mail: emilioiuliano@gmail.com

ELMHURST (PA) - Consular Correspondent
166 Front Street
Elmhurst, PA 18416
Tel.: (570) 842-8932
Fax.: (570) 842-4726
e.mail: stoppinima@aol.com

TOMS RIVER (NJ) - Consular Correspondent
106 Sun Valley Rd.
Toms River, NJ 08755
Tel.: (732) 914-0351
Cell: (732) 773-7223
e.mail: marioamarano@juno.com

WILMINGTON (DE) -   Consular Correspondent
3034 Maple Shade Ln.
Wilmington, DE 19810
Tel.: (302) 478-5730
e.mail: finizio1@udell.edu

RED HILL (PA) - Consular Correspondent
325 Wexford Rd.
Red Hill, PA 18076
Cell: (215)290-8513
e.mail: chiarostm@gmail.com

ATLANTIC CITY (NJ) - Consular Correspondent
1624 Pacific Avenue
Atlantic city, NJ 08401
Tel: (609)347-7000
Cell: (609)335-1882
e.mail: tom@subranni.com

==

Italian Consulate General HOUSTON
1300 Post Oak Blvd., Suite 660
Houston, TX 77056
Tel.: (713) 850-7520
Fax: (713) 850-9113
Homepage: http://www.conshouston.esteri.it
E-mail: italcons.houston@esteri.it
Jurisdiction: Arkansas, Louisiana, Oklahoma, Texas

HOUSTON ADJUNCT CONSULAR OFFICES

NEW ORLEANS (LA) – Honorary Consulate
3501 N. Causeway Blvd., Suite 300
Metairie, LA 70002
Tel.: (504) 836-7444
Fax: (504) 836-7411
E-mail: arnaldo@kensingtonbc.com
Jurisdiction: Louisiana

SAN ANTONIO (TX) - Consular Correspondent
2255 W. Mistletoe Avenue
SAN ANTONIO TX 78201
Tel. Ufficio: 210 731 4216
Fax:210 735 8210
e.mail: cardigno@sbcglobal.net

BATON ROUGE (LA) - Consular Correspondent
c/o Louisiana State University Program
 in Comparative Literature
 Prescott Hall
222 BATON ROUGE LA 70803
Tel.: 225 578 5175
e.mail: ricapito@lsu.edu

===

Italian Consulate General LOS ANGELES
12400 Wilshire Blvd., Suite 300
Los Angeles, CA 90025
Tel.: (310) 820-0622
Tel.: (310) 826-6207
Fax: (310) 820-0727
Homepage: http://www.conslosangeles.esteri.it
E-mail: consolato.losangeles@esteri.it
Jurisdiction: Arizona, California (The following counties: Imperial Valley, Kern,

Los Angeles, Orange, Riverside, Santa Barbara, San Bernardino, San Diego, San Luis Obispo, Ventura), New Mexico, Nevada.

LOS ANGELES ADJUNCT CONSULAR OFFICES

LAS VEGAS (NV) - Honorary Vice Consulate
3084 Red Arrow Dr.
Las Vegas, NV 89135
Tel: (702) 538-5162
Fax (702) 801-0495
e-mail: montivegas@aol.com
Jurisdiction: NEVADA

PHOENIX (AZ) - Honorary Vice Consulate
7509 N.12th Street,
Phoenix, AZ 85020
Tel.: (480) 304 4620
e-mail: viceconsolato.az@live.com

SAN DIEGO (CA)- Honorary Vice Consulate
7607 Family Circle Dr.
San Diego, CA
Tel.(619)517.1406
Fax: (432)225-5441
e-mail: viceconsolatoitalia@italianlegalservices.com

RENO (NV) - Consular Correspondent
c/o University of Nevada
Foreign Languages Dept.
Italian Studies Program
Mail Stop 100
Reno, NV 89557
Tel: 775-784-6055 ext 313 (office hours)

ALBUQUERQUE (NM) - Consular Correspondent
3005 May Circle, Rio Rancho
New Mexico 87124
Tel. (505) 891.8456
Cell. (505) 507.9715
Fax. (505) 891.8456
e-mail: rosegma@yahoo.com

===

Italian Consulate General MIAMI
4000 Ponce de León Blvd., Suite 590
Coral Gables, FL 33146
Tel.: (305) 374-6322 main number
Fax: (305) 374-7945
Homepage: http://www.consmiami.esteri.it
E-mail: italconsulmiami@gmail.com
Jurisdiction: Alabama, British Virgin Islands, Cayman Islands, Florida, Georgia, Island of Saba, Mississippi, Puerto Rico, St. Maarten, St. Eustatius, South Carolina, Turks and Caicos, U.S. Virgin Islands.

MIAMI ADJUNCT CONSUALR OFFICES

ATLANTA (GA) – Honorary Consulate General
133 Luckie St., NW
Atlanta, GA 30303
Tel. (404) 262-0609
Fax: (404) 262-0604
e-mail: italconsulmiami@gmail.com
Jurisdiction: Georgia

SAN JUAN (P R) – Honorary Consulate
Calle Interamericana, 266
Urb. University Gardens
Guaynabo, PR 00927-4133
Tel.: (787) 767-5855
Fax: (787) 767-5855
E-mail: aps161@yahoo.com
Jurisdiction: Puerto Rico, U.S. Virgin Islands, British Virgin Islands, St. Maarten, Island of Saba, St. Eustatius.

BAHAMAS - Honorary Vice Consulate
c/o Quality Service Ltd
West Queen's Highway
Freeport, Grand Bahama
The Bahamas
Tel.: (242) 351-2662
Fax: (242) 351-2682
e.mail: info@gariboldi.org
Jurisdiction: The Bahamas

ORLANDO (FL) - Honorary Vice Consulate
101 Cedar Point Ln.
Longwood, FL 32779
Tel./Fax: (407) 869-9702
E-mail: clmedia205@aol.com
Jurisdiction: The following counties: Volusia, Lake, Seminole, Orange, Brevard, Osceola, Indian River, Polk (central-eastern Florida)

CHARLESTON (SC) – Honorary Consular Agency
C/O Mediterranean Shipping Co.
550 Long Point Road
Mount Pleasant, SC 29464
Tel.: (843) 971-4100 ext. 46030
Fax: (843) 971-1155
E-mail: sfedelini@msc.us

GREENVILLE (SC) - Consular Correspondent
1324 East North St
Greenville, SC 29607
Tel:(864) 233-7703
e.mail: renato@travelvantage.com

SARASOTA(FL) - Consular Correspondent
707 South Gulfstream Avenue # 307
SARASOTA, FL 34236
Tel: (941) 957-0851
Fax: (941) 954-0111
e-mail: consularcorrespondentsarasota@gmail.com

TAMPA (FL) - Consular Correspondent
1714 Curlew Rd.
Dunedin FL 34698
Tel:(727) 449-0300
Fax: (859) 222-7294

TALLAHASSEE (FL)- Consular Correspondent
1351 N. Gadsden Street
Tallahassee FL 32305
Cell:(850) 545-7125
Fax: (859) 222-7294
e.mail: todd@attglobal.net

VERO BEACH (FL) - Consular Correspondent
P.O. Box 651337
Vero Beach FL 32965
Tel:(772) 567-8521

HATTIENSBURG - Consular Correspondent
P.O. Box 15334, Hattiesburg
Mississippi 39404
Tel.:(601) 268-3191 e.mail: davidmgratta@mac.com

PENSACOLA (FL) - Consular Correspondent
3026 Marcus Pointe Blvd.
Pensacola, FL 32505
Tel:(850) 474-9766
e.mail: shasoc@bellsouth.net

BRITISH VIRGIN ISLANDS - Consular Correspondent
c/o La dolce vita, Waterfront
British Virgin Islands
e-mail: virginpi@yahoo.com
Tel.:(284)-4432910

TURKS & CAICOS ISLANDS - Consular Correspondent
Grace Bay Road or P.O. BOX 543
Providenciales - Turks & Caicos Islands
Tel (649) 946-5214
e-mail: dantetripodi@gmail.com

NAPLES - Consular Correspondent
PMB 104 6017 Pine Ridge Rd.
Naples, FL 34119
Tel/Fax (239)353-1842
e-mail: conaida@aol.com

==

Italian Consulate NEWARK
One Gateway Center - Suite 100
Newark, NJ 07102
Tel.: (973) 643-1448
Fax: (973) 643-3043
Homepage: http://www.consnewark.esteri.it
E-mail: consolato.newark@esteri.it
Jurisdiction: The Consulate of Italy in Newark provides services to residents in the following counties: Bergen, Essex, Hudson, Hunterdon, Mercer, Middlesex, Monmouth, Morris, Passaic, Somerset, Sussex, Union, Warren.

NEWARK ADJUNCT CONSULAR OFFICES

TRENTON (NJ) - Consular Correspondent
284 Edinburg Road
Trenton NJ 08619
Tel: (609) 587-7000
Fax: (609) 631-9116

JERSEY CITY (NJ) - Consular Correspondent
C/O Italian Educational & Cultural Center
380 Monmouth Street
Jersey City, NJ 07302
Tel: (201)963-6332
Fax: (201)963-7804
e-mail: info@casacolombo.org

===

Italain Consulate General NEW YORK
690 Park Ave.New York, NY 10065
Tel.: (212) 737-9100
Fax: (212) 249-4945
Homepage: http://www.consnewyork.esteri.it
E-mail: info.newyork@esteri.it
Jurisdiction: The Consulate General in New York provides services to residents in the States of New York and Connecticut and the British Territories of Bermuda Islands.

It can issue visas also for a portion of New Jersey (Counties of Bergen, Essex, Hudson, Hunterdon, Mercer, Middlesex, Monmouth, Morris, Passaic, Somerset, Sussex, Union, Warren).

NEW YORK ADJUNCT CONSULAR OFFICES

HAMILTON - Honorary Consulate
60 South Road
Paget PG 04
Bermuda
Tel.: (441) 295-5291
Fax: (441) 295-5327
E-mail: italia@northrock.bm
Jurisdiction: Bermuda

MINEOLA (NY) - Honorary Consulate
300 Glen St.
Glen Cove, NY 11542
Tel.: (516) 671-9364
Fax: (516) 671-9623
E-mail: gcitalianconsul@yahoo.com
Jurisdiction: Nassau e Suffolk counties

BUFFALO (NY) - Honorary Vice Consulate
160 Court St.
Buffalo, NY 14202
Tel.: (716) 856-3626
Fax: (716) 856-6922
e-mail: lccullens1@verizon.net
Jurisdiction: The following counties: Allengany, Cattaraugus, Chautauqua, Erie, Genesee, Niagara, Orleans.

HARTFORD (CT) - Honorary Vice Consulate
133 Allen Place
Hartford, CT 06106
Mailbox nr.: 702604
Tel: (860) 297-5270
Fax: (860) 297-5260
e-mail: viceconsulateCT@gmail.com
Jurisdiction: Connecticut

ROCHESTER (NY)– Honorary Vice Consulate
2740 Monroe Ave.
Rochester, NY 14618
Tel.: (585) 271-4840
Fax: (585) 271 3750
E-mail: rocitalianviceconsul@yahoo.com
Jurisdiction: The following counties: Cayuga, Chemumg, Cortland, Jefferson, Livingston, Monroe, Onondaga, Ontario, Seneca, Schuyler, Steuben, Yates, Tioga, Tompkins, Wayne.

WESTCHESTER (NY) - Honorary Vice Consulate
131 Alta Avenue, Park Hill
Yonkers, N.Y. 10705
Tel. (914) 966-3180 ext. 110
Fax: (914) 966-3264
e-mail: sa@cinn.com
Jurisdiction: Ulster, Dutchess, Sullivan, Orange, Rockland, Putnam (Mid-Hudson Region); Schenectady/Troy, Warren, Washington, Saratoga, Renselaer, Columbia, Greene (Albany Capital Region); Hamilton, Herkimer, Oneida, Fulton, Montgomery, Schohaire (Mohawk Region); Oswego, Onondaga, Cayuga, Cortland, Madison (Central Region), Delaware, Otsego, Chittenango, Tiuga, Chemung, Schuyler, Steuben, Broome (Southern Region); Essex, Clinton, Franklin, St. Lawrence, Lewis, Jefferson (North Region).

==

Italian Consulate General SAN FRANCISCO
2590 Webster St.
San Francisco, CA 94115
Tel.: (415) 292-9210
Tel.: (415) 931-4924
Fax: (415) 931-7205
Homepage: http://www.conssanfrancisco.esteri.it
E-mail: visti.sanfrancisco@esteri.it
Jurisdiction: Alaska, California (except the following counties: Imperial Valley, Kern, Los Angeles, Orange, Riverside, San Diego, Santa Barbara, San Bernardino,

San Luis Obispo and Ventura, which fall within the jurisdiction of the Consulate General in Los Angeles), Idaho, Montana, Oregon, Utah, Washington, Hawai'i. Also, the following American territories of: Guam, Northern Mariana Islands, Samoa, Wake Island, Midways Islands, Johnston Atoll.

SAN FRANCISCO ADJUNCT CONSULAR OFFICES

FRESNO (CA) - Honorary Vice Consulate
2125 Merced St.
Fresno, CA 93721
Tel.: (559) 268-8776
Fax: (559) 268-5701
E-mail: e.d.fanucchi@qkffirm.com
Jurisdiction: The following counties: Fresno, Madera, Merced, King, Tulare, Inyo, Mono.

HONOLULU (HI) - Honorary Consulate
735 Bishop Street, Suite 201
Honolulu, Hawaii 96814
Tel: (808) 271-3560
Fax: (808) 734-6929
e-mail: info@italianconsulatehawaii.com
Jurisdiction: Hawaii

PORTLAND (OR) - Honorary Vice Consulate
121 S.W. Salmon St., Suite 1030
Portland, OR 97204
Tel.: (503) 287-2578
Fax: (503) 227-0739
Tel.: (503) 225.0702 law office
E-mail: ab@bartoloni.com
Jurisdiction: Oregon

SACRAMENTO (CA)- Honorary Vice Consulate
1420 - 54th StreetSuite 4
Sacramento, CA 95891
Tel.: 916-456-1950
Fax: 916-456-1950
e-mail: avirgadamo@aol.com
Jurisdiction: Sacramento County (CA)

SAN JOSE' (CA) - Honorary Vice Consulate
95 South Market Street - Suite 300
San Jose, CA 95113-2350
Tel.: 408-971-9170
Tel.: 408-995-3266 law office
Fax: 408-995-3277
e-mail: sraviola@ix.netcom.com
Jurisdiction: Santa Clara County (CA)

SALT LAKE CITY (UT) - Honorary Vice Consulate
8 East Broadway - suite 200
Salt Lake City, UT 84111-2204
Tel.: 801-865-4305
Tel.: 801-532-7300 law office
Fax: 801-532-7355
e-mail: italianconsul@sautah.com
Jurisdiction: Utah

SEATTLE (WA) - Honorary Vice Consulate
23718 Bothell-Everett Hwy, Suite H
Bothell, WA 98021
Tel: 206-851-8023
Fax: 425-489-0271
e-mail: viceconsole@hotmail.com
Jurisdiction: Washington state

MODESTO (CA) - Consular Correspondent
1225 West Roseburg Avenue
Modesto, CA 95350-4928
Tel.: 209-524-5583
Fax: 209-578-5541
e- mail: joe-dot_simile@msn.com

BOISE (ID) - Consular Correspondent
3411 Cassia Street
Boise, Idaho 83705
Tel: 208-412-9321
e-mail: italianconsul@cableone.net
Jurisdicton: Idaho

ANCHORAGE (AS) - Consular Agency
P.O. Box 242241
Anchorage, Alaska 99524
Tel: 907-762-7664
Fax: 907-762-7663
e-mail: victormontemezzani@gci.net
Jurisdiction: Alaska

CHAPTER 32
YOUR
FAMILY TREE.

CHAPTER 32 | YOUR FAMILY TREE.

For each person in your line you will need the following information (Not all information will related to each person. Leave blanks where applicable):

YOURSELF:

Full Name at Birth: _____

Alternate Names Used:_____

Date of Birth: _____

Place of Birth: _____

Parents Name (Maiden):_____

Date of Marriage: _____

Place Marriage License Issued:_____

Place of Marriage: _____

Name of Spouse (Maiden):_____

Place of Residence in USA:_____

ADDITIONAL INFORMATION:

You will need to know names, dates and locations of additional marriages and spouses.

You will also need names, place of and dates of court proceedings related to name changes.

Notes:

SPOUSE:

Full Name at Birth: _____

Alternate Names Used:_____

Date of Birth: _____

Place of Birth: _____

Parents Name (Maiden):_____

Date of Marriage: _____

Place Marriage License Issued:_____

Place of Marriage: _____

Name of Spouse (Maiden):_____

Place of Residence in USA:_____

ADDITIONAL INFORMATION:

You will need to know names, dates and locations of additional marriages and spouses.

You will also need names, place of and dates of court proceedings related to name changes.

Notes:

FATHER:

Full Name at Birth: _____

Alternate Names Used:_____

Date of Birth: _____

Place of Birth: _____

Parents Name (Maiden):_____

Date of Marriage: _____

Place Marriage License Issued:_____

Place of Marriage: _____

Name of Spouse (Maiden):_____

Place of Residence in USA:_____

ADDITIONAL INFORMATION:

You will need to know names, dates and locations of additional marriages and spouses.

You will also need names, place of and dates of court proceedings related to name changes.

Notes:

MOTHER:

Full Name at Birth: _____

Alternate Names Used:_____

Date of Birth: _____

Place of Birth: _____

Parents Name (Maiden):_____

Date of Marriage: _____

Place Marriage License Issued:_____

Place of Marriage: _____

Name of Spouse (Maiden):_____

Place of Residence in USA:_____

ADDITIONAL INFORMATION:

You will need to know names, dates and locations of additional marriages and spouses.

You will also need names, place of and dates of court proceedings related to name changes.

Notes:

GRANDFATHER:

Full Name at Birth: _____

Alternate Names Used:_____

Date of Birth: _____

Place of Birth: _____

Parents Name (Maiden):_____

Date of Marriage: _____

Place Marriage License Issued:_____

Place of Marriage: _____

Name of Spouse (Maiden):_____

Place of Residence in USA:_____

ADDITIONAL INFORMATION:

You will need to know names, dates and locations of additional marriages and spouses.

You will also need names, place of and dates of court proceedings related to name changes.

Notes:

GRANDMOTHER:

Full Name at Birth: _____

Alternate Names Used:_____

Date of Birth: _____

Place of Birth: _____

Parents Name (Maiden):_____

Date of Marriage: _____

Place Marriage License Issued:_____

Place of Marriage: _____

Name of Spouse (Maiden):_____

Place of Residence in USA:_____

ADDITIONAL INFORMATION:

You will need to know names, dates and locations of additional marriages and spouses.

You will also need names, place of and dates of court proceedings related to name changes.

Notes:

GREAT GRANDFATHER:

Full Name at Birth: _____

Alternate Names Used:_____

Date of Birth: _____

Place of Birth: _____

Parents Name (Maiden):_____

Date of Marriage: _____

Place Marriage License Issued:_____

Place of Marriage: _____

Name of Spouse (Maiden):_____

Place of Residence in USA:_____

ADDITIONAL INFORMATION:

You will need to know names, dates and locations of additional marriages and spouses.

You will also need names, place of and dates of court proceedings related to name changes.

Notes:

GREAT GRANDMOTHER:

Full Name at Birth: _____

Alternate Names Used:_____

Date of Birth: _____

Place of Birth: _____

Parents Name (Maiden):_____

Date of Marriage: _____

Place Marriage License Issued:_____

Place of Marriage: _____

Name of Spouse (Maiden):_____

Place of Residence in USA:_____

ADDITIONAL INFORMATION:

You will need to know names, dates and locations of additional marriages and spouses.

You will also need names, place of and dates of court proceedings related to name changes.

Notes:

CHILD 1:

Full Name at Birth: _____

Alternate Names Used:_____

Date of Birth: _____

Place of Birth: _____

Parents Name (Maiden):_____

Date of Marriage: _____

Place Marriage License Issued:_____

Place of Marriage: _____

Name of Spouse (Maiden):_____

Place of Residence in USA:_____

ADDITIONAL INFORMATION:

You will need to know names, dates and locations of additional marriages and spouses.

You will also need names, place of and dates of court proceedings related to name changes.

Notes:

CHILD 2:

Full Name at Birth: _____

Alternate Names Used: _____

Date of Birth: _____

Place of Birth: _____

Parents Name (Maiden): _____

Date of Marriage: _____

Place Marriage License Issued: _____

Place of Marriage: _____

Name of Spouse (Maiden): _____

Place of Residence in USA: _____

ADDITIONAL INFORMATION:

You will need to know names, dates and locations of additional marriages and spouses.

You will also need names, place of and dates of court proceedings related to name changes.

Notes:

CHILD 3:

Full Name at Birth: _____

Alternate Names Used:_____

Date of Birth: _____

Place of Birth: _____

Parents Name (Maiden):_____

Date of Marriage: _____

Place Marriage License Issued:_____

Place of Marriage: _____

Name of Spouse (Maiden):_____

Place of Residence in USA:_____

ADDITIONAL INFORMATION:

You will need to know names, dates and locations of additional marriages and spouses.

You will also need names, place of and dates of court proceedings related to name changes.

Notes:

CHILD 4:

Full Name at Birth: _____

Alternate Names Used:_____

Date of Birth: _____

Place of Birth: _____

Parents Name (Maiden):_____

Date of Marriage: _____

Place Marriage License Issued:_____

Place of Marriage: _____

Name of Spouse (Maiden):_____

Place of Residence in USA:_____

ADDITIONAL INFORMATION:

You will need to know names, dates and locations of additional marriages and spouses.

You will also need names, place of and dates of court proceedings related to name changes.

Notes:

CHAPTER 33
ITALIAN CITIZENSHIP LAW.

CHAPTER 33 | ITALIAN CITIZENSHIP LAW.

The following is a summary and a <u>very broad interpretation</u> of Italian citizenship law. You are not required to read it or remember any of it. However, some of you may find it interesting and even useful depending on your individual circumstance. If specific questions arise related to your individual circumstance you should consult the Italian consulate of your jurisdiction.

Historically.

March 17, 1861

Italian Unification Day: Vittorio Emanuele II officially became King of the newly formed nation of Italy. Prior to this date there were no Italian citizens because there was no Italy. (Also see July 16, 1920, below.) Consequently, while the research may be interesting for family history reasons, your jure sanguinis application should never require official records too much older than this date.

The earliest Italian ancestor in your chain must have been alive at any moment when Italy was actually a nation. Then-current citizens of most of Italy's antecedent states -- for example, citizens of the Kingdom of Sicily -- living anywhere in the world automatically acquired Italian citizenship on this date.

Italy did not actually enact its first civil code regulating citizenship until 1865, but that code is retroactive to March 17, 1861.

July 1, 1912

A major citizenship law (Law no. 555 of June 13, 1912) takes effect. Before July 1, 1912, if an Italian citizen became a citizen of another country through naturalization, he, his wife and all his minor children (see March 10, 1975, below) lost Italian citizenship together. But if the Italian father naturalized on or after July 1, 1912, all his previously born or adopted children retained their Italian citizenship even if they were minors, provided that the children did not acquire or possess a foreign citizenship other than one which was granted automatically by virtue of being born in the same foreign country with which their father naturalized.

Example: Giovanni, an Italian citizen, emigrated to the United States in 1931. He had two children: Marina and Peter. Marina was born in Italy in 1928, and Peter was born in the U.S. in 1933. Giovanni naturalized as a U.S. citizen in 1940 when both his children were still minors. When Giovanni naturalized, Marina lost her Italian citizenship. However, because Peter was born in same country (the United States) with which his father naturalized, and because the U.S. is a jure soli country and Peter automatically acquired that country's citizenship at birth by being born in that country, under Italy's 1912 law (Article 7) Peter retained his Italian citizenship.

July 16, 1920

On this date Italy officially annexed certain northern territories (Veneto, Friuli V.Giulia, and Trentino) that were previously part of Austria. Citizens of these territories became Italian citizens on this date. Except for these former Austrian territory citizens, all jure sanguinis Italians, regardless of historical fact (Rome and Venice actually joined after 1861) are legally considered Italian citizens from birth or from March 17, 1861, whichever is later.

January 1, 1948

Italy's new post-war constitution takes effect. Starting on this day, Italian mothers could pass Italian citizenship to their children independently of the father. Sons and daughters born or adopted prior to this day had to have an Italian father in order to acquire Italian citizenship jure sanguinis.

Also, starting on this day, Italian women could no longer lose their Italian citizenship solely through marriage to a foreign husband. (Although for many years, until as late as 2001, the Ministry of Foreign Affairs incorrectly interpreted the 1948 constitution and still treated many Italian women as losing their Italian citizenship when they married foreign husbands.) If you are a woman who lost Italian citizenship when you married a foreigner because your husband's country automatically granted you citizenship, today you can immediately reclaim your Italian citizenship by making a simple declaration at your local consulate. However, descendants of such women only retain their Italian citizenship if the marriage to a foreigner occurred on or after January 1, 1948.

Example: Paulina, an Italian citizen, emigrated to the United States in 1938 and never naturalized. She married a U.S. citizen in 1944, but the U.S. stopped granting foreign women automatic citizenship through marriage in 1922. Paulina had two children: Alice, born in 1946, and George, born in 1948. George was born an Italian citizen, but Alice was not.

March 10, 1975

Italy lowered its age of majority from 21 to 18 (Law no. 39 of March 8, 1975; effective March 10, 1975). Before this date, any Italian citizen who had not reached his 21st birthday was a minor. On or after this date, any Italian citizen who had reached his 18th birthday was an adult.

Minors are not legally competent to act on their own, independent of their parents, so they enjoy certain legal protections which can affect jure sanguinis citizenship cases. See April 27, 1983, below.

April 27, 1983

Automatic Italian citizenship through marriage ended (Law no. 123). Prior to this date foreign women who married Italian men automatically and instantly became Italian citizens. Starting on this date, foreign women and foreign men are treated equally when marrying their Italian spouse: they do not receive automatic and immediate Italian citizenship.

In some jure sanguinis cases an Italian male ancestor naturalized with another country (usually his wife's) after marriage but before the birth or adoption of their child. Since the wife gained automatic Italian citizenship (in addition to her own previous citizenship) if the marriage was before this date, she retained Italian citizenship even when her husband naturalized. If her child was born or adopted after the marriage and on or after January 1, 1948, the child was born as an Italian citizen.

Example: Giuseppe, an Italian citizen, emigrated to Canada in 1947. He married Beatrice, a Canadian citizen, in 1950. Giuseppe naturalized as a Canadian citizen in 1953. They had a child, Karen, in 1955. Karen was born an Italian citizen because her mother, Beatrice, acquired Italian citizenship automatically in 1950 when she married Giuseppe. While Karen's father was no longer an Italian citizen when Karen was born, Beatrice could pass Italian citizenship on her own to Karen because Karen was born after 1947.

Law no. 123 also changed the treatment of minors (see March 10, 1975, above) when one or more Italian parents lose their Italian citizenship through naturalization. According to the Ministry of Foreign Affairs (Circular no. 9 of July 4, 2001), these rules govern whether an Italian minor lost his/her citizenship:

1. If the Italian father naturalized as the citizen of another country prior to July 1, 1912 (see above), he, his wife, and his minor children all lost Italian citizenship.

2. If an Italian minor attained the legal age of majority on or before April 27, 1983, he/she lost his/her Italian citizenship only if both these conditions were met:

(a) The minor acquired or possessed a foreign citizenship other than one which was granted automatically by virtue of being born in a foreign country.

(b) Either the "controlling" parent or the only Italian parent lost Italian citizenship, the minor was living with the parent who lost Italian citizenship, and the parent did not reacquire Italian citizenship before the minor attained the legal age of majority.

3. If an Italian minor attained the legal age of majority after April 27, 1983, and before August 15, 1992, he/she lost his/her Italian citizenship only if both these conditions were met:

(a) The minor acquired or possessed a foreign citizenship other than one which was granted automatically by virtue of being born in a foreign country.

(b) Either both parents or the only Italian parent lost Italian citizenship, and no parent reacquired Italian citizenship before the minor attained the legal age of majority.

Note that any parent who died while still an Italian citizen never lost Italian citizenship, so orphan minors are better protected in Italian citizenship law. Note also that the "controlling" parent is the minor's primary legal guardian and, prior to April 27, 1983, was with only rare exceptions the father if he was alive.

At certain times in history Italian minors could independently naturalize as foreign citizens under other countries' citizenship laws. Australia is a fairly common example, since Australia required children as young as 16 to naturalize on their own if they wanted Australian citizenship. Minors who joined the U.S. Armed Forces and acquired near-instant U.S. citizenship during World War I represent another cohort. If an Italian minor naturalized on his own in these and similar situations, he would retain his Italian citizenship unless the MFA's conditions were met.

August 15, 1992

Italy substantially revised its citizenship laws (Law no. 91 of February 5, 1992) to make dual citizenship more accepted. Prior to August 15, 1992, adult Italian citizens who naturalized with another country lost their Italian citizenship, and often they could also jeopardize even their previously born (or adopted) children's Italian citizenship. Starting on August 15, 1992, Italians naturalizing with another country retain their Italian citizenship.

Also, living Italians who previously renounced their citizenship can quickly reestablish their Italian citizenship by declaring their intention at an Italian embassy or consulate, taking up residence in Italy, and then applying. However, citizenship regained is not retroactive for the period when citizenship was lost. Children born or adopted during the non-Italian citizenship interval are not Italian citizens jure sanguinis.

———

* The laws on adoption in relation to citizenship are at least somewhat complex, and adoption was not specifically mentioned in many early citizenship-related laws. Consulates are likely (but certainly not guaranteed) to treat adoptees as follows:

(1) Adopted children (and their descendants) may still make jure sanguinis

citizenship claims through a biological Italian parent. However, in some jurisdictions original birth records are sealed or marked with phrases such as "not legal" and "for informational purposes only," presenting special challenges in discovering or proving biological parentage. Also, the consulate is likely to record the surname from the adoptee's old birth certificate, not the adoptee's current surname. Changing the surname (if desired) may require additional legal action in Italy subsequent to jure sanguinis citizenship recognition.

(2) If the adoption was legally recorded in Italy while the adoptee was still a minor, there should be no problem: the citizenship link was established at that point. (But if the adoption was legally recorded in Italy the adoptee is almost certainly already recognized as an Italian citizen.)

(3) If the adoption was not legally recorded in Italy while the adoptee was still a minor, then at least some consulates are not recognizing any citizenship link.

(4) If the adoption occurred while the adoptee was an adult (see March 10, 1975, above), then there is no citizenship link.

Fundamental Principals

Fundamental Principals of Italian Citizenship. Italian citizenship is mainly based on "jus sanguinis" (right of blood), according to which a child born to an Italian mother or father is Italian; at present the issue of citizenship is governed by Law No. 91 of 5th February 1992, as subsequently amended and complemented, and by related implementing regulations, as well as by the provisions of Law No. 94 of 15th July 2009.

LEGGE 5 FEBBRAIO 1992, N.91

Nuove norme sulla cittadinanza.

(pubblicata nella Gazzetta Ufficiale n. 38 del 15-2-1992)

1 - Il D.P.R. 18 aprile 1994, n. 362 (in S.O. n. 91 alla G.U. 13/6/1994 n. 136) ha abrogato l'art. 7, comma 1. 2 - La L. 22 dicembre 1994, n. 736 (in G.U. 4/1/1995 n. 3) ha modificato l'art. 17. 3 - La L. 23 dicembre 1996, n. 662 (in S.O. n. 233 relativo alla G.U. 28/12/1996 n. 303) ha modificato l'art. 17. La Camera dei deputati ed il Senato della Repubblica hanno approvato;

IL PRESIDENTE DELLA REPUBBLICA PROMULGA

la seguente legge:

Art. 1.

E' cittadino per nascita: a) il figlio di padre o di madre cittadini; b) chi è nato nel territorio della Repubblica se entrambi i genitori sono ignoti o apolidi, ovvero se il figlio non segue la cittadinanza dei genitori secondo la legge dello Stato al quale questi appartengono. 2. E' considerato cittadino per nascita il figlio di ignoti trovato nel territorio della Repubblica, se non venga provato il possesso di altra cittadinanza.

Art. 2.

Il riconoscimento o la dichiarazione giudiziale della filiazione durante la minore età del figlio ne determina la cittadinanza secondo le norme della presente legge. 2. Se il figlio riconosciuto o dichiarato è maggiorenne conserva il proprio stato di cittadinanza, ma può dichiarare, entro un anno dal riconoscimento o dalla dichiarazione giudiziale, ovvero dalla dichiarazione di efficacia del provvedimento straniero, di eleggere la cittadinanza determinata dalla filiazione. 3. Le disposizioni del presente articolo si applicano anche ai figli per i quali la paternità o maternità non può' essere dichiarata, purchè sia stato riconosciuto giudizialmente il loro diritto al mantenimento o agli alimenti.

Art. 3.

Il minore straniero adottato da cittadino italiano acquista la cittadinanza. 2. La disposizione del comma 1 si applica anche nei confronti degli adottati prima della data di entrata in vigore della presente legge. 3. Qualora l'adozione sia revocata per fatto dell'adottato, questi perde la cittadinanza italiana, sempre che sia in possesso di altra cittadinanza o la riacquisti. 4. Negli altri casi di revoca l'adottato conserva la cittadinanza italiana. Tuttavia, qualora la revoca intervenga durante la maggiore età dell'adottato, lo stesso, se in possesso di altra cittadinanza o se la riacquisti, potrà comunque rinunciare alla cittadinanza italiana entro un anno dalla revoca stessa.

Art. 4.

Lo straniero o l'apolide, del quale il padre o la madre o uno degli ascendenti in linea retta di secondo grado sono stati cittadini per nascita, diviene cittadino: a) se presta effettivo servizio militare per lo Stato italiano e dichiara preventivamente di voler acquistare la cittadinanza italiana; b) se assume pubblico impiego alle dipendenze dello Stato, anche all'estero, e dichiara di voler acquistare la cittadinanza italiana; c) se, al raggiungimento della maggiore età, risiede legalmente da almeno due anni nel territorio della Repubblica e dichiara, entro un anno dal raggiungimento, di voler acquistare la cittadinanza italiana.

Lo straniero nato in Italia, che vi abbia risieduto legalmente senza interruzioni fino al raggiungimento della maggiore età, diviene cittadino se dichiara di voler acquistare la cittadinanza italiana entro un anno dalla suddetta data.

Art. 5.

Il coniuge, straniero o apolide, di cittadino italiano acquista la cittadinanza italiana quando risiede legalmente da almeno sei mesi nel territorio della Repubblica, ovvero dopo tre anni dalla data del matrimonio, se non vi è stato scioglimento, annullamento o cessazione degli effetti civili e se non sussiste separazione legale.

Art. 6.

Precludono l'acquisto della cittadinanza ai sensi dell'articolo 5: a) la condanna per uno dei delitti previsti nel libro secondo, titolo I, capi I, II e III, del codice penale; b) la condanna per un delitto non colposo per il quale la legge preveda una pena edittale non inferiore nel massimo a tre anni di reclusione; ovvero la condanna per un reato non politico ad una pena detentiva superiore ad un anno da parte di una autorità giudiziaria straniera, quando la sentenza sia stata riconosciuta in Italia; c) la sussistenza, nel caso specifico, di comprovati motivi inerenti alla sicurezza della Repubblica. 2. Il riconoscimento della sentenza straniera è richiesto dal procuratore generale del distretto dove ha sede l'ufficio dello stato civile in cui è iscritto o trascritto il matrimonio, anche ai soli fini ed effetti di cui al comma 1, lettera b). 3. La riabilitazione fa cessare gli effetti preclusivi della condanna. 4. L'acquisto della cittadinanza è sospeso fino a comunicazione della sentenza definitiva, se sia stata promossa azione penale per uno dei delitti di cui al comma 1, lettera a) e lettera b), primo periodo, nonché per il tempo in cui è pendente il procedimento di riconoscimento della sentenza straniera, di cui al medesimo comma 1, lettera b), secondo periodo.

Art. 7.

Ai sensi dell'articolo 5, la cittadinanza si acquista con decreto del Ministro dell'interno, a istanza dell'interessato, presentata al sindaco del comune di residenza o alla competente autorità consolare. 2. Si applicano le disposizioni di cui all'articolo 3 della legge 12 gennaio 1991, n. 13.

Art. 8.

Con decreto motivato, il Ministro dell'interno respinge l'istanza di cui all'articolo 7 ove sussistano le cause ostative previste nell'articolo 6. Ove si tratti di ragioni inerenti alla sicurezza della Repubblica, il decreto è emanato su conforme parere del Consiglio di Stato. L'istanza respinta può essere riproposta dopo cinque anni dall'emanazione del provvedimento.

L'emanazione del decreto di rigetto dell'istanza è preclusa quando dalla data di presentazione dell'istanza stessa, corredata dalla prescritta documentazione, sia decorso il termine di due anni.

Art. 9.

La cittadinanza italiana può essere concessa con decreto del Presidente della Repubblica, sentito il Consiglio di Stato, su proposta del Ministro dell'interno: a) allo straniero del quale il padre o la madre o uno degli ascendenti in linea retta di secondo grado sono stati cittadini per nascita, o che è nato nel territorio della Repubblica e, in entrambi i casi, vi risiede legalmente da almeno tre anni, comunque fatto salvo quanto previsto dall'articolo 4, comma 1, lettera c); b) allo straniero maggiorenne adottato da cittadino italiano che risiede legalmente nel territorio della Repubblica da almeno cinque anni successivamente alla adozione; c) allo straniero che ha prestato servizio, anche all'estero, per almeno cinque anni alle dipendenze dello Stato; d) al cittadino di uno Stato membro delle Comunità europee se risiede legalmente da almeno quattro anni nel territorio della Repubblica; e) all'apolide che risiede legalmente da almeno cinque anni nel territorio della Repubblica; f) allo straniero che risiede legalmente da almeno dieci anni nel territorio della Repubblica. 2. Con decreto del Presidente della Repubblica, sentito il Consiglio di Stato e previa deliberazione del Consiglio dei Ministri, su proposta del Ministro dell'interno, di concerto con il Ministro degli affari esteri, la cittadinanza può essere concessa allo straniero quando questi abbia reso eminenti servizi all'Italia, ovvero quando ricorra un eccezionale interesse dello Stato.

Art. 10.

1. Il decreto di concessione della cittadinanza non ha effetto se la persona a cui si riferisce non presta, entro sei mesi dalla notifica del decreto medesimo, giuramento di essere fedele alla Repubblica e di osservare la Costituzione e le leggi dello Stato.

Art. 11.

1. Il cittadino che possiede, acquista o riacquista una cittadinanza straniera conserva quella italiana, ma puo' ad essa rinunciare qualora risieda o stabilisca la residenza all'estero.

Art. 12.

1. Il cittadino italiano perde la cittadinanza se, avendo accettato un impiego pubblico od una carica pubblica da uno Stato o ente pubblico estero o da un ente internazionale cui non partecipi l'Italia, ovvero prestando servizio militare per uno Stato estero, non ottempera, nel termine fissato, all'intimazione che il Governo italiano può rivolgergli di abbandonare l'impiego, la carica o il servizio militare. 2. Il cittadino italiano che, durante lo stato di guerra con uno Stato estero, abbia accettato o non abbia abbandonato un impiego pubblico od una carica pubblica, od abbia prestato servizio militare per tale Stato senza esservi obbligato, ovvero ne abbia acquistato volontariamente la cittadinanza, perde la cittadinanza italiana al momento della cessazione dello stato di guerra.

Art. 13.

1. Chi ha perduto la cittadinanza la riacquista: a) se presta effettivo servizio militare per lo Stato italiano e dichiara previamente di volerla riacquistare; b) se, assumendo o avendo assunto un pubblico impiego alle dipendenze dello Stato, anche all'estero, dichiara di volerla riacquistare; c) se dichiara di volerla riacquistare ed ha stabilito o stabilisce, entro un anno dalla dichiarazione, la residenza nel territorio della Repubblica; d) dopo un anno dalla data in cui ha stabilito la residenza nel territorio della Repubblica, salvo espressa rinuncia entro lo stesso termine; e) se, avendola perduta per non aver ottemperato all'intimazione di abbandonare l'impiego o la carica accettati da uno Stato, da un ente pubblico estero o da un ente internazionale, ovvero il servizio militare per uno Stato estero, dichiara di volerla riacquistare, sempre che abbia stabilito la residenza da almeno due anni nel territorio della Repubblica e provi di aver abbandonato l'impiego o la carica o il servizio militare, assunti o prestati nonostante l'intimazione di cui all'articolo 12, comma 1. 2. Non è ammesso il

riacquisto della cittadinanza a favore di chi l'abbia perduta in applicazione dell'articolo 3, comma 3, nonché dell'articolo 12, comma 2. 3. Nei casi indicati al comma 1, lettera c), d) ed e), il riacquisto della cittadinanza non ha effetto se viene inibito con decreto del Ministro dell'interno, per gravi e comprovati motivi e su conforme parere del Consiglio di Stato. Tale inibizione può intervenire entro il termine di un anno dal verificarsi delle condizioni stabilite.

Art. 14.

I figli minori di chi acquista o riacquista la cittadinanza italiana, se convivono con esso, acquistano la cittadinanza italiana, ma, divenuti maggiorenni, possono rinunciarvi, se in possesso di altra cittadinanza.

Art. 15.

L'acquisto o il riacquisto della cittadinanza ha effetto, salvo quanto stabilito dall'articolo 13, comma 3, dal giorno successivo a quello in cui sono adempiute le condizioni e le formalità richieste.

Art. 16.

L'apolide che risiede legalmente nel territorio della Repubblica è soggetto alla legge italiana per quanto si riferisce all'esercizio dei diritti civili ed agli obblighi del servizio militare. 2. Lo straniero riconosciuto rifugiato dallo Stato italiano secondo le condizioni stabilite dalla legge o dalle convenzioni internazionali è equiparato all'apolide ai fini dell'applicazione della presente legge, con esclusione degli obblighi inerenti al servizio militare.

Art. 17.

Chi ha perduto la cittadinanza in applicazione degli articoli 8 e 12 della legge 13 giugno 1912, n. 555, o per non aver reso l'opzione prevista dall'articolo 5 della legge 21 aprile 1983, n.123, la riacquista se effettua una dichiarazione in tal senso entro due anni dalla data di entrata in vigore della presente legge. 2. Resta fermo quanto disposto dall'articolo 219 della legge 19 maggio 1975, n. 151.

Art. 18.

Le persone già residenti nei territori che sono appartenuti alla monarchia austro-ungarica ed emigrate all'estero prima del 16 luglio 1920 ed i loro discendenti in linea retta sono equiparati, ai fini e per gli effetti dell'articolo 9, comma 1, lettera a), agli stranieri di origine italiana o nati nel territorio della Repubblica.

Art. 19.

Restano salve le disposizioni della legge 9 gennaio 1956, n. 27, sulla trascrizione nei registri dello stato civile dei provvedimenti di riconoscimento delle opzioni per la cittadinanza italiana, effettuate ai sensi dell'articolo 19 del Trattato di pace tra le potenze alleate ed associate e l'Italia, firmato a Parigi il 10 febbraio 1947.

Art. 20.

Salvo che sia espressamente previsto, lo stato di cittadinanza acquisito anteriormente alla presente legge non si modifica se non per fatti posteriori alla data di entrata in vigore della stessa.

Art. 21.

Ai sensi e con le modalità di cui all'articolo 9, la cittadinanza italiana può essere concessa allo straniero che sia stato affiliato da un cittadino italiano prima della data di entrata in vigore della legge 4 maggio 1983, n. 184, e che risieda legalmente nel territorio della Repubblica da almeno sette anni dopo l'affiliazione.

Art. 22.

Per coloro i quali, alla data di entrata in vigore della presente legge, abbiano già perduto la cittadinanza italiana ai sensi dell'articolo 8 della legge 13 giugno 1912, n. 555, cessa ogni obbligo militare.

Art. 23.

Le dichiarazioni per l'acquisto, la conservazione, il riacquisto e la rinunzia alla cittadinanza e la prestazione del giuramento previste dalla presente legge sono rese all'ufficiale dello stato civile del comune dove il dichiarante risiede o intende stabilire la propria residenza, ovvero, in caso di residenza all'estero, davanti all'autorità diplomatica o consolare del luogo di residenza. 2. Le dichiarazioni di cui al comma 1, nonché gli atti o i provvedimenti attinenti alla perdita, alla conservazione e al riacquisto della cittadinanza italiana vengono trascritti nei registri di cittadinanza e di essi viene effettuata annotazione a margine dell'atto di nascita.

Art. 24.

Il cittadino italiano, in caso di acquisto o riacquisto di cittadinanza straniera o di opzione per essa, deve darne, entro tre mesi dall'acquisto, riacquisto o opzione, o dal raggiungimento della maggiore età, se successivo, comunicazione mediante dichiarazione all'ufficiale dello stato civile del luogo di residenza, ovvero, se residente all'estero, all'autorità consolare competente. 2. Le dichiarazioni di cui al comma 1 sono soggette alla medesima disciplina delle dichiarazioni di cui all'articolo 23. 3. Chiunque non adempia agli obblighi indicati nel comma 1 è assoggettato alla sanzione amministrativa pecuniaria da lire duecentomila a lire duemilioni. Competente all'applicazione della sanzione amministrativa è il prefetto.

Art. 25.

Le disposizioni necessarie per l'esecuzione della presente legge sono emanate, entro un anno dalla sua entrata in vigore, con decreto del Presidente della Repubblica, udito il parere del Consiglio di Stato e previa deliberazione del Consiglio dei Ministri, su proposta dei Ministri degli affari esteri e dell'interno, di concerto con il Ministro di grazia e giustizia.

Art. 26.

Sono abrogati la legge 13 giugno 1912, n. 555, la legge 31 gennaio 1926, n. 108, il regio decreto-legge , dicembre 1934, n.1997, convertito dalla legge 4 aprile 1935, n. 517, l'articolo 143- ter del codice civile, la legge 21 aprile 1983, n. 123, l'articolo 39 della legge 4 maggio 1983, n. 184, la legge 15 maggio 1986, n. 180, e ogni altra disposizione incompatibile con la presente legge. 2. E' soppresso l'obbligo dell'opzione di cui all'articolo 5, comma secondo, della legge 21 aprile 1983, n. 123, e all'articolo 1, comma 1, della legge 15 maggio 1986, n. 180. 3. Restano salve le diverse disposizioni previste da accordi internazionali.

Art. 27.

La presente legge entra in vigore sei mesi dopo la sua pubblicazione nella Gazzetta Ufficiale. La presente legge, munita del sigillo dello Stato, sarà inserita nella Raccolta ufficiale degli atti normativi della Repubblica italiana. E' fatto obbligo a chiunque spetti di osservarla e di farla osservare come legge dello Stato.

Data a Roma, addì 5 febbraio 1992

LEGGE 5 FEBBRAIO 1992, N.91

The law 91/1992 reformulated preceding legislation on nationality, bringing it in line with current realities. It reconfirms the principle of ius sanguinis ("blood rights"), and introduces various fundamental principles - such as the equality of both marriage partners in terms of their right to pass nationality to their children, and the opportunity for foreign nationals to choose Italian nationality on the basis of their birth, their residence, or their origins.

ART.1

1. Citizen by birth is:

a) the child of a father or a mother, who are Italian citizens;

b) a person who was born in the territory of the Republic if both parents are unknown or stateless, or if the child does not follow the citizenship of the parents according to the law of the State to which the parents belong.

2. The child of unknown parents who is found abandoned in the territory of the Republic shall, unless possession of another citizenship is proved, be deemed citizen by birth.

ART.2

1. Recognition or judicial statement of filiation, occurred when the child is a minor (or: during the age of minority of the child), determines the citizenship of the child pursuant to the provisions of this statute.

2. If the recognized or judicially stated child is of full age, he keeps his own citizenship. Nevertheless he is entitled to choose the citizenship determined by filiation within one year after-

(a) recognition or judicial statement; or

(b) declaration of effectiveness of the foreign provision. 3. The provisions of this article also apply to children in respect of whom paternity or maternity may not be declared, provided their right to maintenance or alimony has been judicially recognized.

ART.3

1. An alien, who is a minor, shall acquire Italian citizenship if he is adopted by an Italian citizen.

2. Paragraph 1 also applies to persons who were adopted before this statute came into force.

3. When revocation of the adoption is based on a fact of the adopted, he loses Italian citizenship if he possesses another citizenship or he regains it.

4. In the other cases of revocation the adopted maintains Italian citizenship. Nevertheless, if revocation occurs when the adopted is of full age, the latter will be entitled to renounce Italian citizenship within one year after the revocation itself, if he possesses another citizenship or he regains it.

ART.4

1. An alien or a stateless person, whose father or mother or one of the ascendants in second degree were Italian nationals by birth, shall become Italian national:

a) if he serves in the Italian army and preventively declares that he wants to acquire Italian citizenship;

b) if he works for the State in the Civil Service (or: if he works as an employee of the State), even abroad, and he declares that he wants to acquire Italian citizenship;

c) if, when he becomes of full age, he had his legal place of residence in Italy for at least two years and he declares, within one year after reaching the age of majority, that he wants to acquire Italian citizenship.

2. An alien born in Italy, who had his legal place of residence in Italy uninterruptedly until the reaching of full age, becomes Italian national if he declares he wants to acquire Italian citizenship within one year after that date.

ART.5

The spouse, who is alien or stateless, of an Italian national acquires Italian citizenship when he has had legal residence in the Republic for at least six months, or after three years since the date of the marriage, unless dissolution, annulment, divorce, or separation has taken place.

ART.6

1. Acquisition of citizenship pursuant to art.5 is precluded by:

a) conviction for one of the offences provided by book II, title I, capi I, II, III, of the Penal Code;

b) conviction for a non-reckless offence for which law provides imprisonment for a term of at least three years; or conviction for a non-political crime to imprisonment longer than one year inflicted by a foreign court if the judgment has been recognized in Italy;

c) the existence, in the specific case, of relevant grounds concerning public security.

2. Recognition of foreign judgment is required by the General Public Attorney of the district in which the Office of "civil status" - where the marriage is registered - resides.

3. Rehabilitation avoids the results of the sentence.

4. Acquisition of citizenship is suspended till the communication of the final judgment, if the penal action for one of the offences provided by para.1, lett.a) and b), first phrase, has been brought; as well as during the proceeding of recognition of the foreign judgment (para.1, lett.b), second phrase).

ART.7

1. Pursuant to art.5, citizenship is acquired by means of a decree given by the Minister of Internal Affairs, on petition of the person concerned. This petition shall be submitted to the mayor of the commune of residence or to the competent consular authority.

2. Article 3 of statute 12 January 1991, n.13 shall be applied.

ART.8

1. The Minister of Internal Affairs rejects the petition provided by art.7 with a justified decree where the causes provided by art.6 are present. The decree is enacted with the agreement of the State of Council where public security is concerned. The rejected petition may be submitted again after 5 years from the issue of the provision.

2. The petition - equipped with the requested documentation - may not be rejected after 2 years from its submission.

ART.9

1. The President of the Republic, after consulting the State Council, on the recommendation of the Minister of Internal Affairs, grants Italian citizenship to:

a) an alien, whose father or mother or one of the direct ascendants in II degree were Italian nationals by birth, or who was born in the territory of the Republic and, in both cases, has had his legal residence in Italy for at least 3 years, saving art.4, comma1, lett.c);

b) an alien of full age, adopted by an Italian citizen, who has had his legal residence in the territory of the Republic for at least five years after the adoption;

c) an alien, who has been a civil servant - even abroad - for at least five years;

d) a citizen of a EC-Member State if he has had his legal residence in the territory of the Republic for at least four years;

e) a stateless person who has had his legal residence in the territory of the Republic for at least five years;

f) an alien who has had his legal residence in the territory of the Republic for at least ten years.

2. The President of the Republic, after consulting the State Council and after the decision of the Council of Ministers, taken on the proposal of the Minister of Internal Affairs with the agreement of the Minister of Foreign Affairs, grants Italian citizenship to an alien who rendered distinguished services to Italy, or whenever outstanding public interests are concerned.

ART.10

The decree which grants Italian citizenship has no effects unless the person concerned takes the oath of fidelity to the Republic, the Constitution and the national law, within six months after the notification of the decree.

ART.11

The citizen who possesses, acquires or regains a foreign citizenship shall keep the Italian one. Nevertheless he may renounce the Italian citizenship if he resides or settles down abroad.

ART.12

1. Whenever an Italian citizen accepted a public office from a foreign State or a foreign public body or an international body - to which Italy does not belong - or he is in a foreign Army, he shall lose Italian citizenship, unless he obeys, within the fixed term, to the order of the Government to abandon the office or the military service.

2. An Italian citizen shall lose the Italian citizenship when the state of war ceases, if, during the state of war against a foreign State-

a) he accepted or did not abandon a public office; or

b) he was in the Army for this State without being obliged to do so; or

c) he voluntarily acquired the citizenship of this State.

ART.13

1. He who lost the citizenship shall recover it:

a) if he is in the Italian Army and he previously declares he wants to recover it; b) if he accepts or accepted a public office for the State, even abroad, and he declares he wants to recover it;

c) if he declares he wants to recover it and he resided or he resides in the territory of the Republic, within one year from the declaration;

d) after one year from the establishment of the residence in the territory of the Republic, unless he express renounced within the same term;

e) if he lost his citizenship because he did not obey the order of abandoning the military service for a foreign State or the office granted by a State, by a foreign public body or by an international body and he declares he wants to recover it, on condition that he has resided in the territory of the Republic for at least two years and he proves that he abandoned the public office or the military service he has undertaken notwithstanding the order provided by art.12, comma 1.

2. He who lost the Italian citizenship according to art.3, comma 3 and art.12, comma 2 may not recover it.

3. In the cases provided by comma 1, lett.c), d), e), the acquisition of citizenship has no effects if it is forbidden by decree of the Minister of Internal Affairs, for severe reasons and the agreement of the State Council. This prohibition may take place within one year since the established conditions happened.

ART.14

Minor children of a person who acquires or recovers the Italian citizenship acquire Italian citizenship, if they live together with their parent; but, once they became of full age, they are entitled to renounce it, if they possess another citizenship.

ART.15

1. Save what provided by art.13, comma 3, acquisition or recovering of citizenship produces effect from the day after the fulfilment of the required conditions and formalities.

ART.16

1. A stateless person who has his legal residence in the territory of the Republic is subject to Italian law as to the exercise of civil rights and of military duties.

2. An alien recognized as a refugee by Italian State according to the provisions provided by law or by international conventions is considered a stateless person as to the application of this statute except for military duties.

ART.17

1. He who lost citizenship pursuant artt.8 and 12 of statute 13 June 1912, n.555, or for not having taken the option provided by art.5 of statute 21 April 1983, n.123, shall recover it if he declares, within two years from the implementation of this statute, that he wants to recover Italian citizenship.

2. Art.219 of statute 19 May 1975, n.151, is still in force.

.

ART.18

1. The persons who resided in the territories which were under the House of Austria, and who emigrated abroad before 16 July 1920 and their direct descendants - pursuant to art.9, comma 1, lett.a) - are deemed aliens of Italian origin or born in the territory of the Republic.

ART.19

1. Statute 9 January 1956, n.27, on transcription in the registers of civil status of the provisions of recognition of options for Italian citizenship - options taken pursuant to art.19 of Peace Treaty between the Allies and Italy, signed up in Paris on the 10 February 1947 - stays in force

ART.20

1. Unless it has been express provided, the status of citizenship acquired before the issue of this statute shall not be modified unless by facts occured after the date in which this statute came into force.

ART.21

1. Pursuant to article 9, Italian citizenship may be granted to the alien who was affiliated by an Italian citizenship before the date of implementation of statute 4 May 1983, n.184, and who has been having the legal residence in the territory of the Republic for at least seven years after the affiliation.

ART.22

1. The persons, who had already lost Italian citizenship pursuant to art. 8 of statute 13 June 1912, n.555, are not subject to military duties.

ART.23

1. The statements for acquiring, keeping, recovering and renouncing citizenship and the swearing provided by this statute are set out before the registrar of the commune where the declarant resides or intends to settle down, or, in case he resides abroad, before the diplomatic or consular authority of the place of residence.

2. Statements provided by comma 1, and acts or provisions concerning the lost, the keeping and the recovering of Italian citizenship shall be transcribed in the citizenship-registers and shall be annotated in the birth-certificate.

ART.24

1. An Italian citizen, in case he acquires or regains or chooses foreign citizenship, must communicate it by statement to the registrar of the place of residence or, if he resides abroad, to the entitled consular authority, within three months from the acquisition, recovering or option, or from the achievement of full age, if it is subsequent.

2. Statements provided by comma 1 follow the same rules as the statements provided by art.23.

3. Whoever does not fulfil the obligations provided by comma 1 is subject to a fine for an amount which can vary between 200.000 and 2.000.000 Lire. The prefect is entitled to the application of the fine mentioned above.

ART.25

1. The provisions which are necessary for the enactment of this statute are promulgated, within one year since it came into force, by means of a decree of the President of the Republic, with the advice of the State Council and after the deliberation of the Council of Ministers, on the proposal of the Minister of

Foreign Affairs and of the Minister of Internal Affairs, with the agreement of the Minister of Justice.

ART.26

1. Statute 13 June 1912, n.555, statute 31 January 1926, n.108, royal decreto-legge 1 December 1934, n.1997, converted by statute 4 April 1935, n.517, art.143-ter civil code, statute 21 April 1983, n.123, art.39 of statute 4 May 1983, n.184, statute 15 May 1986, n.180, and every other provision which is incompatible with this statute are repealed.

2. The duty of option provided by art.5, comma 2, of statute 21 April 1983, n.123, and art.1, comma 1, of statute 15 May 1986, n.180 is abolished.

3. Different provisions provided by international agreements shall be applied.

ART.27

1. This statute shall come into force after six months from its publication in the Gazzetta Ufficiale.

MINISTERO DELL'INTERNO *CIRCOLARE N° 28 (2002)

OGGETTO: Iscrizione anagrafica dei discendenti di cittadini italiani per nascita, per il riconoscimento della cittadinanza italiana.

E' stato da più parti rappresentato a questo Dipartimento il differente comportamento tenuto dagli Uffici demograficl comunali in merito alla iscrizione anagrafica dei discendenti di cittadini italiani per nascita in possesso di un valido permesso dl soggiorno, condizione indispensabile per avviare in Italia la procedura per il riconoscimento della cittadinanza "jure sanguinis".

Pertanto, dopo un approfondito esame della problematica si ritiene di dover impartire la seguente disposizione, ai fine di garantire la parità di trattamento dei soggetti interessati e di evitare agli stessi ulteriori disagi, velocizzando le procedure previste.

E pertanto, ribadendo l'orientamento già espresso in altre occasionl, si ritiene che si debba procedere all'iscrizione nei registri anagrafici del discendenti di cittadini italiani per nascita in possesso di un valido permesso di soggiorno, indipendentemente dalla durata dello stesso e dal titolo per il quale viene concesso.

D'altra parte dal contesto generale del d.lgs. 25 luglio 1998, n. 286 e del regolamento di attuazione dello stesso adottato con il d.P.R. 31 agosto 1999 n. 394 emerge che gli stranieri in possesso dl regolare permesso dl soggiorno possono essere iscritti nell'anagrafe della popolazione residente, a prescindere dalla durata dei permesso stesso, come si evince dall'articolo 6, c. 7 del citato d.lgs n. 286/1998.

Ai Signori Prefetti si chiede di voler comunicare ai Sindaci il contenuto della presente circolare.

IL DIRETTORE CENTRALE (Ciclosi)

Articolo 6 - Facoltà ed obblighi inerenti al soggiorno - D.lgs n. 286/1998

Il permesso di soggiorno rilasciato per motivi di lavoro subordinato, lavoro autonomo e familiari può essere utilizzato anche per le altre attività consentite. Quello rilasciato per motivi di studio e formazione può essere convertito, comunque prima della sua scadenza, e previa stipula del contratto di soggiorno per lavoro ovvero previo rilascio della certificazione attestante la sussistenza dei requisiti previsti dall'articolo 26, in permesso di soggiorno per motivi di lavoro nell'ambito delle quote stabilite a norma dell'articolo 3, comma 4, secondo le modalità previste dal regolamento di attuazione.

Fatta eccezione per i provvedimenti riguardanti attività sportive e ricreative a carattere temporaneo e per quelli inerenti agli atti di stato civile o all'accesso a pubblici servizi, i documenti inerenti al soggiorno di cui all'articolo 5, comma 8, devono essere esibiti agli uffici della pubblica amministrazione ai fini del rilascio di licenze, autorizzazioni, iscrizioni ed altri provvedimenti di interesse dello straniero comunque denominati.

Lo straniero che, a richiesta degli ufficiali e agenti di pubblica sicurezza, non esibisce, senza giustificato motivo, il passaporto o altro documento di identificazione, ovvero il permesso o la carta di soggiorno è punito con l'arresto tino a sei mesi e l'ammenda fino a lire ottocentomila.

Qualora vi sia motivo di dubitare della identità personale dello straniero, questi è sottoposto a rilievi fotodattiloscopici e segnaletici.

Per le verifiche previste dal presente testo unico o dal regolamento di attuazione, l'autorità di pubblica sicurezza, quando vi siano fondate ragioni, richiede agli stranieri informazioni e atti comprovanti la disponibilità di un reddito, da lavoro o da altra fonte legittima, sufficiente al sostentamento proprio e dei familiari conviventi nel territorio dello Stato.

Salvo quanto è stabilito nelle leggi militari, il Prefetto può vietare agli stranieri il soggiorno in comuni o in località che comunque interessano la difesa militare dello Stato. Tale divieto è comunicato agli stranieri per mezzo della autorità locale di pubblica sicurezza o col mezzo di pubblici avvisi. Gli stranieri, che trasgrediscono al divieto, possono essere allontanati per mezzo della forza pubblica.

Le iscrizioni e variazioni anagrafiche dello straniero regolarmente soggiornante sono effettuate alle medesime condizioni dei cittadini italiani con le modalità previste dal regolamento di attuazione. In ogni caso la dimora dello straniero si considera abituale anche in caso di documentata ospitalità da più di tre mesi presso un centro di accoglienza. Dell'avvenuta iscrizione o variazione l'ufficio da comunicazione alla questura territorialmente competente.

Fuori dei casi di cui al comma 7, gli stranieri che soggiornano nel territorio dello Stato devono comunicare al questore competente per territorio, entro i quindici giorni successivi, le eventuali variazioni del proprio domicilio abituale.

Il documento di identificazione per stranieri è rilasciato su modello conforme al tipo approvato con decreto del Ministro dell'interno. Esso non è valido per l'espatrio, salvo che sia diversamente disposto dalle convenzioni o dagli accordi internazionali.

Contro i provvedimenti di cui all'articolo 5 e al presente articolo è ammesso ricorso al tribunale amministrativo regionale competente.

Ministry of the Interior

*CIRCULAR n° 28 (2002)

RE: Vital Records registration of descendents of Italians who are citizens by birth, for citizenship purposes.

This Department has received several reports on the differences in the behavior of the various municipal Offices of Vital Records regarding the registration of those descendants of Italian citizens by birth who have a valid residence permit, which is an indispensable condition for starting in Italy the proceedings for obtaining citizenship by right of descent (jure sanguinis).

Therefore, after a thorough investigation of the problem we deem necessary to issue the following guidelines in order to ensure that the interested parties are treated equally and can avoid further inconvenience, by speeding up the established procedures.

In addition, reiterating the previously indicated opinion, we deem it necessary to proceed with the registration in the Vital Records registers of those descendants of Italian citizens by birth who have a valid residence permit, regardless of the duration of such residence and the title under which it was granted.

On the other hand, from the general context of Legislative Decree 25 July 1998, n. 286 and of the rule governing its implementation that was adopted with (d.P.R) Decree by the President of the Republic 31 August 1999 n. 394, it emerges that aliens in possession of a regular residence permit may be registered in the resident population register of Vital Records, regardless of the duration of such permit, as indicated by <u>article 6, c. 7 of the cited Legislative Decree n. 286/1998.</u>

We ask the Prefects to inform the Mayors of the contents of this circular.

THE CENTRAL DIRECTOR (Ciclosi)

Article 6 – Rights and obligations inherent in residence – Legislative Decree n. 286/1998

The residence permit issued for employment, self-employment and family members can also be used for other permitted activities. A permit issued for study or training purposes can be converted into a residence permit for employment within the scope of the quotas established under article 3, par. 4, in accordance with the methods established in the rule governing implementation, as long as said permit is not expired, and after the contract of residence for employment purposes is completed, and after the issuance of certification attesting to the presence of the requirements prescribed in article 26.

Except for the provisions regarding sports and recreational activities of a temporary nature and the provisions inherent in the civil status records or access to public services, the documents related to residence described in article 5, par. 8, must be presented to the public administration offices when seeking the issuance of licenses, permits, registrations and any other documents of interest to the alien.

The alien resident who, without justification, upon the request by police officers and agents, does not show his passport or other identification document or his residence permit or card, will be punished by imprisonment for up to six months and payment of a fine of up to eight hundred thousand lire.

Whenever there is reason to doubt the identity of an alien resident, he will have to undergo photodactyloscopic and identification checks.

For the checks prescribed in this document or in the current regulations, the public safety authorities, whenever there is compelling reason, shall ask alien residents for information and documents demonstrating the availability of income, whether from employment or other legitimate source, sufficient for the support of the individual and the family members living with him within the territory of the State.

Except for the provisions of military law, the Prefect can prohibit an alien to reside in a municipality or locality that is in any way involved in the defense of the State. Such prohibition will be communicated to the alien through the local police authority or by public notices. Aliens who violate the prohibition may be removed by the police.

The registration of and changes in the personal data of the legally residing aliens will be made under the same conditions as for the Italian citizens, in the manner established in the rule governing implementation.

In any case, the domicile of the alien shall be considered habitual even in the event of a documented stay of more than three months in a reception center. The office shall notify the competent police station of the registrations or changes.

Aside from the cases in paragraph 7, the aliens who reside in the territory of the State must notify the area's chief of police within 15 days of any changes in his habitual domicile.

The identification document for aliens is modeled in conformity with the type approved by decree by the Ministry of the Interior. This document is not valid outside the country, unless otherwise provided by international conventions or agreements.

Claims against the provisions of article 5 and in this article may be submitted to the competent regional administrative court.

*CIRCOLARE N° 28.1 (1991)

* La Circolare K.28.1 per i Sindaci in materia di cittadinanza Circolare n. K. 28.1 - 8 aprile 1991 del Ministero dell'Interno

Riconoscimento del possesso dello status civitatis italiano ai cittadini stranieri di ceppo italiano

Si è avuto modo di rilevare come pervengano sempre più numerose richieste di chiarimenti circa le modalità che debbono essere adottate al fine di definire la situazione di cittadinanza di persone provenienti da Paesi esteri (in particolar modo dall'Argentina ma anche dal Brasile o dagli Stati Uniti) e munite di passaporto straniero, le quali rivendicano la titolarità dello status civitatis italiano.

Come è noto, infatti, in virtù della contemporanea operatività del combinato disposto dagli artt. 1 e 7 della Legge 13 giugno 1912, n.555 e delle disposizioni vigenti in materia di cittadinanza di numerosi Paesi esteri d'antica emigrazione italiana (ad es. tutti gli Stati del continente americano, l'Australia, ecc.) attributivi iure soli dello status civitatis. La prole nata sul territorio dello Stato d'emigrazione (Argentina, Brasile, Uruguay, Stati Uniti d'America, Canada, Australia, Venezuela, ecc.) da padre cittadino italiano acquisiva dalla nascita il possesso tanto della cittadinanza italiana (in derivazione paterna) quanto della cittadinanza dello Stato di nascita e permaneva nella condizione di bipolidia anche nel caso in cui il genitore, durante l'età minorile, mutasse cittadinanza naturalizzandosi. straniero.

Nel contempo, anche i soggetti nati in uno Stato estero il quale attribuisce la cittadinanza iure soli e riconosciuti dal padre cittadino o la cui paternità sia stata dichiarata giudizialmente risultano versare nella medesima situazione di doppia cittadinanza.

Da ciò deriva la concreta possibilità che i discendenti di seconda terza e quarta generazione ed oltre di nostri emigrati siano investiti della cittadinanza italiana. Detta eventualità si è ancor più estesa per gli appartenenti a famiglie di antica origine italiana i quali siano nati dopo il 1° gennaio 1948 in quanto, a partire da tale data, debbono essere considerati, secondo il dettato della sentenza n. 30 del 9 febbraio 1983 della Corte Costituzionale, cittadini italiani all'epoca della loro nascita ovvero riconosciuti dalla madre o la cui maternità sia stata giudizialmente dichiarata.Ne consegue che pure i discendenti di nostra emigrante sono da reputarsi cittadini italiani iure sanguininis in derivazione materna purché nati dopo il I° gennaio 1948, data di entrata in vigore della Costituzione repubblicana.

Si fa, tuttavia, presente che il riconoscimento del possesso dello status civitatis italiano all'anzidetta categoria di persone deve essere subordinato al verificarsi di determinate condizioni ed al documentato accertamento di alcune essenziali circostanze.

Condizioni preliminari per il riconoscimento della cittadinanza italiana. Innanzi tutto occorre chiarire che, dovendo l'eventuale possesso dello status civitatis italiano essere certificato dal Sindaco del Comune italiano di residenza, potrà essere avviato il relativo procedimento su istanza degli interessati, solo ove costoro risultino iscritti nell'anagrafe della popolazione residente di un Comune italiano. Peraltro, l'iscrizione anagrafica di queste persone, entrate in Italia con passaporto straniero, deve seguire le modalità disciplinanti l'iscrizione nell'anagrafe della popolazione residente degli stranieri e presuppone, da parte degli interessati, l'espletamento degli adempimenti di cui alle disposizioni vigenti in materia. Si soggiunge, altresì, che qualora l'iscrizione anagrafica delle anzidette persone non risultasse possibile in quanto costoro non possono annoverarsi tra la popolazione residente secondo la nozione di cui all'art. 3 del D.P.R. 30 maggio 1989, n.123, la procedura di riconoscimento del possesso dello status civitatis italiano dovrà essere espletata, su apposita istanza, dalla Rappresentanza consolare italiana competente in relazione alla località straniera di dimora abituale dei soggetti rivendicanti la titolarità della cittadinanza italiana.

Procedura per il riconoscimento della cittadinanza italiana. Le istanze di riconoscimento della cittadinanza italiana ex articolo 1 della legge 13 giugno 1912, n.555 dovranno essere indirizzate al Sindaco del Comune italiano di residenza, ovvero al Console italiano nell'ambito della cui circoscrizione consolare risieda l'istante straniero originario italiano.Le stesse dovranno essere corredate dalla seguente documentazione:

estratto dell'atto di nascita dell'avo italiano emigrato all'estero rilasciato dal Comune italiano dove egli nacque;

atti di nascita, muniti di traduzione ufficiale italiana, di tutti i suoi discendenti in linea retta, compreso quello della persona rivendicante il possesso della cittadinanza italiana;

atto di matrimonio dell'avo italiano emigrato all'estero, munito di traduzione ufficiale italiana se formato all'estero;

atti di matrimonio dei suoi discendenti, in linea retta, compreso quello dei genitori della persona rivendicante il possesso della cittadinanza italiana;

certificato rilasciato dalle competenti Autorità dello Stato estero di emigrazione, munito di traduzione ufficiale in lingua italiana, attestante che l'avo italiano a suo tempo emigrato dall'Italia non acquistò la cittadinanza dello Stato estero di emigrazione anteriormente alla nascita dell'ascendente dell'interessato;

certificato rilasciato dalla competente Autorità consolare italiana attestante che né gli ascendenti in linea diretta né la persona rivendicante il possesso della cittadinanza italiana vi abbiano mai rinunciato ai termini dell'art. 7 della legge 13 giugno 1912, n. 555;

certificato di residenza.

Si precisa che l'istanza, presentata in Italia, dovrà essere redatta su carta legale e che i certificati forniti a corredo della medesima, ove rilasciati in Italia da Autorità italiane, dovranno essere prodotti in conformità con le disposizioni vigenti in materia di bollo. I certificati rilasciati da Autorità straniere dovranno essere redatti su carta semplice ed opportunamente legalizzati salvo che non sia previsto l'esonero dalla legalizzazione in base a convenzioni internazionali ratificate dall'Italia. I medesimi documenti dovranno essere muniti di traduzione ufficiale in lingua italiana la quale, se gli stessi sono esibiti in Italia, dovrà essere redatta su carta da bollo. Si fa, ancora, presente che, allo scopo di poter accertare in modo compiuto il mancato esercizio - da parte dei soggetti reclamanti il possesso della cittadinanza italiana - della facoltà di rinunziarvi ex art.7 della richiamata Legge n. 555/1912 si rende necessario, da un lato, svolgere adeguate indagini presso il comune italiano d'origine o di ultima residenza dell'avo italiano emigrato all'estero ovvero presso il Comune di Roma e, dall'altro lato, contattare direttamente tutte le Rappresentanze consolari italiane competenti per le varie località estere ove gli individui in questione abbiano risieduto o, se del caso, consultare opportunamente il Ministero degli Affari Esteri - Direzione Generale dell'Emigrazione e degli Affari Sociali - Ufficio VIII perché interpelli i dipendenti Uffici Consolari interessati. I Signori Sindaci, verificata altresì la fondatezza della pretesa avanzata dagli istanti a vedersi attribuita iure sanguinis la cittadinanza italiana, disporranno la trascrizione degli atti di stato civile relativi ai soggetti riconosciuti nostri connazionali e potranno procedere al rilascio dell'apposita certificazione di cittadinanza nonché agli altri conseguenti incombenti di competenza. I Signori Sindaci vorranno, infine, dare comunicazione delle determinazioni assunte alle SS.LL. alle locali Autorità di P.S. ed a questo Ministero. Nel caso in cui, invece, insorgessero dubbi circa l'effettiva situazione di cittadinanza dei richiedenti il nostro status civitatis. i Signori Sindaci sono pregati di interpellare questo Ministero trasmettendo il relativo carteggio. Si prega di diramare le opportune istruzioni ai Sindaci dei Comuni della Provincia e di fornire assicurazione.

*CIRCULAR N° 28.1 (1991)

* Circular K.28.1 sent to town Mayors on the matter of citizenship Circular no. K. 28.1 – April 8, 1991, by the Ministry of the Interior

Recognition of Italian citizenship for citizens of other countries who are descendents of Italians

We have been made aware of the increasing number of requests for clarification regarding how to define the matter of citizenship for individuals from foreign countries (especially Argentina, but also Brazil and the United States) who hold a foreign passport and are claiming the right to Italian citizenship.

It is known that, due to the simultaneous application of the combined provisions of articles 1 and 7 of the Law of June 13, 1912, no. 2555, and the regulations concerning citizenship currently in effect in several countries that in the past were the destination of Italian emigrants (for example, all the countries on the American continent, Australia, etc.) and which confer citizenship by birth in the territory. A child whose father is an Italian citizen and is born within the territory of the country to which the parents emigrated (Argentina, Brazil, Uruguay, United States, Canada, Australia, Venezuela, etc.), at the time of birth he/she holds both the Italian citizenship (from the father) as well as the citizenship of the country of birth, and retains the dual citizenship status even if the father becomes a naturalized citizen of the foreign country while the child is a minor.

At the same time, individuals who are born in a foreign country which confers citizenship based on birth on its territory and are acknowledged by the father who is a citizen, or such paternity is judicially established, are in the same status of double citizenship.

This gives rise to the concrete possibility that second-, third- and fourth-generation or later descendents of our emigrants acquire Italian citizenship.

Such eventuality has been additionally extended to individuals from families who in the far past originated in Italy. and were born after January 1, 1948, because starting on that date, according to decision no. 30 dated February 9, 1983, issued by the Constitutional Court, they must be considered Italian citizens at the time of their birth, that is, acknowledged by the mother or whose maternity was established judicially.

Consequently, even the descendents of our emigrant women must be considered Italian citizens by maternally derived right of blood, as long as they are born after January 1st, 1948, the date in which the republic's Constitution became effective.

However, it must be noted that the acknowledgment of the acquisition of Italian citizenship by the above category of individuals must be subordinated to the verification of certain conditions and the documented verification of certain essential circumstances.

Preliminary conditions for the granting of Italian citizenship.

First of all, it is necessary to clarify that, since the eventual possession of Italian citizenship must be certified by the Mayor of the Italian town where the petitioner resides, the procedure may be started upon request by the interested parties only when they are registered in the Register of Vital Records (Anagrafe) of the Italian population residing in said Italian town. In addition, the registration of persons who entered Italy with a foreign passport must follow the rules that govern the registration of resident aliens, with the assumption that such interested parties will fulfill the requirements of the pertinent regulations in effect. In addition, in the event such registration of the above persons should not be possible because they do not fall under the category of resident population according to article 3 of D.P.R. May 30, 1989, no. 123, the procedure for the granting of Italian citizenship shall be carried out, upon appropriate request, by the Consular Representative with jurisdiction in the area of the foreign country where is located the habitual domicile of the individuals claiming the right to Italian citizenship. .

Procedure for obtaining Italian citizenship

According to article 1 of Law June 13, 1912, no. 555, the petition for Italian citizenship must be addressed to the Mayor of the Italian municipality where the petitioner resides, or to the Italian Consul for the consular territory where resides the foreign national of Italian origin submitting the petition.. To the petitions shall be attached the following documents:

2. abstract of the birth certificate of the Italian ancestor who emigrated, issued by the Italian municipality where he was born;

3. birth certificates with their official translation in Italian for all his/her direct descendents, including the birth certificate of the person claiming Italian citizenship;

4. marriage certificate of the Italian ancestor who emigrated, with its translation in Italian if issued in a foreign country;

5. marriage certificates for his direct descendents, including the certificate for the parents of the person claiming Italian citizenship;

6. certificate issued by the Authorities of the foreign State of emigration, together with its official Italian translation, attesting that the Italian ancestor who emigrated from Italy did not become a citizen of the foreign State where he emigrated prior to the birth of the ancestor of the interested party;

7. certificate issued by the competent Italian Consulate Authorities attesting that neither the direct ancestors nor the person claiming to have Italian citizenship ever renounced their Italian citizenship under the conditions of article 7 of Law of June 13, 1912, no. 555;

8. certificate of residence.

We point out that the request presented in Italy must be prepared on legal paper, and the certificates provided in support of the same, if issued in Italy by Italian authorities, must be prepared in accordance with the current regulation related to tax stamps. The certificates issued by foreign Authorities must be prepared on plain paper properly legalized unless exempt from legalization based on international conventions ratified by Italy. The same documents shall be accompanied by the official translation in the Italian language which, if submitted in Italy, shall be prepared on paper bearing the tax stamp.

In addition, please note that in order to be able to fully confirm that the persons claiming to have Italian citizenship did not exercise their choice to renounce said citizenship according to article 7 of the cited Law no. 555/1912, first of all it is necessary to carry out adequate research in the Italian municipality of origin, or in the last residence of the Italian ancestor who emigrated to a foreign country, or at the Municipality of Rome (Comune di Roma); also, contact directly all the Italian consular authorities competent in the various foreign localities where the individuals in question resided, or, if necessary, consult the Ministry of Foreign Affairs – General Management Office for Emigration and Social Affairs – Office VIII, so that it may contact the Consular Offices involved.

The Mayors, after having verified the solid foundation of the request submitted by the petitioners requesting Italian citizenship by right of birth, will order the transcription of the civil status records pertaining to the individuals acknowledged to be our countrymen, and will proceed with the issuance of the appropriate citizenship certification as well as other consequent responsibilities.

Finally, the Mayors shall give notice to you, to the local police authorities and to this Ministry regardung the decisions taken.

In case of doubts regarding the actual citizenship status of the persons requesting our citizenship, the Mayors should contact this Minister and send the documentation involved.

Please provide the necessary instructions to the Mayors of the Provincial Municipalities and provide assurance.

CHAPTER 34
THE
EUROPEAN UNION.

CHAPTER 34 | THE EUROPEAN UNION.

Technically, to gain your Italian dual citizenship, you do not need to know anything about Italy or the European Union to obtain Italian citizenship by Descent. You do not need to even be able to speak Italian. However, I personally feel an obligation to suggest a thirty-thousand foot fly by on these topics. You can read this when you get a chance and might find some of the information exceptionally useful. You don't have to read it at all and may elect to skip this chapter all together and that is just fine. It will not impact your application what so ever.

So lets begin.

The European Union, or EU, is a collaborative effort between 28 European countries to form a mutually beneficial economic and policy community. Since 1993, the EU has worked to increase economies and spread human rights advances worldwide. The goals of the European Union include uniting Europe toward common goals and providing aid to developing nations.

After World War II, Europe was a fractured area, divided by political and cultural differences. Several attempts to promote a regional governing body met with varying success, including the European Coal and Steel Community and the European Community. Because of the powerful ideological and political differences between Western and Eastern Europe, a true community could not be formed until after the end of the Cold War.

In 1992, the Maastricht Treaty was signed by member nations, bringing the European Union into effect. The treaty outlined three pillars of the union: European Communities, Common Foreign and Security Policy, and Justice and Home Affairs. The treaty also made provisions to admit many of the nations of Eastern Europe. In 2001, the Treaty of Nice further expanded provisions for new nations.

To become a member of the European Union, a nation must be in conformance with a series of standards called the Copenhagen criteria. These detail geographic and political necessities for member nations. Included standards dictate human rights laws, democracy, protective law for minorities, and a market economy. As of 2019, five states are candidates: Albania, Montenegro, Turkey, the Republic of North Macedonia and Serbia. All except Albania and

North Macedonia have started accession negotiations. Kosovo, Bosnia and Herzegovina are recognized as postential candidates for membership by the EU.

One of the greatest achievements of the European Union is the establishment of a single market economy. Between member nations, trade is largely unrestricted. While nations maintain separate laws on taxation and trade standards, EU members agree to basic trade laws between their countries. Almost all products created by one nation are legal for trade in all of the other countries.

Most nations belonging to the EU have adopted a common currency, called the Euro. The Euro is overseen by the European Central Bank, in an effort to promote all economies that incorporate the use of the currency. As of 2019, 23 nations use the Euro, collectively called the Eurozone. Other EU members must meet specific financial and economic standards before being allowed to adopt the currency. Slovenia was the first of the countries from the 2004 expansion to meet euro criteria.

In addition to increasing economic stability, the European Union sets member policy on a variety of social and political issues. Agriculture, energy policy, anti-terrorism efforts, environmental issues, and education are among the serious areas covered by various EU committees. The EU's goal of creating a neighborhood community of nations is still in its infancy, but measurable impacts are already apparent in the economic and social arenas.

BASIC TIMELINE OF THE EUROPEAN UNION

1948 Plans for a peaceful Europe

In the wake of World War II nationalism is out of favour in large

Parts of continental Europe and support for federalism is high. The European Union of Federalists organizes a Congress at The Hague in 1948 in the hope of drawing up a European constitution. But the UK rejects the federal approach and the result is the Council of Europe a loose grouping that becomes a guardian of Europe's human rights.

1949 Nato is born

The Washington Treaty is signed by the USA Canada and 10 Western European states Britain France the Benelux countries Iceland Italy Norway and Portugal. The key feature of the pact is a mutual defense clause if one country is attacked the others will come to its defense. The US is supportive of European integration but it is another year before real progress is made in this field.

1950 The Schuman Declaration

French Foreign Minister Robert Schuman announces a plan for France and Germany to pool coal and steel production and invites other states to join them. His plan is based on the idea that European unity is the key to peace. Solidarity in production he said would make war between France and Germany "not merely unthinkable but materially impossible."

1951 Treaty of Paris establishes European Coal and Steel Community ECSC

Six countries sign the treaty France Germany the Benelux states and Italy. It sets up a High Authority to manage the coal and steel industries and a Common Assembly a precursor of the European parliament. The Dutch supported by the Germans also insist on the creation of a Council of Ministers made up of ministers from member states to counterbalance the supranational High Authority.

1952 The ECSC begins work with Jean Monnet at its head

The first president of the High Authority is Jean Monnet the inspiration behind the Schuman Declaration. The ECSC guarantees German coal to the French steel industry. It also provides funds to upgrade Belgian and Italian coal mines. Germany agrees to this and to the dismantling of its steel cartels in order to gain international respectability.

1954 The rise and fall of the European Defense Community

In response to the Korean War the USA insists that Europe must contribute more to its own defense and that Germany must rearm. In 1952 the six ECSC members agree to create a European Defense Community which envisages German soldiers joining a European army. But the French parliament delays ratification and ultimately rejects the idea in 1954.

1957 The Treaty of Rome a first step towards the common market

The six members of the ECSC sign the Treaty of Rome setting up the European Economic Community EEC and the European Atomic Energy Community Euratom. The EEC aims to create a common market a customs union plus free movement of capital and labor. To please France it also promises subsidies to farmers. Euratom's goal is the joint development of nuclear energy.

1958 The EEC takes off dominating the other European communities

The EEC starts work and quickly establishes itself as the most important of the European communities. It has a commission a council of ministers and an advisory parliamentary assembly whose members are drawn from national parliaments. At the same time the European Court of Justice comes into existence to interpret the Treaty of Rome and rule in disputes over Community decisions.

1960 EFTA is launched another kind of Europe

An alternative to the EEC emerges when Austria Denmark Norway Portugal Sweden Switzerland and the UK set up EFTA the European Free Trade Association. Like the EEC EFTA aims to establish free trade but it opposes uniform external tariffs and sees no need for supranational institutions.

1961 Britain, Denmark and Ireland apply to join the EEC

The UK's decision to apply for membership of the EEC was taken by the government of Harold Macmillan a Conservative. It was not welcomed by French President Charles de Gaulle who saw it as a threat to his goal of using the EEC to amplify France's voice in world affairs. He was also concerned about the UK's close ties with the US.

1963 French President Charles de Gaulle vetoes British membership

France's nationalist leader Charles de Gaulle refuses to back the UK's application to join the EEC saying that the British government lacks commitment to European integration.

1967 Treaty creating a single Council and a Commission for the three communities comes into effect

1968 The European Community customs union is completed

1973 Britain, Denmark and Ireland join the European Community

The three countries and Norway had failed to join 10 years earlier because of General de Gaulle's veto on British membership. This time all sign an accession treaty in 1972 but Norwegians reject it in a referendum later in the year. Denmark and Ireland hold successful referendums. The UK does not hold a referendum until 1975 after renegotiating its entry terms the result is two-tone in favour.

1979 The road to the euro begins with the EMS

The European Monetary System EMS introduces the European currency unit Ecu and the exchange rate mechanism ERM. The Ecu a unit for the community's internal budget also takes on some of the features of a real currency it is used for travellers cheques and bank deposits. The ERM gives national currencies an exchange rate band denominated in Ecus. All EC members join except the UK.

1981 Greece becomes the ECs 10th member

1984 The UK wins its budget rebate

1985 Jacques Delors becomes president of the European Commission

Jacques Delors proposes that the European Community should by the end of 1992 remove a series of barriers to free trade and free movement of capital and labour creating a "single market". Delors believes the single market programme will revive European integration by spilling over from the economic into the political arena. It is widely seen as a necessity if Europe is to compete with the United States.

1986 Portugal and Spain join the EC and the European flag is unveiled

1987 The Single European Act enters into force

The SEA modifies the Treaty of Rome aiming to complete the formation of a common market which the earlier treaty had begun. It abolishes national vetoes in a host of areas relating to the single market increases the legislative powers of the European parliament and makes the first commitment by member states to create a "European Union".

1988 Regional aid is doubled

Market liberalisation is seen to work to the benefit of the more developed northern European member states so the poorer southern states demand compensation. This comes in the form of agreement to double the allocations for structural funds paid to poorer regions.

1990 Britain enters the ERM

1991 Maastricht turns the Community into a Union

The Maastricht treaty on European Union is signed in December. It paves the way for monetary union and includes a chapter on social policy. The UK negotiates an opt out on both. The treaty also introduces European citizenship giving Europeans the right to live and vote in elections in any EU country and launches European cooperation in foreign affairs security asylum and immigration.

1992 The UK is forced out of the ERM

Volatile currency markets put the Exchange Rate Mechanism ERM under pressure. The ERM was intended to harmonize currency values ahead of creating a single currency. In an effort to bolster the £ which had been devalued by the unstable market the UK government raises base rates in an effort to prompt currency traders to buy £s. Traders keep selling however forcing the government to pull the £ out of the ERM.

1993 The Treaty on European Union comes into effect

The Maastricht Treaty had a rough ride in national referendums. Danes rejected it in June 1992 and only accepted it in a second vote in May 1993 after receiving an opt out on monetary union like the UK. In France it squeaked home by just

50.4 to 49.7. There was also evidence of public discontent in other countries including Germany and the UK.

1995 Borders come down as a result of the Schengen pact

France, Germany, Portugal, Spain and the Benelux countries are the first to drop border controls except on the EUs external borders followed later by Austria Italy Denmark Finland Sweden and Greece but not the UK or Ireland. Austria Finland and Sweden joined the EU at the start of 1995 taking membership to 15. Norway would have joined if voters had not rejected the move in a second referendum.

1997 The Amsterdam Treaty is signed

The treaty starts to get the EU ready for its eastward expansion. More national vetoes are abolished. Laws on employment and discrimination are strengthened and the social chapter of the Maastricht treaty becomes an official part of EU law. The Schengen agreement also becomes law though Ireland and the UK maintain their opt outs. This gives the EU more say on immigration and asylum.

1998 First big steps towards enlargement

Accession negotiations open with Cyprus the Czech Republic Estonia Hungary Poland and Slovenia. A year later another group of countries gets its foot in the European door as the EU opens membership talks with Romania Slovakia Latvia Lithuania Bulgaria and Malta.

1999 Crisis at the commission fraud and resignation

The EU faces its darkest hour as revelations of fraud nepotism and mismanagement undermine the commission. All 20 commissioners including President Jacques Santer resign before the parliament sacks them. In September Romano Prodi becomes the new president of the commission promising radical change in the way it is run. Only a handful of the old commissioners are reappointed.

2002 National currencies replaced by euro notes and coins

The euro came into existence in 1999 as the official currency of 11 countries. Greece adopted the currency two years later though Sweden Denmark and the UK stayed out. On 1 January 2002 euro notes and coins were introduced in the 12 participating states and over the next few months their national currencies were phased out.

2003 Plans for a European constitution suffer a setback

A convention headed by former French President Valery Giscard destining has spent much of 2002 and 2003 drafting the EUs first constitution. Its goals are to simplify the EU treaties to make the EU more easily understood by its citizens and to help it work efficiently after enlargement. But an intergovernmental conference ends in disarray as heads of state and government fail to agree a final text.

2004 The EU enlarges and a new constitution is signed

Enlargement goes ahead on 1 May 2004. Elections to the European parliament in June 2004 the sixth since European polls began in 1979 are held in 25 countries from Ireland to Cyprus and Malta to Finland. On 29 October EU leaders sign a new constitution in the same room where the Treaty of Rome was signed to establish the EU.

2005 No votes plunge constitution into crisis

Voters in referendums in both France and the Netherlands reject their governments plans to ratify the EU constitution. As the constitution cannot come into effect unless it is ratified by all 25 member states many commentators declare it dead. The European Union continues to function on the basis of existing treaties but its future direction has been thrown dramatically into question.

2006 Turkeys EU bid stalls

Negotiations on Turkey's entry to the European Union run into problems in December 2006. EU foreign ministers decide to suspend accession talks with Turkey in eight of the 35 areas that candidates are required to complete. The decision follows Turkey's refusal to open its sea and air ports to ships and planes from EU member Cyprus.

2007 New candidates admitted

Romania and Bulgaria become member states on 1 January 2007. Privately many European politicians question whether they are ready. But harsh penalties are threatened if the countries fail to continue making progress in curbing organized crime and corruption and ensuring food safety and the proper use of EU funds.

COUNTRIES OF THE EUROPEAN UNION

The European Union (EU) is the biggest single developed market in the world, with more than 450 million consumers. This is a list of the countries of the EU.

- Austria
- Belgium
- Bulgaria
- Cyprus
- Czech Republic
- Denmark
- Estonia
- Finland
- France
- Germany
- Greece
- Hungary
- Ireland
- Italy
- Latvia
- Lithuania
- Luxembourg
- Malta
- Netherlands
- Poland
- Portugal
- Romania
- Slovakia
- Slovenia
- Spain
- Sweden
- United Kingdom
- Croatia

WHAT IS EUROPA? Oh boy, you're going to love it .....

EUROPA is the European Union's web portal accessible via the address http://europa.eu. It is managed by the European Commission (DG COMM) in co-ordination with all EU institutions.

Given the central role of the Commission, the name EUROPA is also widely used to refer to both this portal and the European Commission's own website hosted at the address http://ec.europa.eu.

DG Communication has direct responsibility for the top-level pages of Europa, such as the homepage and a number of general information sites directly accessible from it, as well as for the Commission's homepage and the overall co-ordination of the sites of the Commission's directorates-general and services. Each institution and each directorate general or service are responsible for the individual style and contents of their own site.

EUROPA provides a vast array of information on European integration concerning the European Union's objectives, policies and institutional set-up. It is designed to be as user-friendly as possible in line with the EU institutions' commitment to openness and one of its main objectives is to make information accessible to the greatest number of people possible.

The EUROPA site was launched in February 1995 on the occasion of the G7 ministerial meeting on the information society organized by the Commission in Brussels. Although it was originally designed for that particular event, EUROPA expanded rapidly and the Commission decided to turn it into a useful information resource for everyone, specializing in all matters covered by the EU Treaties and the work of the European Institutions. The general public makes great use of EUROPA and statistics show an average of 165 million page viewings per month

EXPLORE: Your Amazing Life in the European Union

Information and legal advice on your rights to live, work and study abroad, including access to healthcare and consumer rights.

Gateway to the European Union online: europa.eu

BASIC TIMELINE FOR ITALY

A chronology of key events:

1915 - Italy enters World War I on side of Allies.

1919 - Gains Trentino, South Tyrol, and Trieste under peace treaties.

1922 - Fascist leader Mussolini forms government after three years of political and economic unrest.

1926 - Suppression of opposition parties.

1929 - Lateran Treaty creates state of Vatican City.

1935 - Italy invades Ethiopia.

1936 - Mussolini forms axis with Nazi Germany.

1939 - Albania annexed.

1940 - Italy enters World War II on German side. Italian forces occupy British Somaliland in East Africa.

1941 - Italy declares war on USSR.

1943 - Sicily invaded by Allies. King Victor Emmanuel III imprisons Mussolini. Armistice signed with Allies. Italy declares war on Germany.

1944 - Allied armies liberate Rome.

1945 - Mussolini, who had been rescued from prison by Germans, is captured and executed by Italian partisans.

1946 - Referendum votes for republic to replace monarchy.

1947 - Italy cedes land and territories under peace treaty.

1948 - New constitution. Christian Democrats win elections.

1951 - Italy joins European Coal and Steel Community.

1955 - Italy joins United Nations.

1957 - Founder member of European Economic Community.

1963 - Italian Socialist Party joins Christian Democrat-led coalition under Prime Minister Aldo Moro.

1972 - Giulio Andreotti becomes prime minister - a post he will hold seven times in 20 years.

1976-78 - Communist election gains lead to voice in policy making.

1978 - Former Prime Minister Aldo Moro kidnapped and murdered by fanatical left-wing group, the Red Brigades. Abortion legalized.

1980 - Bombing of Bologna station kills 84, linked to right-wing extremists.

1983 - Bettino Craxi becomes Italy's first Socialist prime minister since war.

1984 - Roman Catholicism loses status as state religion.

1991 - Communists rename themselves Democratic Party of the Left.

1992 - Revelations of high level corruption spark several years of arrests and investigations.

1993 - Bribery scandal leads to Craxi's resignation as leader of Socialist Party. He later flees the country, is tried and sentenced in absentia to imprisonment but dies in Tunisia in 2000.

1994 March - Freedom Alliance wins election. The coalition, which includes Silvio Berlusconi's Forza Italia, the Northern League and the neo-Fascist National Alliance, collapses by end of year following clashes with anticorruption magistrates and a battle with trade unions over pension reform.

1995-96 - Lamberto Dini heads government of technocrats. Austerity budget.
1996 - Centre-left Olive Tree alliance wins election. Romano Prodi becomes prime minister.

1997 - Earthquakes strike Umbria region, causing extensive damage to Basilica of St Francis of Assisi. Four killed.

Prodi government loses confidence vote. Massimo D'Alema becomes prime minister.

1999 - Carlo Ciampi becomes president.

2000 April - D'Alema resigns after poor regional election results and is replaced by Giuliano Amato.

2001 May/June - A centre-right coalition, led by Silvio Berlusconi of the Forza Italia party, wins the general elections.

2001 Oct - First constitutional referendum since 1946 sees vote in favour of major constitutional change giving greater autonomy to the country's 20 regions in tax, education and environment policies.

2002 Jan - Euro replaces the lira.
Foreign Minister Renato Ruggiero resigns in protest at the Eurosceptical views of right-wing cabinet colleagues.

2002 February-March - Controversy as parliament approves bill enabling Berlusconi to keep control of his businesses.

2002 October - Lower house of parliament passes controversial criminal reform bill which critics allege is intended to help PM Berlusconi avoid trial on corruption charges.

2003 May-June - Prime Minister Silvio Berlusconi appears in Milan court at his own trial on corruption charges relating to business dealings in the 1980s. He asserts that he is the victim of a conspiracy by a politically-motivated judiciary.

2003 June - Mr Berlusconi's trial halted after parliament passes law granting immunity from prosecution to five holders of key state posts, including the prime minister.

2003 November - Italy declares national day of mourning after 19 of its servicemen are killed in a suicide bomb attack on their base in southern Iraq.

Multi-billion euro fraud uncovered at Parmalat food-manufacturing giant. The company is declared insolvent.

2004 January - Constitutional Court throws out law granting Mr Berlusconi and other top state post holders immunity from prosecution. Mr Berlusconi's trial resumes in April.

2004 October - Forced expulsion from island of Lampedusa of hundreds of African asylum seekers is criticized by UN.

2004 December - After a four-year trial Prime Minister Berlusconi is cleared of corruption.

2005 March - Italian secret service officer shot dead during operation to free hostage in Iraq.

2005 April - Parliament ratifies EU constitution.
Government coalition collapses after suffering a crushing defeat in regional polls. Berlusconi resigns. Days later, he forms a new government after receiving a presidential mandate.

2005 December - Antonio Fazio resigns as governor of Bank of Italy following a scandal over the sale of Banca Antonveneta. He denies acting improperly.

2006 January - Defense minister says Italian troops will leave Iraq. The mission ends in September 2006.
Prodi in, then out

2006 April - Centre-left leader Romano Prodi wins closely-fought general elections. He is sworn in as prime minister in May.

2004: Face-to-face with Michelangelo's genius
Ten things about David

2006 May - Giorgio Napolitano, a former communist, is elected as president.

2006 June - National referendum rejects reforms intended to boost the powers of the prime minister and regions. The changes were proposed during Silvio Berlusconi's premiership.

2006 August - Hundreds of Italian peacekeepers leave for Lebanon. Italy is set to become the biggest contributor to the UN-mandated force.

2007 February - Prime Minister Prodi resigns after the government loses a Senate vote on its foreign policy. The president asks him to stay on and Mr Prodi goes on to win confidence votes in both houses of parliament.

2008 January - A no-confidence vote forces Mr Prodi's government to resign.
Berlusconi back again

2008 April - Berlusconi wins general elections, securing a third term as premier after two years in opposition.

2008 August - Berlusconi apologizes to Libya for damage inflicted by Italy during the colonial era and signs a five billion dollar investment deal by way of compensation.
Italy's national airline, Alitalia, files for bankruptcy.

2008 November - After posting two consecutive quarters of negative growth, Italy is declared to be officially in recession.

2009 April - Earthquake strikes towns in the mountainous Abruzzo region, leaving hundreds of people dead and thousands homeless.

2009 May-July - Parliament approves controversial law criminalizing illegal immigration and allowing citizens' patrols.

2009 October - Constitutional court overturns law that granted Premier Berlusconi immunity while in office.

2009 December - Prime Minister Silvio Berlusconi is assaulted at a rally in Milan. A man said to have a history of mental illness flings a model of Milan cathedral at the premier's face, breaking his nose and two teeth.

2010 January - Pope Benedict calls on Italians to respect the rights of illegal migrants. The call came after a wave of violence against African farm workers in southern Italy which left some 70 people injured.

2010 March - Mr Berlusconi's coalition makes strong gains from the centre-left in regional polls.
Coalition splits

2010 July - Government survives confidence vote on austerity package meant to bolster the country's finances.

Mr Berlusconi splits with his former political ally, speaker of parliament Gianfranco Fini, who sets up rival centre-right party Future and Freedom for Italy (FLI).

2010 August - Mr Berlusconi's coalition loses majority in lower house of parliament after more than 30 deputies break away from his Party of Freedom and join Mr Fini's FLI.
2010 November - Four members of Mr Berlusconi's coalition government resign.

2010 December - Mr Berlusconi wins two confidence votes - brought after scandals in his private life and corruption allegations - by slender margin.

2011 February - A Milan judge orders Mr Berlusconi to stand trial on 6 April for abuse of power and paying for sex with an under-age prostitute.

2012 January – Former President Oscar Luigi Scalfaro dies.

2013 January – Former Prime Minister Giulia Andretti dies at 94 years old in Rome.

2015 January – President Giorgio Napolitano resigned.

2015 January – Sergio Mattarella is the new President of the Italian Republic.

2016 September- Former President Carlo Azeglio Ciampi Died in Rome.

2018 March – Italian general election 2018.

2018 August – The Ponte Miranda viaduct collapses on the A10 motorway in Genoa, Italy. Local news agencies reported that the number of deaths reached 42.

CHAPTER 35
REGIONS, PROVINCES
& TOWN REFERENCES.

ITALIAN REGIONS

ABR	Abruzzo	PUG	Apulia	BAS	Basilicata	CAL	Calabria
CAM	Campania	EMI	Emilia Romagna	FRI	Friuli-Venezia Giulia	LAZ	Latium
LIG	Liguria	LOM	Lombardy	MAR	The Marches	MOL	Molise
PIE	Piedmont	SAR	Sardinia	SIC	Sicily	TRE	Trentino Alto Adige
TOS	Tuscany	UMB	Umbria	VAL	Val d'Aosta	VEN	Veneto

ITALIAN PROVINCES

AG	Agrigento	AL	Alessandria	AN	Ancona	AO	Aosta
AP	Ascoli Piceno	AQ	L'Aquila	AR	Arezzo	AT	Asti
AV	Avellino	BA	Bari	BG	Bergamo	BI	Biella
BL	Belluno	BN	Benevento	BO	Bologna	BR	Brindisi
BS	Brescia	BZ	Bolzano	CA	Cagliari	CB	Campobasso
CE	Caserta	CH	Chieti	CL	Caltanisetta	CN	Cuneo
CO	Como	CR	Cremona	CS	Cosenza	CT	Catania
CZ	Catanzaro	EN	Enna	FE	Ferrara	FG	Foggia
FI	Firenze	FO	Forlì-Cesena	FR	Frosinone	GE	Genova
GO	Gorizia	GR	Grosseto	IM	Imperia	IS	Isernia
KR	Crotone	LC	Lecco	LE	Lecce	LI	Livorno
LO	Lodi	LT	Latina	LU	Lucca	MC	Macerata
ME	Messina	MI	Milano	MN	Mantova	MO	Modena
MS	Massa Carrara	MT	Matera	NA	Napoli	NO	Novara
NU	Nuoro	OR	Oristano	PA	Palermo	PC	Piacenza
PD	Padova	PE	Pescara	PG	Perugia	PI	Pisa
PN	Pordenone	PO	Prato	PR	Parma	PT	Pistoia
PU	Pesaro-Urbino	PV	Pavia	PZ	Potenza	RA	Ravenna
RC	Reggio Calabria	RE	Reggio Emilia	RG	Ragusa	RI	Rieti
RN	Rimini	RO	Rovigo	RM	Roma	SA	Salerno
SI	Siena	SO	Sondrio	SP	La Spezia	SR	Siracusa
SS	Sassari	SV	Savona	TA	Taranto	TE	Teramo
TN	Trento	TO	Torino	TP	Trapani	TR	Terni
TS	Trieste	TV	Treviso	UD	Udine	VA	Varese
VB	Verbano	VC	Vercelli	VE	Venezia	VI	Vicenza
VR	Verona	VT	Viterbo	VV	Vibo Valentia		

ITALIAN TOWNS

(ALSO CALLED MUNICIPALITIES AND COMUNES)

http://en.wikipedia.org/wiki/list_of_italian_communes

MAP OF ITALY

CHAPTER 36
SAMPLE FORMS.

SAMPLE FORM INDEX

NARA Request	340
County Clerk Request	341
G1041 Index Search Request USCIS	342
G1041 Instructions	343
G1041A Records Request USCIS	344
G1041A Instructions	345
BC 600 Census Request	346
1910 Census	351
1920 Census	352
1930 Census	353
Sample Affidavit	354
Application Form 1	355
Application Form 2	356
Application Form 3	357
Application Form 4	358
Spouse Application	359
A.I.R.E Registration Form	361
N-565 Naturalization Replacement Form	362
G-639 FOIA Request	366
Certificate of Clerk or No Appeal	371
Italian Vital Records Request	372
Comune Declaration	373
Correction to Vital Records Example	374
Affidavit to Request Marriage Records	375
Affidavit to Request Death Records	376
Apostille Cover Letter	377
USCIS Cover Letter – Non Existence	378
Sample Naturalization Documents	379
Arrival Record	386
Military Draft Card	387
Certificate of Non Existence	388
Sample Apostille	389

(**NOTE: Most sample forms are available for download online. Be sure to check the Italian Consulate web site and Google the form title and number for most current version available.***)

YOUR NAME
ADDRESS
CITY, STATE ZIP
TELEPHONE

NARA Great Lakes Region
7358 South Pulaski Road
Chicago, IL 60629-5898
Phone: 773-948-9001

June 7, 2011

RE: CERTIFICATE OF NATURALIZATION / STATEMENT OF NO RECORD

Dear Archive Specialist:

I am writing to request a certified copy of the following individuals Naturalization or certificate
No Record/Nonexistence. The information is listed below:

Alfonso Pasquale Comito

Born: 6 Nov 1856

Place of Birth: Italy

Spouse: Francesca Maria Amadeo

Residence: Des Moines, Iowa

Dates of Search: 1898 - 1910

I have enclosed a prepaid return envelope for your reply.

Please contact me at the telephone number listed above if you have any questions.

Thank you for your kind attention to this matter.

Sincerely,

YOUR NAME

YOUR NAME
ADDRESS
CITY, STATE ZIP
TELEPHONE NUMBER

Kings County Clerk
Supreme Court Building
360 Adams Street
Room 189
Brooklyn, NY 11201
Phone: 718-643-5771

August 1, 2011

RE: CERTIFICATE OF NATURALIZATION OR CERTIFICATE OF
NON-EXISTENCE RECORD FOR DUAL US-ITALIAN CITIZENSHIP

Dear Archive Specialist:

I am writing to request a certified copy of my ancestor's Certificate of
Naturalization or Certificate of Nonexistence. The information required for the
search is shown below:

>   Nicola Soccodato
>   AKA: Nicholas or Nick Soccodato
>   Born: 26 June 1878
>   Born in Italy
>   Spouse: Giovanna or Giovannina Soccodato
>   Residence: New York, New York
>   Dates of Search: 1880 - 1920

I have enclosed a prepaid return envelope and a $10 money order for the
associated search fee. Please contact me at the above telephone number if you
have any questions or require any additional information.

Thank you in advance for your kind attention to this matter.

Sincerely,

YOUR NAME

OMB 1615-0096; Expires 04/30/2012

G-1041, Genealogy
Index Search Request

Department of Homeland Security
U.S. Citizenship and Immigration Services

START HERE - Type or print in black ink and read all instructions before completing this form.

Part I. Information About You

Full Name   Salutation: ☐ Mr.   ☐ Mrs.   ☐ Ms.

Last Name	First Name	Middle Name	Suffix (Jr., Sr.)

Address (Number and Street Name, (P.O. Box Number or Route Number))			Apartment No.

City	State/Province	Country (if other than U.S.)	Zip/Postal Code

E-Mail Address: (if available)	Daytime Telephone Number: (include Area/Country Code, ext.)

Would you prefer to receive your search results via e-mail or postal mail?   ☐ E-mail   ☐ Postal mail

Part II. Information Needed to Search the Index

A. Required Information

Immigrant's Full Name (If appropriate, enter religious salutation before the first name - Example: father, sister, etc.)

Last Name	First Name	Middle Name

Other names used, maiden names, aliases, or variant spellings (if any)

*Immigrant's Date of Birth (Check only one): Day Month Full Year ☐ Actual ☐ Estimated __ __ / __ __ / __ __ __ __	Immigrant's Country of Birth (Include Country, Province, Town/Village, if known)

B. Additional Information Useful to Identify a Given Immigrant From Others With the Same Name

Date of immigrant's exact arrival in the United States: (mm/dd/yyyy) _____ (If unsure or unknown of date range, check additional choices below) Before 1906 _____ 1924 to 1940 _____ 1906 to 1924 _____ After 1940 _____	Where did the immigrant live in the United States? (State, city, or exact street address-Example: in Pennsylvania until 1938, then lived in Madison, Wisconsin)

Other information about the immigrant that may prove useful in the index search (name of spouse and/or children, date of immigrant's death, military service, date of naturalization, date of female immigrant's marriage, occupation):

* **Important:** If the immigrant's date of birth is **less than** 100 years prior to the date of this request, you must attach documentary proof of death to the request form. Do not attach original records because we will **not** return them. See instructions on **Page 1** for examples of acceptable documentary proof of death.

NOTE: The fee for an Index Search Request is **$20**.

G-1041 (Rev. 04/30/09)Y

Department of Homeland Security
U.S. Citizenship and Immigration Services

Instruction for G-1041, Genealogy Index Search Request

Instructions
Please read all instructions carefully before completing this form.

What Is the Purpose of This Form?

Use this Form G-1041 to request a search of U.S. Citizenship and Immigration Services (USCIS) historical indices. (To obtain copies of USCIS historical records, use Form G-1041A, Genealogy Records Request.)

Requests for searches of USCIS historical indices are used to determine whether any USCIS records exist on the subject and, if such records exist, to capture the file number and/or other identifier of each record.

Who Should Use This Form?

Use this form if you are a:

1. Researcher seeking records of your ancestors for genealogical/family history purposes;

2. Historian or social scientist seeking historical records of persons you can identify by name, date of birth, and place of birth;

3. Researcher involved in heir location.

When Should This Form Not Be Used?

This form should not be used to request a copy of a USCIS historical record or a copy of any record.

Do not use this form to request index searches for:

1. Records of naturalization prior to September 27, 1906. Consult Federal records stored at the National Archives and Records Administration (NARA) Record Group 21, or write to the clerk of the court where the naturalization occurred; or

2. Sea, land, or air passenger manifest lists recording arrivals prior to December 1982. For these documents, contact the NARA.

NOTE: For any records not specifically mentioned in this Form G-1041 or not available through any other USCIS program, use Form G-639, Freedom of Information/Privacy Act Request.

What Information Is Required To Begin an Index Search?

The following information is required to initiate a search of USCIS historical indices:

1. Required Information:

    A. Immigrant's full name (last, first, and middle);

    B. Alias names or variant spellings, if any;

    C. Date of birth (state whether date given is exact or an estimated year);

    D. Country or place of birth;

2. Additional data will help identify a certain immigrant from others with the same name, such as:

    A. Date of immigrant's arrival in the United States (state whether the date is actual or estimated); and/or

    B. Immigrant's residence(s) in the United States (State, city, or exact street address - Example: "in Pennsylvania until 1938, then lived in Madison, Wisconsin.")

3. If the immigrant's date of birth is less than 100 years before today's date, you must attach documentary proof of death to this request form. Examples of acceptable documentary proof of death include:

    A. Death certificate (uncertified copy);

    B. Printed obituaries, funeral programs, or photographs of gravestones;

    C. Bible, church, or other religious records;

    D. U.S. Social Security Death Index records (individual records only, not lists);

    E. Records relating to the payment of death benefits; and/or

    F. Other documents demonstrating that the immigrant subject of the request is deceased.

Submit copies of these items with this request form. Do not include original records because such documents will not be returned.

OMB 1615-0096; Expires 04/30/09

Department of Homeland Security
U.S. Citizenship and Immigration Services

G-1041A, Genealogy
Records Request

START HERE - Please type or print in black ink and read all instructions before completing this form.

Part I. Information About You

Full Name

Salutation (Mr., Mrs., Ms.) Last Name	First Name	Middle Name	Suffix (Jr., Sr.)

Address (Number and Street Name, P.O. Box Number or Route Number)			Apartment No.

City	State/Province	Country (If other than U.S.)	Zip/Postal Code

E-Mail Address: (If available.)	Daytime Telephone Number: (Include Area/Country Code, ext.)

If the record(s) requested are available in electronic format, would you prefer to received them via e-mail or printed and postal mail?   ☐ E-mail   ☐ Postal mail

Part II. Information Needed to Release a Historical Record

Immigrant's Full Name (If appropriate, please enter Religious Salutation before first name - Example: Father, Sister, etc.)

Is the file information provided below the result of a previous Genealogy Index Search Request? ☐ Yes ☐ No	If Yes, provide the Genealogy Index Search Request case number(s): # _____

Last Name	First Name	Middle Name

Other names used, maiden names, aliases or variant spellings (if any).

Immigrant's Date of Birth* Check only one: ☐ Actual ☐ Estimated	Day Month Full Year _ _ / _ _ / _ _ _ _	Immigrant's Country of Birth (Include Country, Province, Town/Village, if known)

*Important: If the immigrant's date of birth is **less than 100 years** prior to the date of this request, you **must** attach documentary evidence showing that the immigrant is deceased. Do not attach original records because we will **not** return them.

Examples of acceptable documentary proof of death include: Death certificates (uncertified copy), printed obituaries, funeral programs or photographs of gravestones, Bible records, Social Security Death Index records (individual records only, **not** lists), records relating to payment of death benefits, or other documents demonstrating the subject of the request is deceased. Do **not** attach original records because we will not return them to you.

G-1041A (Rev. 06/16/08)Y

Part III. Identification of Requested Record(s)

Type of File(s) Requested	File Number/File Information	Fee
		Check one or both fees
Naturalization Certificate File 1906-1956	Certificate Number (up to 7 digits): C _ _ _ _ _ _ Date of Naturalization: Day Month Full Year __ / __ / ____ Court City/County State	☐ $20M* ☐ $35HC**
Non-standard C-Files (B, D, OM, OS, A, AA, OL)	Number as Shown on Certificate: - __ __ _____ Date of Issuance: Day Month Full Year __ / __ / ____	
Alien Registration Record (AR-2), 1940-1944	Alien Registration Number (must be 7 digits): A- or AR- _ _ _ _ _ _ _	☐ $20 M*
A-File numbered below 8 million	A-File Number (must be 7 digits): A- _ _ _ _ _ _ _	☐ $35 HC**
Visa File 1924-1944	Visa Number (up to 7 digits): Visa # _ _ _ _ _ _ _ Date of Entry: Day Month Full Year _ _ / _ _ / _ _ _ _ Port of Entry: Ship (seaport arrivals only):	☐ $35 HC**
Registry File 1929-1944	Registry File Number (up to 6 digits): R _ _ _ _ _ _	☐ $35 HC**

NOTE:

Total Fees Due/Attached: $_____

If you are a researcher providing a C-file number below C-6500000 obtained from any source other than the USCIS Genealogy Program, you may not know the format of the file (microfilm or hard copy). Therefore, you will be unable to determine the fee. In this case, submit the **$20** fee. If the C-file is found in hard copy format, we will notify you to remit the additional **$15**.

*The fee for a copy of a microfilm record (M) is **$20** per request.

The fee for a copy of a textual hard copy file (HC) file is **$35 per request.

Department of Homeland Security
U.S. Citizenship and Immigration Services

G-1041A, Genealogy
Records Request

Instructions
Please read all instructions carefully before completing this form.

What Is the Purpose of This Form?

Use Form G-1041A to obtain copies of U.S. Citizenship and Immigration Services (USCIS) historical records. (To request an index search of USCIS historical records, use Form G-1041, Genealogy Index Search Request.)

Who Should Use This Form?

Use this form if you are a:

1. Researcher requesting a copy of a USCIS historical record by file number. (See descriptions of USCIS historical records on **Page 2** of these instructions.);

2. Researcher who has received file numbers resulting from the Genealogy Index Search Request (G-1041);

3. Researcher seeking records for genealogical/family history purposes or heir location, and who can provide a precise historical record series file number and can identify the immigrant by name and/or other information.

When Should This Form Not Be Used?

Do not use this form to request:

1. Records of naturalization prior to September 27, 1906. For such records, consult Federal court records stored at the National Archives and Records Administration (NARA) Record Group 21, or write to the clerk of the court where the naturalization occurred;

2. Copies of sea, land, or air manifest lists prior to December, 1982. For these lists, write to NARA;

3. The return of original documents. For such documents, use Form G-884, Request for Return of Original Documents.

NOTE: For any records not specifically mentioned in this Form G-1041A or not available through any other USCIS program, use Form G-639, Freedom of Information/Privacy Act Request.

How Are Historical Records and Files Identified?

Records and files are identified by file numbers.

To help identify historical USCIS file numbers, review the chart on **Page 2** of these instructions, which lists available series of USCIS historical files and shows sample file numbers.

Requests for copies of USCIS historical records or files must identify the record by the file number or another file identifier. No record can be retrieved without a file number. If you do not have the file number as described in the chart on **Page 2**, you should submit Form G-1041, Genealogy Index Search Request.

What Are the Fees?

You must submit the appropriate fee with this form for a genealogy records request. The fee for a copy from microfilm is $20 per request. The fee for a copy of a hard copy file is $35 per request.

Send payment with your request form. Payment may be in the form of a cashier's check or money order. **Personal checks will not be accepted**, and they will be returned to you. If the form is submitted from outside the United States, remittance may be made with a bank international money order or foreign draft drawn in U.S. dollars and payable through a U.S. bank. Make all payments payable in U.S. currency to the **Department of Homeland Security. Do not send cash** with your form.

If the file number provided does not match the immigrant named on this form, and there is **no** previous Genealogy Index Search case identification number provided, we will not refund any fee.

Where Should You Mail the Request?

Mail your request to:

USCIS Genealogy Program
PO Box 805925
Chicago, IL 60680-4120

G-1041A (Rev. 06/16/08)

FORM **BC-600**
(9-25-2008)

U.S. DEPARTMENT OF COMMERCE
Economics and Statistics Administration
U.S. CENSUS BUREAU

APPLICATION FOR SEARCH OF CENSUS RECORDS

IMPORTANT INFORMATION

PLEASE READ AND FOLLOW CAREFULLY

This application is for use in requesting a search of census records.* Copies of these census records often are accepted as evidence of age, citizenship, and place of birth for employment, social security benefits, insurance, and other purposes.

If the applicant is located, an official transcript will be provided including the following information:

Personal Census Information	Available for census year(s)
• Census year	1910–2000
• County where taken	1910–1980
• State where taken	1910–2000
• Name	1910–2000
• Relationship to head of household	1910–2000
• Name of person in whose household you were counted	1910–2000
• Age at the time of the census	1910–1950, 1970–2000
• Date of birth	
Year and quarter	1960
Month and year	1970–1980
Year	1990
Month/day/year	2000
• Place of birth	1910–1950
• Citizenship if requested or if foreign born	1910–1950
• Occupation (if requested)	1910–1950

The U.S. Census Bureau's records are arranged according to the address at the time of the census. Censuses are taken primarily for statistical, not legal, purposes. Attention is called to the possibility that the information shown in the census record may not agree with that given in your application. **The record must be copied exactly as it appears on the census form.** The U.S. Census Bureau CANNOT make changes even though it realizes that enumerators may have been misinformed or made mistakes in writing down the data they collected. Those agencies that accept census transcripts as evidence of age, relationship, or place of birth usually overlook minor spelling differences but would be reluctant to consider a record that was changed years later at an applicant's request.

If you authorize the U.S. Census Bureau to send your record to someone other than yourself, you must provide the name and address, including ZIP Code, of the other person/agency.

Birth certificates, including delayed birth certificates, are **not issued** by the U.S. Census Bureau. You can obtain the birth certificate from the Health Department or the Department of Vital Statistics of the state in which the applicant was born.

The average time it should take you to fill out the BC-600, "Application for Search of Census Records", including the time spent reading instructions is 12 minutes.

Send comments regarding this burden estimate or any other aspect of this collection of information, including suggestions for reducing this burden, to: Paperwork Project 0607–0117, U.S. Census Bureau, 4600 Silver Hill Road, AMSD-3K138, Washington, D.C. 20233. You may e-mail comments to Paperwork@census.gov; use "Paperwork Project 0607-0117" as the subject.

Respondents are not required to respond to any information collection unless it displays a valid approval number from the Office of Management and Budget. This 8-digit number appears in the top right corner of page 3 of this form.

* Information from 1930 and earlier censuses is public information and is available from the National Archives.

The completed application should be mailed to the U.S. Census Bureau, P.O. Box 1545, Jeffersonville, IN 47131, together with a money order or check payable to "Commerce–Census."

USCENSUSBUREAU

347

PLEASE FOLLOW NUMBERED INSTRUCTIONS

1. Purpose

The purpose for which the information is desired must be shown so that a determination may be made under 13 U.S.C. 8(a) that the record is required for proper use. For proof of age, most agencies require documents closest to date of birth; therefore we suggest you complete information for the EARLIEST CENSUS AFTER DATE OF BIRTH.

2. Signature

Each application requires a signature. The signature should be the same as that shown on the line captioned "full name of person whose census record is requested." When the application is for a census record concerning another person, the requester must sign the application, and the authority of the requester must be furnished as stated in instruction 3 below. If signed by marking (X), please indicate the name of the person whose mark it is and have witnesses sign as instructed. IF SIGNATURE IS PRINTED, please indicate that is the usual signature.

3. Confidential information given to other than person to whom it relates

(a) Census information is confidential and ordinarily will not be furnished to another person unless the person to whom it relates authorizes this in the space provided or if there is other proper authorization as indicated in 3(b), 3(c), and 3(d).

(b) Minor children - Information regarding a child who has at this time not reached the legal age of 18 may be obtained upon the written request of either parent or guardian.

(c) Mentally incompetent persons – Information regarding persons who are mentally incompetent may be obtained upon the written request of the legal representative, supported by a certified copy of the court order naming such legal representative.

(d) Deceased persons - If the record requested relates to a deceased person, the application MUST be signed by (1) a blood relative in the immediate family (parent, brother, sister, or child), (2) the surviving wife or husband, (3) the administrator or executor of the estate, or (4) a beneficiary by will, or insurance. IN ALL CASES INVOLVING DECEASED PERSONS, a certified copy of the death certificate MUST be furnished, and the relationship to the deceased MUST be stated on the application. Legal representatives MUST also furnish a certified copy of the court order naming such legal representatives; and beneficiaries MUST furnish legal evidence of such beneficiary interest.

4. Fee required

The $65.00 fee is for a search of one census for one person only. The time required to complete a search depends upon the number of cases on hand at the particular time and the difficulty encountered in searching a particular case. The normal processing time is 3 to 4 weeks. The fee covers return postage of your search results by regular mail. You do not need to include a return envelope for normal processing. For an additional fee of $20 the search can be completed in one business day after we receive it. If you want your search results returned to you by express mail you must include a self-addressed, prepaid express mail envelope with your application. You may also submit your application by express mail for faster service.

No more than one census will be searched and the results furnished for one fee. Should it be necessary to search more than one census to find the record, you will be notified to send another fee before another search is made. Tax monies are not available to furnish the information. **If a search has been made, the fee cannot be returned even if the information is not found.**

5. Full schedules

The full schedule is the complete one-line entry of personal data recorded for that individual ONLY. The names of other persons will not be listed. If the applicant specifies "full schedule," the Census Bureau will furnish, in addition to the regular transcript, whatever other information appears on the named person's record in the original schedule, but only for THAT PERSON. In this case the information is typed on a facsimile of the original census schedule and verified as a true copy. There is an additional charge of $10.00 for EACH full schedule requested.

The Census Bureau also will provide "full schedule" information for those other members of the same household for whom authorizations are furnished. (See instruction 3 for authorization requirements). A fee of $10.00 is required for each person listed on the full schedule.

LIMITATIONS – Certain information, such as place of birth, citizenship, and occupation, is available only for census years 1910 through 1950. Full schedule information is not available for census years 1970, 1980, 1990, and 2000.

6. Census years 1910–1920–1930–1940– 1950– 1960–1970–1980–1990–2000

The potential of finding an individual's census record is increased when the respondent provides thorough and accurate address information FOR THE DAY THESE CENSUSES WERE TAKEN. If residing in a city AT THE TIME THESE CENSUSES WERE TAKEN, it is necessary to furnish the house number, the name of the street, city, county, state, and the name of the parent or other head of household with whom residing at the time of the census. If residing in a rural area, it is VERY IMPORTANT to furnish the township, district, precinct or beat, AND the direction and number of miles from the nearest town.

1990 and 2000 Request - It is VERY IMPORTANT to provide a house number and street name or rural route and box number. Always include a ZIP Code.

7. Locator Map (optional)

Box 7 is provided for a sketch of the area where the applicant lived at the time of the requested census.

IF YOU NEED HELP FILLING OUT THIS APPLICATION, PLEASE CALL 812-218-3046, MONDAY THROUGH FRIDAY 7:00 A.M. THROUGH 4:30 P.M. EASTERN TIME

FORM BC-600 (9-26-2008)

OMB No. 0607-0117

-600

U.S. DEPARTMENT OF COMMERCE
Economics and Statistics Administration
U.S. CENSUS BUREAU

APPLICATION FOR SEARCH OF CENSUS RECORDS

URN TO: U.S. Census Bureau, P.O. Box 1545, Jeffersonville, IN 47131

ose for which record is to be used (See Instruction 1)

☐ Passport (date required) _____   ☐ Proof of age
☐ Genealogy   ☐ Other – Please specify

certify that information furnished about anyone other than the applicant will
not be used to the detriment of such person or persons by me or by anyone
lse with my permission.

ature – Do not print (Read Instruction 2 carefully before signing)

Number and street

City   State   ZIP Code

phone number (Include area code)

IF SIGNED BY MARK (X), TWO WITNESSES MUST SIGN HERE

re _____   Signature _____

E – Intentionally falsifying this application may result in a fine of
$10,000 or 5 years of imprisonment, or both (title 18, U.S. Code,
section 1001).

First name	Middle name

ME OF
N WHOSE
S RECORD
ESTED

Date of birth (If unknown, estimate)	Place of birth (City, county, State)

ne of father (Stepfather, guardian, etc.)

iden name of mother (Stepmother, etc.)

arriage (Name of husband or wife of applicant) | Year married (Approximate) | Second marriage (Name of husband or wife of applicant) | Year married (Approximate)

of brothers and sisters

and relationship of all other persons living in household (Aunts, uncles, grandparents, lodgers, etc.)

DO NOT USE THIS SPACE – OFFICIAL USE ONLY

Case number

$ _____ (Fee)

☐ Money Order
☐ Check
☐ Other

Papers received (itemize)   Returned

Received by	Date	Returned by	Date

3. If the census information is to be sent
to someone other than the person
whose record is requested, give the
name and address, including ZIP Code,
of the other person or agency.

This authorizes the U.S. Census Bureau
to send the record to: (See Instruction 3)

4. FEE REQUIRED: (See instructions 4 and 5)
A check or money order (DO NOT SEND
CASH) payable to "Commerce – Census"
must be sent with the application. This
fee covers the cost of a search of no
more than one census year for one
person only.

5. Fee required . . . . $ 65.00
   ____ extra copies @ $2.00 $ ____
   ____ full schedules @ $10.00 $ ____
   ____ expedited fee @ $20.00 $ ____
   TOTAL amount enclosed $ ____

Present last name	Nicknames

Race	Sex	Nicknames

Maiden name (If any) | Nicknames

PLEASE COMPLETE REVERSE SIDE

349

6. GIVE PLACE OF RESIDENCE FOR APPROPRIATE CENSUS DATE *(SEE INSTRUCTIONS 1 AND 6)*

Census date	Number and street *(Read instruction 6 first)*	City, town, township *(Read instruction 6 first)*	County and State	Name of person with whom living *(Head of household)*	Relationship of head of household
April 15, 1910 *(See instruction 6)*					
Jan. 1, 1920 *(See instruction 6)*					
April 1, 1930 *(See instruction 6)*					
April 1, 1940 *(See instruction 6)*					
April 1, 1950 *(See instruction 6)*					
April 1, 1960 *(See instruction 6)*					
April 1, 1970 *(See instruction 6)*					
April 1, 1980 *(See instruction 6)*					
April 1, 1990 *(See instruction 6)*	ZIP Code				
April 1, 2000 *(See instruction 6)*	ZIP Code				

7. LOCATOR MAP (Optional)
PLEASE DRAW A MAP OF WHERE THE APPLICANT LIVED, SHOWING ANY PHYSICAL FEATURES, LANDMARKS, INTERSECTING ROADS, CLOSEST TOWNS, ETC., THAT MAY AID IN LOCATING THE APPLICANT FOR THE CENSUS YEAR REQUESTED.

HAVE YOU SIGNED THE APPLICATION AND ENCLOSED THE CORRECT FEES?

350

1910 United States Federal Census

State: _____
County: _____
City, township: _____

Call Number/URL: _____

Enumeration District: _____
Sheet Number: _____
Enumeration Date: _____

To search the 1910 census online, visit www.ancestry.com

Ancestry Census Form 013

351

1920 United States Federal Census

State: _____ County: _____ Enumeration District: _____ City / Township: _____

Call Number/URL: _____ Sheet Number: _____ Enumeration Date: _____

Line Number	Place of Abode				Name of each person whose place of abode on January 1, 1920 was in this family	Relation	Tenure		Personal Description					Citizenship			Education	
	Street, avenue, road, etc.	House number or farm	Dwelling number	Number of family, in order of visitation		Relationship of this person to the head of the family	Home owned or rented	If owned, free or mortgaged	Sex	Color or Race	Age at last birthday	Single, married, widowed or divorced	Year of immigration to the United States	Naturalized or alien	If naturalized, year of naturalization	Attended school anytime since Sept. 1, 1919	Able to read	Able to write
	1	2	3	4	5	6	7	8	9	10	11	12	13	14	15	16	17	18

Nativity and Mother Tongue

Place of birth of each person and parents of each person enumerated. If born in the United States, give state or territory. If foreign birth, give the place of birth, and, in addition, the mother tongue.

Line Number	Person		Father		Mother		Able to speak english	Occupation			
	Place of Birth	Mother Tongue	Place of Birth	Mother Tongue	Place of Birth	Mother Tongue		Trade, profession or particular kind of work done	Industry, business or establishment of work done	Employer, salary or wage worker, or working on own account	No. of farm schedule
	19	20	21	22	23	24	25	26	27	28	29

Ancestry® Census Form 014

To search the 1920 census online, visit www.ancestry.com

©The Generations Network, Inc. 2007

1930 United States Federal Census

State: _____

County: _____

City, township: _____

Call Number/URL: _____

Enumeration District: _____

Sheet Number: _____

Enumeration Date: _____

Line number	PLACE OF ABODE				NAME	RELATION	HOME DATA				PERSONAL DESCRIPTION					EDUCATION		PLACE OF BIRTH		
	Street, avenue, road, etc.	House number (in cities or towns)	Number of dwelling house in order of visitation	Number of family in order of visitation	of each person whose place of abode on April 1, 1930, was in this family. Enter surname first, then the given name and middle initial, if any. Include every person living on April 1, 1930. Omit children born since April 1, 1930.	Relationship of this person to the head of the family	Home owned or rented	Value of home, if owned, or monthly rental, if rented	Radio set	Does this family live on a farm?	Sex	Color or race	Age at last birthday	Marital condition	Age at first marriage	Attended school or college any time since Sept.1,1929	Whether able to read and write	PERSON	FATHER	MOTHER
	1	2	3	4	5	6	7	8	9	10	11	12	13	14	15	16	17	18	19	20

Place of birth of each person and parents of each person enumerated. If born in the United States, give the State or Territory. If of foreign birth, give the country of birth. See instructions for additional entries required for certain countries

Line number	MOTHER TONGUE (OR NATIVE LANGUAGE) OF FOREIGN BORN	CODE (For office use only. Do not write in these columns)			CITIZENSHIP			OCCUPATION AND INDUSTRY		CODE (For office use only. Do not write in this column)	EMPLOYMENT			VETERANS		
	Language spoken in home before coming to the United States	State or M.T.	Country		Year of immigration to the United States	Naturalized or alien	Whether able to speak English	OCCUPATION Trade, profession, or particular kind of work, as spinner, salesman, riveter, etc.	INDUSTRY Industry or business, as cotton mill, dry goods store, shipyard, public school, etc.		Whether actually at work	Yes or No	Line number for unemployed	Whether a veteran of the U.S. military or naval forces mobilized for any war or expedition	Yes or No	What war or expedition	No. of farm schedule
	21	A	B	C	22	23	24	25	26	D	27	28	29		30	31	32

NOTES:

To search the census online, visit www.ancestry.com

© The Generations Network 2007

ancestry.com

Ancestry Census Form 015

GENERAL AFFIDAVIT

State Of Florida
County of Pinellas

Before me, the undersigned notary public, personally appeared

MONICA IZZO DALTON, known to me or proven, who being duly sworn

deposes and says:

Regarding her mother, Rachela Di Taranto, on the marriage certificate

Last name changed from:	DiTaranto to DeTaranto
First name changed from:	Rachela to Lena
Date of Birth changed from:	11 January, 1918 to
	31 December, 1917

and further depondent sayeth not.

_____
Signature of Affiant

Subscribed and sworn before me, this
23 day of June, 2008

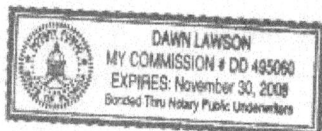

_____
Notary

APPLICATION FOR ITALIAN CITIZENSHIP *JURE SANGUINIS*

*THE UNDERSIGNED Last/First/ Middle Name*_____
City of birth:_____Date of birth (DD/MM/YYYY:_____
State/Province of birth:_____ -----
Current Address:_____.
Telephone (Home)_____(Business)_____(Cell)_____
Married (YES/NO)_____ Divorced (YES/NO)_____
City and Date of Marriage_____
Spouse's Full Name (Please use maiden name)_____-
Spouse's City and date of birth_____

CHILDREN UNDER 18 YEARS OLD

Name	City of Birth	Date of Birth (DD/MM/YYYY)
1)_____	_____	_____
2)_____	_____	_____
3)_____	_____	_____

Requests that his/her right to Italian citizenship be recognized and, therefore, declares to be a descendant of:

GREAT GRANDFATHER	GREAT GRANDMOTHER
Last Name:_____	Last Name:_____
First Name/s:_____	First Name/s:_____
City of Birth:_____	City of Birth:_____
Date of Birth (DD/MM/YYYY):_____	Date of Birth (DD/MM/YYYY):_____
Date and City of Marriage:_____	Date and City of Marriage:_____
NATURALIZATION	NATURALIZATION
Certificate No.:	Certificate No.:
City:	City:
Date of Naturalization (DD/MM/YYYY):	Date of Naturalization (DD/MM/YYYY):
GRANDFATHER	GRANDMOTHER
Last Name:_____	Last Name:_____
First Name/s:_____	First Name/s:_____
City of Birth:	City of Birth:_____
Date of Birth (DD/MM/YYYY):_____	Date of Birth (DD/MM/YYYY):_____
Date and City of Marriage:_____	Date and City of Marriage:_____
NATURALIZATION	NATURALIZATION
Certificate No.:	Certificate No.:
City:	City:
Date of Naturalization (DD/MM/YYYY):	Date of Naturalization (DD/MM/YYYY):
FATHER	MOTHER
Last Name:_____	Last Name:_____
First Name/s:_____	First Name/s:_____
City of Birth:_____	City of Birth:_____
Date of Birth (DD/MM/YYYY):_____	Date of Birth (DD/MM/YYYY):_____
Date and City of Marriage:_____	Date and City of Marriage:_____
NATURALIZATION	NATURALIZATION
Certificate No.:	Certificate No.:
City:	City:
Date of Naturalization (DD/MM/YYYY):	Date of Naturalization (DD/MM/YYYY):

Attached (please mark appropriate box):

☐ FORM2 (Declaration that I never renounced Italian citizenship, listing all my places of residence);
☐ FORM 3 and/or FORM4 (Declaration that my ☐FATHER ☐MOTHER ☐GRANDFATHER ☐GRANDMOTHER ☐ GREAT GRANDFATHER ☐GREAT GRANDMOTHER never renounced Italian citizenship, listing all places of residence)

DATE (DD/MM/YYYY):_____ SIGNATURE:_____
(MUST BE NOTARIZED)

DECLARATION OF APPLICANT

THE UNDERSIGNED *(Last/First/ Middle Name)*_____
BORN IN (City and State/Province):_____
DATE OF BIRTH (DD/MM/YYYY:_____
CURRENT ADDRESS:_____

Telephone (Home)_____(Business)_____(Cell)_____

IN REFERENCE TO HIS/HER REQUEST FOR RECOGNITION OF ITALIAN CITIZENSHIP *JURE SANGUINIS,*

DECLARES

THAT HE/SHE HAS NEVER RENOUNCED ITALIAN CITIZENSHIP BEFORE ANY ITALIAN AUTHORITY,
THAT HE/SHE, STARTING FROM THE AGE OF EIGHTEEN (18), HAS RESIDED IN:

CITY, STATE/PROVINCE	APPROXIMATE TIME PERIOD (YEARS)
1.	
2.	
3.	
4.	
5.	
6.	
7.	
8.	
9.	
10.	

DATE (DD/MM/YYYY):_____ SIGNATURE:_____

(SIGNATURE MUST BE NOTARIZED. OTHERWISE THIS DECLARATION MUST BE SIGNED BEFORE A CONSULAR OFFICER)

DECLARATION OF LIVING ITALIAN ASCENDANT

*THE UNDERSIGNED (Last/First/ Middle Name)*_____

BORN IN (City and State/Province):_____

DATE OF BIRTH (DD/MM/YYYY:_____

CURRENT ADDRESS:_____
_____

Telephone (Home)_____(Business)_____(Cell)_____

(PLEASE CHECK THE APPROPRIATE BOX)☐FATHER ☐MOTHER ☐GRANDFATHER ☐GRANDMOTHER ☐
GREAT GRANDFATHER ☐GREAT GRANDMOTHER OF THE APPLICANT

(Applicant's last/first/middle name)

IN REFERENCE TO THE APPLICANT'S REQUEST FOR RECOGNITION OF ITALIAN CITIZENSHIP *JURE SANGUINIS*, AND BEING AWARE THAT THE UNDERSIGNED WILL ALSO OBTAIN HIS/HER OWN RECOGNITION OF ITALIAN CITIZENSHIP

DECLARES

THAT HE/SHE HAS NEVER RENOUNCED ITALIAN CITIZENSHIP BEFORE ANY ITALIAN AUTHORITY,
THAT HE/SHE, STARTING FROM THE AGE OF EIGHTEEN (18), HAS RESIDED IN:

CITY, STATE/PROVINCE	APPROXIMATE TIME PERIOD (YEARS)
1.	
2.	
3.	
4.	
5.	
6.	
7.	
8.	
9.	
10.	

DATE (DD/MM/YYYY):_____   SIGNATURE:_____

(SIGNATURE MUST BE NOTARIZED. OTHERWISE THIS DECLARATION MUST BE SIGNED BEFORE A CONSULAR OFFICER)

DECLARATION OF DECEASED ITALIAN ASCENDANT

(If your Italian ancestor was born in Italy, but is deceased, please fill out the following declaration. If alive please have him/her fill FORM3)

THE UNDERSIGNED (Last/First/ Middle Name) _____

BORN IN (City and State/Province): _____

DATE OF BIRTH (DD/MM/YYYY; _____

IN REFERENCE TO THE APPLICANT'S REQUEST FOR RECOGNITION OF ITALIAN CITIZENSHIP *JURE SANGUINIS*

DECLARES THAT

_____

(Name of ancestor)

BORN IN (City and State/Province): _____

DATE OF BIRTH (DD/MM/YYYY: _____

AND RELATED TO THE APPLICANTAS (PLEASE CHECK THE APPROPRIATE BOX)☐FATHER ☐MOTHER ☐ GRANDFATHER ☐GRANDMOTHER ☐ GREAT GRANDFATHER ☐GREAT GRANDMOTHER

NEVER RENOUNCED ITALIAN CITIZENSHIP BEFORE ANY ITALIAN AUTHORITY, and THAT HE/SHE, STARTING FROM THE AGE OF EIGHTEEN (18), RESIDED IN:

CITY, STATE/PROVINCE	APPROXIMATE TIME PERIOD (YEARS)
1.	
2.	
3.	
4.	
5.	
6.	
7.	
8.	
9.	
10.	

DATE (DD/MM/YYYY): _____   SIGNATURE: _____

(SIGNATURE MUST BE NOTARIZED. OTHERWISE THIS DECLARATION MUST BE SIGNED BEFORE A CONSULAR OFFICER)

MODELLO A

Articolo 5 legge 5 febbraio 1992, n. 91 e successive modifiche e integrazioni

---

All'Autorità diplomatico-consolare di
_____

_L_ sottoscritt_(cognome)_____

(nome)_____

sesso (M/F)_____ nat_ il ___/___/____ a (città)_____

(Stato)_____

cittadin_____
(indicare la cittadinanza o la condizione di apolidia)

figlio di

(paternità) _____
(Cognome, nome e cittadinanza)

e figlio di

(maternità) _____
(Cognome, nome e cittadinanza)

residente a (città)_____prov._____

via_____n._____dal___/___/____

tel. _____ cell._____

coniugato/a con cittadin_ italian_ in data ___/___/____

atto di matrimonio trascritto presso il Comune italiano di_____

in possesso del seguente titolo di studio_____

attività svolta_____
(1) (indicare come riportato in nota)

(1): agricoltore, agronomo, architetto, artigiano, artista, autista, avvocato, bracciante, cameriere, casalinga, chimico, collaboratore domestico, commercialista, commerciante, consulente commerciale, consulente turistico, cuoco, disegnatore, farmacista, fotografo, geometra, giornalista, impiegato, industriale, infermiere, ingegnere, insegnante, interprete, manovale, marittimo, meccanico, medico, operaio, pensionato, perito, pittore, portiere, prof. universitario, ragioniere, rappresentante, regista, religioso, ricercatore, sportivo, studente, altro.

Indirizzi all'estero a partire dall'età di 14 anni:

1)(Stato, città, via e numero civico) _____

_____ *per il periodo dal* ___ / ___ / ___ *al* ___ / ___ /____

2)(Stato, città, via e numero civico) _____

_____ *per il periodo dal* ___ / ___ / ___ *al* ___ / ___ /____

CHIEDE

*di poter acquistare la cittadinanza italiana ai sensi dell' **Art. 5** della legge 5 febbraio 1992, n. 91 e successive modifiche e integrazioni essendo in possesso dei requisiti prescritti dalla legge.*

Al riguardo, _l_ sottoscritt_ (cognome) _____

(nome) _____

DICHIARA

di essere residente _____

Qualunque variazione di residenza o domicilio, anche temporanea, deve essere tempestivamente comunicata all' Autorità diplomatico-consolare presso la quale è stata presentata l'istanza.

2

CONSOLATO GENERALE D'ITALIA IN MIAMI
4000 Ponce de Leon Blvd, Suite 590 – Coral Gables, FL 33146
www.consmiami.esteri.it

modulo integrato

POS. N_____

DICHIARAZIONE SOSTITUTIVA DI CERTIFICAZIONE E DI ATTO DI NOTORIETA'
Iscrizione / Aggiornamento AIRE, Trascrizione atto di Nascita / Matrimonio, Rilascio / Rinnovo Passaporto
Personal Declaration of Certification and Notoriety Act / Declaración sustitutiva de certificación y acto de notoriedad

IL SOTTOSCRITTO_____
The Applicant/El Declarante   COGNOME (Last Name/Apellido)   NOME (First Name/Nombre)   COGNOME DA NUBILE (Maiden Name/Apellido de Soltera)

NATO IL_____/_____/_____ A _____
Born/Nacido   (dd)   (mm)   (yy)   Place of Birth/ Lugar de nacimiento

COMUNE ITALIANO TRASCRIZIONE ATTO NASCITA (dato obbligatorio)_____
Italian city where birth was registered/Ciudad italiana donde fué registrada la partida de nacimiento (required)   PROVINCIA (Province)

NOME PADRE_____ COGNOME E NOME MADRE DA NUBILE_____
Father's First Name/Nombre del padre   Mother's Maiden & First Name/Apellido y Nombre de soltera de la madre

LUOGO DI RESIDENZA DEL DICHIARANTE: ☐ USA   ☐ ITALIA   ☐ ALTRO (Other/Otros)_____
Place of permanent residence/Lugar permanente de residencia

INDIRIZZO_____
Address/Dirección   VIA (Street/Calle)   CITTA (City/Ciudad)   STATO (State/Estado)   CAP (Zip/Código Postal)

TELEFONO_____-_____-_____ EMAIL_____
Phone   CASA (Home)   LAVORO (Work/Trabajo)

COMUNE DI ISCRIZIONE A.I.R.E. IN ITALIA_____
City of registration in Italy/Ciudad de inscripción en Italia   PROVINCIA (Province)

LUOGO E CONSOLATO DI PROVENIENZA SE GIA' ISCRITTI all'A.I.R.E._____
Place and Consulate of origin if already registered with the AIRE/Lugar y Consulado donde ha sido inscrito en AIRE

ANNO PRIMA EMIGRAZIONE_____ DATA ARRIVO CIRCOSCRIZIONE CONSOLARE_____
Year of first emigration/Año de primera emigración   Date of arrival in the Consular district/Fecha de llegada en esta circunscripción consular

PASSAPORTO N._____ RILASCIATO A_____ IL_____
Italian passport /Pasaporte   Issued by/Expedido por   on/el

RINNOVATO A_____ IL_____ NR.PERMESSO DI SOGGIORNO/ VISTO_____
Renewed by/Renovado por)   on/el   Alien Registration Card/Green Card /Visa

ALTRA CITTADINANZA_____ DATA ACQUISTO CITT. STRANIERA_____ DATA RIACQUISTO CITT. ITALIANA_____
Other citizenship/Otra Ciudadanía   Naturalization Date/Fecha de naturalización   Date of citizenship reacquisition/ Fecha de readquisición

PROFESSIONE_____ STATURA_____ COLORE DEGLI OCCHI_____ FIGLI MINORI: ☐ Si (Yes) ☐ No
Profession/Occupation   Height/Altura   Color of Eyes/Color de ojos   Minor Children. Hijos menores

STATO CIVILE: ☐ libero   ☐ coniugato   ☐ separato   ☐ divorziato   ☐ vedovo   PRECEDENTI MATRIMONI: ☐ Si (Yes) ☐ No
Marital Status/Estado civil: single/soltero married/casado separated divorced widowed/viudo   Previous marriage/Matrimonios precedentes

FAMILIARI (Family members/Miembros familiares)
CONIUGE RESIDENTE NELLA STESSA ABITAZIONE (Spouse living in the same residence/Cónyuge viviendo en la misma residencia)

(dd)   (mm)   (yy)
_____/_____/_____

COGNOME (Maiden Name/Apellido de Soltera)   NOME (First Name/Nombre)   LUOGO E DATA NASCITA (Place and Date of Birth/Lugar y Fecha de nacimiento)

CITTADINANZA DEL CONIUGE (Citizenship of the spouse/Ciudadanía del cónyuge)_____

(dd)   (mm)   (yy)
LUOGO E DATA DEL MATRIMONIO_____   _____/_____/_____
Place and Date of the marriage/Fecha y lugar del matrimonio
COMUNE ITALIANO DI TRASCRIZIONE ATTO DI MATRIMONIO_____
Italian city where marriage was registered/Ciudad italiana donde fué registrada la partida de matrimonio   PROVINCIA (Province)

FIGLI MAGGIORENNI E MINORENNI RESIDENTI NELLA STESSA ABITAZIONE (Child living at the same address/ Hijos viviendo en la misma residencia)

COGNOME (Last Name/Apellido)   NOME (First Name/Nombre)   LUOGO E DATA NASCITA (Place and Date of Birth/Lugar y Fecha de nacimiento)   (dd)   (mm)   (yy)

1 _____ _____/_____/_____

2 _____ _____/_____/_____

3 _____ _____/_____/_____

FIGLI MINORENNI NON RESIDENTI NELLA STESSA ABITAZIONE (Child not living at the same address/ Hijos no viviendo en la misma residencia)

4 _____ _____/_____/_____

5 _____ _____/_____/_____

Il sottoscritto dichiara sotto la propria responsabilità che quanto attestato risponde a verità e richiede il servizio di seguito indicato:
The undersigned declares that the above information is true and request/ El signatario certifica que lo declarado es fidedigno y solicita:

Barrare la casella a lato
Check the appropriate box
Marque la casilla apropiada

☐ **Iscrizione / Aggiornamento AIRE** (Registry of Italian Nationals residing abroad. Italianos residentes en el extranjero)
☐ **Trascrizione Atto di Nascita / Matrimonio** (Certificate registration of Birth/Marriage. Transcripción Partida de Nacimiento/Matrimonio)
☐ **Rilascio / Rinnovo Passaporto** (Passport Application Issuance/Renewal. Solicitud para pasaporte o renovación)

Firma del dichiarante (Sign)_____ Data (Date/Fecha)_____

CONSOLATO GENERALE D'ITALIA MIAMI

4000 Ponce de Leon Blvd, Suite 590, Coral Gables, Florida 33146 - Tel. 305/374 6322 Fax 305/374 7945

DICHIARAZIONE SOSTITUTIVA DI CERTIFICAZIONE E DI ATTO DI NOTORIETA' (LEGGE N.15 DEL 04.01.68)

Personal Declaration of Certification and Notoriety Act (Law n.15 of Jan. 4, 1968)

I SOTTOSCRITTI:

PADRE: COGNOME _____ NOME (Name) _____ CITTADINANZA _____
(Last name) _(Name)_ _(citizenship)_

NATO A _____ IL (giorno/mese/anno) _____
(Place of birth) _(date day/month/year)_

STATO CIVILE: ___Celibe ___Coniugato ___ Divorziato ___ Separato ___ Vedovo
(Single) _(Married)_ _(Divorced)_ _(Separated)_ _(Widow)_

MADRE: COGNOME _____ NOME (Name) _____ CITTADINANZA _____
(Last name) _(Name)_ _(citizenship)_

NATO A _____ IL (giorno/mese/anno) _____
(Place of birth) _(date day/month/year)_

STATO CIVILE: ___Celibe ___Coniugato ___ Divorziato ___ Separato ___ Vedovo
(Single) _(Married)_ _(Divorced)_ _(Separated)_ _(Widow)_

RESIDENTI **PERMANENTEMENTE** AL SEGUENTE INDIRIZZO _(Address of permanent residence)_:

Via _____ Apt. _____ Città _____ Stato _____ Cap ____
(Address) _(Apt)_ _(City)_ _(State)_ _(Zip)_

Tel. (____) _____ Fax (____) _____

ESPRIMONO IL LORO ASSENSO A _(Hereby grant their authorization in favour of)_:
____ RINNOVO del passaporto ai figli minori sotto indicati _(Renewal passport for children under 18 below mentioned)_
____ RILASCIO del passaporto ai figli minori sotto indicati _(Issue passport for children under 18 below mentioned)_
____ ISCRIZIONE dei figli minori sotto indicati su passaporto ____ DELLA MADRE NR. _(Mother)_ _____
(Registration of children on the parents passaport)

____ DEL PADRE NR. _(Father)_ _____

COGNOME _(Last name)_	NOME _(Name)_	LUOGO NASCITA _(Place of birth)_	DATA NASCITA _(D.O.B.)_	STATURA _(Height)_	COLORE OCCHI _(Color of Eyes)_

ALLEGANO I SEGUENTI DOCUMENTI _(Attach the following documents)_:

PER IL RILASCIO _(New passport)_:
Certificato di nascita italiano del minore oppure prova dell'avvenuta trascrizione in Italia dell'atto straniero _(Copy of Italian birth certificate, or proof of birth certificate registration in Italy)_.
Due fotografie formato passaporto _(Two photos, for size see 2nd page)_.
Fotocopia del passaporto dei genitori. Fotocopia notarizzata se cittadini NON EUROPEI (pagine con foto ed eventuale visto USA) _(Copy of parents passports, in the event parents are not European citizen, please provide a notarized copy of passport pages with pictures and the page with visa)_.
Money Order di US$ _____ per ogni anno di marche (massimo 10 anni).
Money Order di US$ _____ per il nuovo libretto passaporto.

PER IL RINNOVO _(Renewal)_:
Passaporto scaduto _(Expired passaport)_.
Una fotografia formato passaporto _(One photo, for size see 2nd page)_.
Fotocopia del passaporto dei genitori. Fotocopia notarizzata se cittadini NON EUROPEI (pagine con foto ed eventuale visto USA) _(Copy of parents passports, in the event parents are not European citizen, please provide a notarized copy of passport pages with pictures and the page with visa)_.
Money Order di US$ _____ per ogni anno di marche (massimo 10 anni).

PER L'ISCRIZIONE SUL PASSAPORTO DEI GENITORI _(For the registration on parents passports)_:
Passaporti di entrambi i genitori _(Parents passports)_.
Due fotografie del minore (una se ha meno di 10 anni) _(Two photos of the child, one if he is under 10, for size see 2nd page)_.
Certificato di nascita italiano del minore oppure prova dell'avvenuta trascrizione in Italia dell'atto straniero _(Copy of Italian birth certificate, or proof of birth certificate registration in Italy)_.

SI PREGA DI COMPILARE ACCURATAMENTE E FIRMARE SUL RETRO SEGUENDO LE ISTRUZIONI

SI PREGA DI INDICARE SE IL PASSAPORTO VERRA' RITIRATO PERSONALMENTE: SI _____ NO _____

Department of Homeland Security
U.S. Citizenship and Immigration Services

N-565, Application for Replacement Naturalization/Citizenship Document

Instructions

Purpose of This Form.

This form is used to apply to the U.S. Citizenship and Immigration Services (USCIS) for a replacement:

- Declaration of Intention, or
- Naturalization Certificate, or
- Certificate of Citizenship, or
- Repatriation Certificate, or to
- Apply for a special certificate of naturalization as a U.S. citizen to be recognized by a foreign country.

NOTE: USCIS is comprised of offices of the former Immigration and Naturalization Service (INS).

Who May File?

You may apply for a replacement:

- If you have been issued a Naturalization Certificate, Certificate of Citizenship, Declaration of Intention or Repatriation Certificate which has been lost, mutilated, or destroyed, or;
- If your name has been changed by marriage or by court order after the document was issued and you seek a document in the new name.
- If you are a naturalized citizen desiring to obtain recognition as a citizen of the United States by a foreign country, you may apply for a special certificate for that purpose.

General Filing Instructions.

Please answer all questions by typing or clearly printing in black ink. Indicate that an item is not applicable with "N/A." If an answer is "none," so state. If you need extra space to answer any item, attach a sheet of paper with your name and your A#, if any, and indicate the number of the item.

Every application must be properly signed and filed with the correct fee. If you are under 14 years of age, your parent or guardian may sign the application in your behalf.

Initial Evidence Requirements.

You must file your application with the following evidence:

- You must submit two standard passport-style photographs in color of yourself taken within 30 days of this application. These photos must be glossy, unretouched and unmounted, and have a white background. The dimension of your full frontal facial position should be about 1 inch from your chin to the top of your hair. Using pencil or felt pen, lightly print your name and A# if any, on the back of each photo. This requirement may be waived by USCIS if you can establish that you are confined because of age or physical infirmity.

- If you are applying for replacement of a mutilated document, you must attach the mutilated document.

- If you are applying for a new document because your name has been changed, you must submit the original USCIS (or former INS) document and a copy of the marriage certificate or court order showing the name change.

- If you are applying for a special certificate of naturalization, you must attach a copy of your naturalization certificate.

Copies.

If these instructions state that a copy of a document may be filed with this application, and you choose to send us the original, we may keep that original for our records.

Where to File.

File this application at the local USCIS office having jurisdiction over your place of residence.

What Is the Fee?

The fee for this petition is **$220.00**, except there is no fee if you check block 2 (d) of Part 2 of the form.

The fee must be submitted in the exact amount. It cannot be refunded. **Do not mail cash.**

All checks and money orders must be drawn on a bank or other institution located in the United States and must be payable in United States currency. The check or money order should be made payable to the **Department of Homeland Security**, except that:

- If you live in Guam, and are filing this application in Guam, make your check or money order payable to the "Treasurer, Guam."

- If you live in the U.S. Virgin Islands, and are filing this application in the U.S. Virgin Islands, make your check or money order payable to the "Commissioner of Finance of the Virgin Islands."

OMB No. 1615-0091; Expires 05/31/2011

Department of Homeland Security
U.S. Citizenship and Immigration Services

Form N-565, Application for Replacement Naturalization/Citizenship Document

START HERE - Please type or print in black ink

For USCIS Use Only

Part 1.   Information about you.

Family Name	Given Name	Middle Name

Address - In care of:

Street Number and Name	Apt. Number

City or Town	State or Province

Country	Zip or Postal Code

Date of Birth *(mm/dd/yyyy)*	Country of Birth

Certificate Number	A-Number

Telephone Number (with area/country codes)	E-Mail Address (if any)

Part 2. Type of application

1. I hereby apply for: (check one)

a. ☐ New Certificate of Citizenship
b. ☐ New Certificate of Naturalization
c. ☐ New Certificate of Repatriation
d. ☐ New Declaration of Intention
e. ☐ Special Certificate of Naturalization to obtain recognition of my U.S. citizenship by a foreign country. (Skip Number 2 and go to Part 3)

2. Basis for application: (Refer to the instructions for additional information.)

a. ☐ My certificate is/was lost, stolen or destroyed (attach a copy of the certificate if you have one.) Explain when, where and how.

b. ☐ My certificate is mutilated (attach the certificate).
c. ☐ My name has been changed (attach the certificate).
d. ☐ My certificate or declaration is incorrect (attach the document(s)).

Part 3. Processing information

Gender	☐ Male ☐ Female	Height	Marital Status	☐ Single ☐ Married	☐ Widowed ☐ Divorced

My last certificate or Declaration of Intention was issued to me by:

USCIS Office or Name of Court:	Date *(mm/dd/yyyy):*

Name in which the document was issued:

Other names I have used (if none, so indicate):

Since becoming a citizen, have you lost your citizenship in any manner?

☐ No   ☐ Yes (attach an explanation)

Part 4. Complete if applying for a new document because of a name change

Name changed to present name by: (check one)

☐ Marriage or divorce on (month/day/year)
  (Attach a copy of marriage or divorce certificate)

For USCIS Use Only

Returned	Receipt
————	
————	
Resubmitted	
————	
————	
Reloc Sent	
————	
————	
Reloc Rec'd	
————	
————	

☐ Applicant Interviewed

☐ Declaration of Intention verified by
————————

☐ Citizenship verified by
————————

Remarks

Action Block

To Be Completed by
Attorney or Representative, if any.

☐ Fill in box if Form G-28 is attached to represent the applicant.

VOLAG#

Part 5. Complete if applying to correct your document

If you are applying for a new certificate or Declaration of Intention because your current one is incorrect, explain why it is incorrect and attach copies of the documents supporting your request.

_____
_____
_____
_____
_____
_____

Part 6. Complete if applying for a special certificate of recognition as a citizen of the U.S. by the government of a foreign country

Name of Foreign Country _____

Information about official of the country who has requested this certificate (if known)

Name   Official Title

Government Agency:

Address: Street Number and Name		Suite Number
City	State/Province	
Country		Zip or Postal Code

Part 7. Signature

Read the information on penalties in the instructions before completing this part. If you are going to file this application at a USCIS office in the United States sign below. If you are going to file this application at a USCIS office abroad, sign it in front of a USCIS or Consular Official.

I certify, or if outside the United States, I swear or affirm, under penalty of perjury under the laws of the United States of America, that this application and the evidence submitted with it is all true and correct. I authorize the release of any information from my records which U.S. Citizenship and Immigration Services needs to determine eligibility for the benefit I am seeking.

Signature   **Date** *(mm/dd/yyyy)*

Signature of USCIS   Print Your Name   Date *(mm/dd/yyyy)*
or Consular Official

NOTE: *If you do not completely fill out this form or fail to submit required documents listed in the instructions, you may not be found eligible for a certificate and this application may be denied.*

Part 8. Signature of person preparing form, if other than the applicant

I declare that I prepared this application at the request of the applicant and it is based on all information of which I have knowledge.

Signature   **Print Your Name**   **Date** *(mm/dd/yyyy)*

Firm Name and Address | Telephone Number (with area code)
                                                        |
                                                        | E-Mail Address (if any)

Department of Homeland Security
U.S. Citizenship and Immigration Services

G-639, Freedom of Information/ Privacy Act Request

Instructions

NOTE: Please read all instructions carefully before completing this form. Applicants making false statements are subject to criminal penalties (Pub. L. 93-579.99 Stat. [5 U.S.C. 552a(i)(3)]).

Are There Cases When You Should Not Use This Form?

Do not use this form:

1. To determine the status of pending applications. For status inquires, write to the USCIS office where the application was filed or call our National Customer Service Center at **1-800-375 5283.**

2. For consular notification of a visa petition approval, use Form I-824 (Application for Action on an Approved Application or Petition).

3. For the return of original documents, use Form G-884 (Request for Return of Original Documents).

4. For records of naturalization prior to September 27, 1906, write to the clerk of court where naturalization occurred.

5. For information on USCIS manifest arrivals prior to December 1982, write to the National Archives.

6. To obtain proof of status (i.e., Social Security benefit, Selective Service requirement).

Where Should USCIS FOIA/PA Requests Be Submitted?

Depending on the type of record you are seeking, Freedom of Information Act (FOIA) or Privacy Act (PA) requests should be submitted by mail to the following locations:

Alien Files -

National Record Center (NRC)
P. O. Box 648010
Lee's Summit, MO 64064-8010

Human Resources and
Procurement Records -

USCIS FOIA/PA
70 Kimball Avenue
South Burlington, Vermont 05403-6813

Remaining USCIS Records
and Border Patrol Records -

USCIS National Record Center
FOIA Division
P.O. Box 648010
Lee Summit, MO 64064-5570

The envelopes containing your request should be clearly marked "Freedom of Information" or "Privacy Act Request."

NOTE: Do not submit your FOIA/PA request to your local USCIS office or Service Center.

What Information Is Needed to Search for USCIS Records?

NOTE: Failure to provide complete and specific information as requested in **Number 5** of the form may result in a delay in processing or USCIS' inability to locate the record(s) or information requested. You may access **www.uscis.gov** for a description of **DHS/USCIS** systems of records.

Verification of Identity in Person.

Requesters appearing in person for access of their records may identify themselves by showing a document bearing a photograph (such as a Permanent Resident Card, Form I-551; Naturalization Certificate or passport) or two items that bear their name and address (such as a driver's license and voter registration card).

Verification of Identity by Mail.

Requesters wanting access of their records should identify themselves by name, current address, date and place of birth, and alien registration or employee identification number.

A notarized example of their signature or sworn declaration under penalty of perjury must also be provided. (This Form G-639 or a U.S. Department of Justice Form 361, Certification of Identity, may also be used).

Verification of Identity of Parents, Guardians, Children or Other Persons.

Parents or legal guardians must establish their own identity as parents or legal guardians and the identity of the child or other person being represented.

Authorization or Consent.

Other parties requesting nonpublic information about an individual usually must have the consent of that person on Form G-639 or by an authorizing letter, together with appropriate verification of identity of the record subject. A notarized or sworn declaration is required from a record subject who is a lawful permanent resident or U.S. citizen, and for access to certain Legalization files.

Form G-639 (Rev. 11/13/06)Y

Can Your Request Be Expedited?

To have your case processed ahead of other requests received previously, you must show a compelling need for your request to be expedited.

How Do You Show a Compelling Need?

A requester who seeks expedited processing must explain in detail the basis of the need and should submit a statement certified to be true and correct to the best of his or her knowledge and belief. The requester must also establish that one of the following situations exists:

1. Circumstances in which the lack of expedited processing could reasonably be expected to pose an imminent threat to the life or physical safety of an individual, or

2. An urgency to inform the public about an actual or alleged federal government activity, if made by a person primarily engaged in disseminating information.

Fees.

No fees are required until you are notified by USCIS during the processing of your request.

Except for commercial requesters, the first 100 pages of reproduction and two hours of search time will be provided without charge. Thereafter, for requests processed under the Privacy Act, there may be a fee of ten cents per page for photocopy duplication.

Other costs for searches and duplication will be charged at the actual direct cost.

Fees will only be charged if the aggregate amount of fees for searches, copy and/or review is more than $14.00. If the total anticipated fees amount to more than $250.00, or the same requester has failed to pay fees in the past, an advance deposit may be requested.

NOTE: If fees for a prior request are outstanding, we will not honor future requests until all fees are paid.

Fee waivers or reductions may be sought for a request that clearly will benefit the public and is not primarily in the personal or commercial interest of the requester. Such requests should include a justification.

When Must You Submit the Fees?

Do not send money with this request. When USCIS instructs you to do so, submit the fees in the exact amount.

Payment may be in the form of a check or U. S. postal money order. If the form is submitted from outside the United States, remittance may be made on a bank international money order or foreign draft drawn on a financial institution based in the United States, made payable in U.S. currency to the "United States Treasury."

A requester residing in the U.S. Virgin Islands should make the remittance payable to the Commissioner of Finance of the Virgin Islands; and, if residing in Guam, to the Treasurer, Guam." **Do not send cash at any time.**

A charge of $30.00 will be imposed if a check in payment of a fee is not honored by the bank on which it is drawn. Every remittance will be accepted subject to collection.

Routine Uses.

Information will be used to comply with requests for information under **Title 5 U.S. Code 552** and **552a.** Information provided to other agencies may be for referrals, consultations and/or to answer subsequent inquiries concerning specific requests.

Effect of Not Providing Requested Information.

Providing the information requested on this form is voluntary. However, failure to furnish the informations may result in our inability to comply with a request when compliance will violate other policies or laws.

General Information.

The Freedom of Information Act (5 U.S.C. 552) allows requesters to have access to Federal agency records, except those exempted by the Act.

Privacy Act Statement.

Authority to collect this information is contained in **Title 5 U.S. Code 552** and **552a.** The purpose of the collection is to enable USCIS to locate applicable records and to respond to requests made under the Freedom of Information and Privacy Acts.

Privacy Act of 1974 (5 U.S.C. 552a).

With certain exceptions, the Privacy Act of 1974 permits persons (U.S. citizens or permanent resident aliens) to gain access to information pertaining to themselves in Federal agency records, to have a copy made of all or any part thereof, to correct or amend such records, and to permit individuals to make requests concerning what records pertaining to themselves are collected, maintained, used or disseminated. The Act also prohibits disclosure of any person's records without their written consent, except under certain circumstances as prescribed by the Privacy Act.

USCIS Forms and Information.

To order USCIS forms, call our toll-free number at **1-800-870-3676**. You can also get USCIS forms and information on immigration laws, regulations and procedures by telephoning our National Customer Service Center at **1-800-375-5283** or visiting our internet website at **www.uscis.gov**.

Use InfoPass for Appointments.

As an alternative to waiting in line for assistance at your local USCIS office, you can now schedule an appointment through our internet-based system, **InfoPass**. To access the system, visit our website at **www.uscis.gov**. Use the **InfoPass** appointment scheduler and follow the screen prompts to set up your appointment. **InfoPass** generates an electronic appointment notice that appears on the screen. Print the notice and take it with you to your appointment. The notice gives the time and date of your appointment, along with the address of the USCIS office.

Public Reporting Burden.

Under the Paperwork Reduction Act (5 U.S.C. 1320), a person is not required to respond to a collection of information unless it displays a currently valid OMB control number.

We try to create forms and instructions that are accurate, can be easily understood and that impose the least possible burden on you to provide us with information. Often this is difficult because some immigration laws are very complex.

The estimated average time to complete and file this application is 15 minutes per response, including the time for reviewing the instructions, searching existing data sources, gathering and maintaining the data needed, and completing and reviewing the collection of information.

If you have comments regarding the accuracy of this estimate or suggestions for making this form simpler, write to U.S. Citizenship and Immigration Services, Regulatory Management Division, 111 Massachusetts Avenue, N.W., 3rd Floor, Suite 3008, Washington, DC 20529; OMB No. 1653-0030. **Do not send your request to this office address.**

OMB No. 1653-0030; Expires 11/30/08

**G-639, Freedom of Information/
Privacy Act Request**

Department of Homeland Security
U.S. Citizenship and Immigration Services

NOTE: The completion of this form is optional. Any written format for a Freedom of Information or Privacy Act request is acceptable.

START HERE - Please type or print in black ink. Read instructions before completing this form.

1. Type of request: *(Check appropriate box.)*

☐ Freedom of Information Act (FOIA). *(Complete all items except **Number 6.**)*

☐ Privacy Act (PA). *(**Number 6** must be completed in addition to all other applicable items.)*

☐ Amendment. *(PA only. **Number 5** must be completed in addition to all other applicable items.)*

2. Requester information.

Name of Requester: (Last, First and Middle Names)	Date (mm/dd/yyyy)	Daytime Telephone:
Address *(Street Number and Name)*:		Apt. Number:
City:	State:	Zip Code:

By my signature, I consent to the following:

Pay all costs incurred for search, duplication and review of materials up to **$25.00**, when applicable. *(See Instructions.)*

Signature of requester:

☐ Deceased Subject - **Proof of death must be attached.** *(Obituary, Death Certificate or other proof of death required.)*

3. Consent to release information. *(Complete if name is different from Requester).* *(**Numbers 7 and 8** must be completed.)*

Print Name of Person Giving Consent:	Signature of Person Giving Consent: *(Original signature required.)*

By my signature, I consent to the following: *(Check applicable boxes.)*

☐ Allow the Requester named in **Number 2** above to review: ☐ All of my records, or ☐ A portion of my records. *(If a portion, specify below what part, i.e. copy of application.)*

(Consent is required for records of U. S. citizens (USC) and Lawful Permanent Residents (LPR).

4. Information needed to search for record(s).

Specific information, document(s) or record(s) desired: *(Identify by name, date, subject matter and location of information.)*

Purpose: *(Optional: You are not required to state the purpose of your request. However, doing so may assist USCIS to locate the records needed to respond to your request.)*

5. Data needed on subject of record. *(If data marked with an asterisk (*) is not provided, records may not be located.)*

* Family Name:	Given Name:	Middle Name:
* Other names used, if any:	* Name at time of entry into the U.S.:	I-94 Admission #:
* Alien Registration Number: (A#)	* Petition or Claim Receipt #:	* Country of Birth:	* Date of Birth (mm/dd/yyyy)

Names of other family members that may appear on requested record(s) *(i.e., Spouse, Daughter, Son):*

Father's Name	First	Middle	Last

Mother's Name	First	Middle	Last (Include Maiden Name)

Form G-639 (Rev. 11/13/06)Y

Country of Origin: *(Place of Departure)*	Port-of-Entry Into the U.S.:		Date of Entry:
Manner of Entry: *(Air, Sea, Land)*	Mode of Travel: *(Name of Carrier)*		U.S. Social Security Number:
Name on Naturalization Certificate:		Certificate #:	Naturalization Date:
Address on Date of Naturalization:		Court and Location:	

6. Verification of subject's identity: *(See Instructions for explanation. Check one box.)*

☐ In-Person With ID ☐ Notarized Affidavit of Identity ☐ Other *(Specify)* _____

7. Signature of subject of record:

(Original signature required) _____ Date: _____

Telephone No.: (   ) _____

8. Notary: *(Normally needed from persons who are the subject of the record sought or for a sworn declaration under penalty of perjury. See below.)*

Subscribed and sworn to before me this _____ Day of _____ in the Year _____

Signature of Notary _____ My Commission Expires on _____

OR

NOTE: *If a declaration is provided in lieu of a notarized signature, it must state at a minimum the following: (Include Notary Seal or Stamp in the appropriate space below.)*

Executed outside U.S.

If executed outside the United States: "I declare (certify, verify or state) under penalty of perjury under the laws of the United States of America that the foregoing is true and correct.

Signature: _____

Executed in U.S.

If executed within the United States, its territories, possessions or commonwealths: "I declare (certify, verify or state) under penalty of perjury that the foregoing is true and correct.

Signature: _____

(Seal/Stamp)   **(Seal/Stamp)**

STATE OF _____)
)
COUNTY OF _____)

CASE NO.: _____

IN THE CIRCUIT COURT OF _____ COUNTY,

THIS IS TO CERTIFY THAT I, _____, CLERK OF THE CIRCUIT COURT, AM THE LEGAL CUSTODIAL OF THE RECORDS OF THIS COURT AND THE KEEPER OF IT'S SEAL.

I FURTHER CERTIFY, THAT AFTER A CAREFUL SEARCH OF THE RECORDS, OF MY OFFICE, I FIND THAT THERE IS NO APPEAL IN THE FINAL DIVORCE DECREE OF:

_____ VS. _____

AND THE DECREE IS IN FULL FORCE AND EFFECT JUST AS THE DATE OF ENTRY.

IN WITNESS WHEREOF, I HEREUNTO SET MY HAND AND THE SEAL OF MY OFFICE THIS _____DAY OF _____ IN THE YEAR OF _____ .

_____
CIRCUIT COURT CLERK
                                                      SEAL

_____
NOTARY PUBLIC
                                                      SEAL

MY COMMISSION EXPIRES ON: _____

FAC-SIMILE RICHIESTA ATTI DI STATO CIVILE DI CITTADINI ITALIANI A COMUNI ITALIANI

La richiesta deve essere inviata **direttamente** dall'interessato al proprio Comune, il cui indirizzo può essere reperito sul web www.comuni.it e dovrà essere riportato sulla busta.
*The request must be **directly** sent from the person concerned to the own Italian "Comune" City Hall, whose direction can be find in the web site www.comuni.it and must be reported on the envelope.*

Al Sindaco del Comune di

....

....

Il sottoscritto/a chiede cortesemente, uso _____, l'invio del/i seguente certificato/i:

    integrale con eventuali annotazioni (**complete** with notes if needed)

☐ **modello internazionale** plurilingue (multilingual **International** form)

Dell'atto di stato civile (of the following certificate):
☐ Estratto per riassunto atto di NASCITA (Birth Certificate)
☐ Estratto per riassunto atto di MATRIMONIO (Marriage Certificate)
☐ MORTE (Death Certificate)

Relativi alla seguente persona: (Pertinent to the following person)

Cognome (Last name):   Nome (First name):

_____

Nome da nubile (Maiden name):

_____

Nato/a a (Birth place): _____

il (Birth date): (day/month/year) _____/_____/_____

Indirizzo per l'invio del certificato (Direction to send and return the certificate):

Cognome richiedente (Applicant's last name):

_____

Nome richiedente (Applicant's name): _____
Via (Full address):

_____

Città (City): _____   Zip _____

Stato (State):_____   Tel. (Phone no.)_____

FAX:_____   E-mail:_____

Osservazioni (Other comments):

Data (Date):_____   Firma (Applicant's signature):_____

ALLEGARE FOTOCOPIA DEL DOCUMENTO D'IDENTITÀ' ED UNA BUSTA VUOTA DI RISPOSTA CON L'INDIRIZZO DEL RICHIEDENTE (AVVERTENZA: I COMUNI POSSONO ESIGERE L'INTEGRAZIONE DELLE RELATIVE SPESE POSTALI O IL PAGAMENTO DEI CERTIFICATI EMESSI)
Il Consolato Generale non si rende responsabile delle mancate risposte
ENCLOSE THE I.D. COPY AND THE SELF-ADDRESSED STAMPED RETURN ENVELOPE.
(IMPORTANT: THE ITALIAN "COMUNI" (City halls) CAN DEMAND A SUPPLEMENT POSTAL FEES OR THE ISSUED CERTIFICATE'S PAYMENT)

EXAMPLE COMUNE DECLARATION

YOUR FULL NAME (MAIDEN)

YOUR STREET ADDRESS

YOUR CITY, STATE ZIP CODE

YOUR TELEPHONE NUMBER

YOUR EMAIL ADDRESS

Date: _____

Dear Sir or Madam,

Please accept this completed packet of documents and affidavits. All have been properly notarized, translated and affixed with Apostilles.

I would like to register my civil status documents in the comune of my Italian ancestor:

Comune Di _____

Thank you for your prompt attention to my application.

Sincerely,

_____

SIGNED BY YOU

NEW YORK STATE DEPARTMENT OF HEALTH
Vital Records Section

Application for Correction
of Certificate of Death

See Reverse Side for Instructions

Deceased	District Number
Date of Death	Register Number
Place of Death	State Number

I, _____ of _____
(name of applicant)

_____
(address of applicant)

request that the following information amend the certificate of death identified above.

ITEM IN ERROR (or omitted)	AS IT APPEARS	AS IT SHOULD BE

Documentary evidence submitted herewith in support of this application includes:

Explain reason for error or omission:

_____
_____
_____
_____
_____

TO BE COMPLETED BY THE APPLICANT

Under the penalties of perjury, I hereby affirm that the statements made herein are true and correct to the best of my knowledge.

Signature of Applicant	Relationship to Deceased	Date

TO BE COMPLETED BY REGISTRAR OF VITAL STATISTICS

The above information has been added to the local record of death on file in this office.

Signature of Registrar	District Number	Date

DOH-299 (6/99) Page 1 of 2

(OVER)

NEW YORK STATE DEPARTMENT OF HEALTH
Vital Records Section

Affidavit to Request Certified Copy of Marriage Certificate

Affidavit for use with Dual Citizenship Application Requests

FOR OFFICE USE
Ref. # _____

I, _____ , swear or affirm under penalty of perjury that the statements made herein and any accompanying documentation are true and correct to the best of my knowledge and belief.

I reside at _____ _____ _____ _____
  (Street Address) *(City)* *(State)* *(ZIP Code)*

and I am requesting a certified copy of the marriage record of _____ and
  (Bride/Maiden Name)

_____ who were married on _____
  (Groom) *(Date of Marriage)*

with a license issued by the City / Town of _____ in New York State.
  (Town or City where license is believed to have been issued)

A certified copy of this record is required for the purpose of obtaining citizenship with _____
  (Name of Country)

I am related to the Bride or Groom as follows: *(Show name and relationship of descendents from yourself to the bride or groom. For example, I, Joseph Kelly, am the son of Mary McCormick, who is the daughter of Simon Green, who is the son of the bride, Alice Faillugh.)*

_____

_____

_____

_____

I also swear or affirm that this affidavit is being made for the sole purpose of obtaining the record of marriage for the purpose stated above and that both the bride and groom on the record are deceased. (Submit photocopies of the bride and groom's death certificates with this affidavit.)

▶ _____
Signature of Applicant

———— *Below to be completed by Notary Public* ————

STATE OF _____ }
                              } SS:
COUNTY OF _____ }

Subscribed and sworn to
(affirmed) before me this _____ day

of _____ , _____ .

▶ _____
Notary Public

DOH-5000 (5/10)

NEW YORK STATE DEPARTMENT OF HEALTH
Vital Records Section

Affidavit to Request Certified Copy of Death Certificate

Affidavit for Use with Dual Citizenship Application Requests

I, _____ , swear or affirm under penalty of perjury that the statements made herein and any accompanying documentation are true and correct to the best of my knowledge and belief.

I reside at _____
          (Street Address)   (City)   (State)   (ZIP Code)

and I am requesting a certified copy of the death record of _____ who
                                                          (Full Name of Deceased - First Middle Last)

was born on _____ and who died on _____
           (MM/DD/YYYY)   (Date of Death or Period to Be Searched)

The death occurred in the City, Town or Village of _____ in New York State.
                                                  (City, Town or Village Where Death Is Believed to Have Occurred)

A certified copy of this record is required for the purpose of obtaining citizenship with _____
                                                                                        (Name of Country)

I am related to the Deceased as follows: *(Show name and relationship of descendents from the deceased to yourself. For example, I, Joseph Kelly, am the son of Mary McCormick, who is the daughter of Simon Green, who is the son of the deceased, Alice Faillugh.)*

_____

_____

_____

_____

I also swear or affirm that this affidavit is being made for the sole purpose of obtaining the death certificate for the purpose stated above. (Submit photocopies of the citizenship requirements as well as any birth and/or marriage records necessary to document your relationship to the deceased.)

▶ _____
Signature of Applicant

——————— *Below to be completed by Notary Public* ———————

STATE OF _____ }
                            } SS:
COUNTY OF _____ }

Subscribed and sworn to
(affirmed) before me this _____ day

of _____ , _____ .

▶ _____
Notary Public

DOH-5001 (5/10)

YOUR NAME

ADDRESS

CITY, STATE, ZIP

TELEPHONE

Date: _____

RE: APOSTILLES FOR USE IN ITALY

Dear Authentication Clerk,

Please find enclosed _____ document(s) for authentication and use in Italy.

I have enclosed the fee of $_____ per document for the authentication and a prepaid return envelope.

Thank you in advance for your kind attention to this matter.

Sincerely,

YOUR NAME

YOUR NAME
ADDRESS
CITY STATE ZIP
TELEPHONE

Date: _____

RE: Certificate of Non Existence of Naturalization

Dear USCIS,

I am in receipt of the response from USCIS Genealogy Program and am writing to request a Certificate of Non-existence for the naturalization of my ancestor.

I have attached a copy of the findings from the Genealogy Program.

My case number is: _____

Thank you very much for your kind attention to this matter.

                                                              Sincerely,

                                                              YOUR NAME

UNITED STATES OF AMERICA

No. 7276

DECLARATION OF INTENTION

(Invalid for all purposes seven years after the date hereof)

THE STATE OF TEXAS } ss: In the .... DISTRICT .... Court

COUNTY OF GALVESTON   of GALVESTON COUNTY of GALVESTON, TEXAS

I, ADOLFO GIUSTI .... Galveston .... Galveston .... Texas
now residing at 911 - 9th St. .... aged 55 .... years, do declare on oath that my personal description is:
occupation Labor .... color White .... complexion Dark .... color of eyes Brown
Sex Male .... height 5 feet 6 inches, weight 150 pounds, visible distinctive marks
color of hair Black & Gray .... None .... nationality Italian
I was born in Lucca, Italy .... on October 18th, 1886
I am married. The name of my wife is Sofia Giusti
we were married on November 22, 1911 .... at Houghton Michigan .... entered the United States
Taspagnano Italy .... on Nov. 22, 1889 .... for permanent residence therein, and now
New York, New York .... on July 18th, 1911 .... I have 8 children, and the name, date and place of birth
resides at Galveston Texas
and place of residence of each of said children are as follows:

All reside in United States

I have heretofore made a declaration of intention: Number 6203 .... March 25, 1923
at Galveston .... Texas .... District Court
my last foreign residence was S Maria Ttlguidicelmona .... Italy
I emigrated to the United States of America from Havre .... France
my lawful entry for permanent residence in the United States was at New York, N. Y.
under the name of Adolfo Giusti .... October 25, 1904
on the vessel SS La Savole

I will, before being admitted to citizenship, renounce forever all allegiance and fidelity to any foreign prince, potentate, state, or sovereignty of which I may be at the time of admission a citizen or subject; I am not an anarchist; I am not a polygamist nor a believer in the practice of polygamy; and it is my intention in good faith to become a citizen of the United States of America and to reside permanently therein; and I certify that the photograph affixed to the duplicate and triplicate hereof is a likeness of me.

I swear (affirm) that the statements I have made and the intentions I have expressed in this declaration of intention subscribed by me are true to the best of my knowledge and belief: So help me God.

adolfo ejiusti

adolfo ejiusti

Subscribed and sworn to before me in the form of oath shown above in the office of the Clerk of said Court, at Galveston, Texas this 24th day of April .... anno Domini, 1940. Certification N17 11479 from the Commissioner of Immigration and Naturalization showing the lawful entry of the declarant for permanent residence on the date stated above, has been received by me. The photograph affixed to the duplicate and triplicate hereof is a likeness of the declarant.

H. H. TREACCAR
DISTRICT Court
Clerk of the
By *Alice Amundson*, Deputy Clerk.

[SEAL]

U. S. DEPARTMENT OF LABOR
IMMIGRATION AND NATURALIZATION SERVICE

[See instructions on reverse hereof]

No. 5135

UNITED STATES OF AMERICA

DECLARATION OF INTENTION

(Invalid for all purposes seven years after the date hereof)

State of California | In the Superior Court

County of Santa Clara | of California at San Jose, Calif.

I, Florigio Ciciarelli

now residing at Route 2, Box 5, Los Gatos, Santa Clara, California

occupation Barber aged 40 years, do declare on oath that my personal description is: sex Male color White complexion Medium color of eyes Blue color of hair Brown height 5 feet 8 inches; weight 155 pounds; visible distinctive marks None

race Italian, North; nationality Italian

I was born in Casal Velino, Italy on October 22, 1892

I am married. The name of my wife or husband is Carmela Ciciarelli

we were married on Oct. 2, 1923 at Casal Velino, Italy; she or he was born at Casal Velino, Italy on July 17, 1900 entered the United States at New York, N. Y. on Jan. 16, 1930, for permanent residence therein, and now resides at Los Gatos, California. I have two children, and the name, date and place of birth, and place of residence of each of said children are as follows: Renato, born Dec. 7, 1929, at Naples, Italy; and Angela, born Apr. 27, 1932, at Los Gatos, Calif.; both residing at Los Gatos, California.

I have heretofore made a declaration of intention: Number on Aug. 3, 1923 at San Francisco, California, in the U. S. District Court.

My last foreign residence was Casal Velino, Italy

I emigrated to the United States of America from Naples, Italy

My lawful entry for permanent residence in the United States was at New York, N. Y. under the name of Florigio Ciciarelli on August 23, 1910 on the vessel Berlin

I will, before being admitted to citizenship, renounce forever all allegiance and fidelity to any foreign prince, potentate, state, or sovereignty, and particularly, by name, to the prince, potentate, state, or sovereignty of which I may be at the time of admission a citizen or subject; I am not an anarchist; I am not a polygamist nor a believer in the practice of polygamy; and it is my intention in good faith to become a citizen of the United States of America and to reside permanently therein; and I certify that the photograph affixed to the duplicate and triplicate hereof is a likeness of me: So help me God.

[signature] Florigio Ciciarelli

[signature] Florigio Ciciarelli

Subscribed and sworn to before me in the office of the Clerk of said Court, at San Jose, Calif. this 7th day of August anno Domini 83. Certification No 22-12153 from the Commissioner of Naturalization showing the lawful entry of the declarant for permanent residence on the date stated above, has been received by me. The photograph affixed to the duplicate and triplicate hereof is a likeness of the declarant.

Henry A. Pfister

[SEAL]

Clerk of the Superior Court.

By *[signature]* R. O'Neil Deputy Clerk.

Form 2202-L-A
U. S. DEPARTMENT OF LABOR
NATURALIZATION SERVICE

380

THE UNITED STATES OF AMERICA

No. 8450407

CERTIFICATE OF NATURALIZATION

·ORIGINAL·

Petition No 738040

Personal description of holder as of date of naturalization Date of birth August 29, 1928 sex female
complexion medium color of eyes brown color of hair brown height 4 feet 11 inches
weight 195 pounds visible distinctive marks none
Marital status married Country of former nationality Italy
I certify that the description above given is true, and that the photograph affixed hereto is a likeness of me

Regina Ambroselli
(Complete and true signature of holder)

UNITED STATES OF AMERICA } SS:
SOUTHERN DISTRICT OF NEW YORK

Be it known, that at a term of the District Court of
The United States
held pursuant to law at New York City
on June 18, 1962 the Court having found that
REGINA AMBROSELLI
then residing at 315 East 11th Street, New York, N.Y.,
intends to reside permanently in the United States (when so required by the
Naturalization Laws of the United States) had in all other respects complied with
the applicable provisions of such naturalization laws, and was entitled to be
admitted to citizenship, thereupon ordered that such person be and (s)he was
admitted as a citizen of the United States of America.
In testimony whereof the seal of the court is hereunto affixed this 18th
day of June in the year of our Lord nineteen hundred and
62

HERBERT A. CHARLSON
Clerk of the U.S. District Court
By Deputy Clerk

It is a violation of the U.S. Code (and
punishable as such) to copy, print, photograph,
or otherwise illegally use this certificate.

DEPARTMENT OF JUSTICE

...D STATES OF AMERICA

No. 4074

PETITION FOR NATURALIZATION

[Under General Provisions of the Nationality Act of 1940 (Public, No. 853, 76th Cong.)]

Honorable the ___DISTRICT___ Court of ___GALVESTON COUNTY___ at ___GALVESTON, TEXAS___

...tion for naturalization, hereby made and filed, respectfully shows:

...full, true, and correct name is ___ADOLFO GIUSTI___

...present place of residence is ___911-9th Street, Galveston, Galveston,___ ...

...___57___ years old. (5) I was born on ___October 18 1882___ , in ___Lucca Toscana Italy___ (3) My occupation is ___Laborer___

...personal description is as follows: Sex ___male___, color ___white___, complexion ___dark___ ...

___5___ feet ___6___ inches, weight ___158___ pounds, visible distinctive marks ___nail deformed right ring finger___ color of eyes ___brown___, color of hair ___blk-grey___, race ___white___

...nationality ___Italy___ (7) I am ___ married; the name of my wife or husband is ___Sofia___

...married on ___November 22 1911___ , at ___Hancock___

...was born at ___Tempagnano Toscana Italy___ ___New York New York___ ... ___November 22 1889 Michigan___

...resides at ___911-9th Street, Galveston, Galveston, Texas___ on ___July 11 1911___ for permanent residence in the United States

...___8___ children; and the name, sex, date and place of birth, and present place of residence of each of said children who is living, are as follows:

___All born in and reside in the United States___

...place of foreign residence was ___Sta. Maria del Guidice, Toscana, Italy___

___Lucca Italy___ (10) I emigrated to the United States from

___New York___ ___New York___ (11) My lawful entry for permanent residence in the United States was

___October 20 1906___ on the ___SS La Savoie___ under the name of ___ADOLFO GUISTI___

... the certificate of my arrival attached to this petition.

...my lawful entry for permanent residence I have ___not___ been absent from the United States, for a period or periods of 6 months or longer, as follows:

DEPARTED FROM THE UNITED STATES			RETURNED TO THE UNITED STATES		
PORT	DATE (Month, day, year)	VESSEL OR OTHER MEANS OF CONVEYANCE	PORT	DATE (Month, day, year)	VESSEL OR OTHER MEANS OF CONVEYANCE

...ed my intention to become a citizen of the United States on ___April 24 1940___ in the ___District___

___Galveston County___ at ___Galveston___ ___Texas___ (14) It is my intention in good faith to become a

...ed States and to renounce absolutely and forever all allegiance and fidelity to any foreign prince, potentate, State, or sovereignty of whom or which at ...ect or citizen, and it is my intention to reside permanently in the United States. (15) I am not, and have not been for the period of at least 10 years ...ding the date of this petition, an anarchist; nor a believer in the unlawful damage, injury, or destruction of property, or sabotage; nor a disbeliever in ...nized government; nor a member of or affiliated with any organization or body of persons teaching disbelief in or opposition to organized government. ...speak the English language (unless physically unable to do so). (17) I am, and have been during all of the periods required by law, attached to the ...Constitution of the United States and well disposed to the good order and happiness of the United States. (18) I have resided continuously in the ...ed for the term of 5 years at least immediately preceding the date of this petition, to wit, since ___October 20 1906___

...the State in which this petition is made for the term of 6 months at least immediately preceding the date of this petition, to wit, since ___14 1921___ (19) I have ___not___ heretofore made petition for naturalization: No. ___—___

... at ___ ... in the ___ (Name of court)

...petition was dismissed or denied by that Court for the following reasons and causes, to wit:

... and the cause of such dismissal or denial has since been cured or removed. ...made a part of this, my petition for naturalization, are my declaration of intention to become a citizen of the United States (if such declara... ...required by the naturalization law), a certificate of arrival from the Immigration and Naturalization Service of my said lawful entry into the United ...residence (if such certificate of arrival be required by the naturalization law), and the affidavits of at least two verifying witnesses required by law.

...your petitioner for naturalization, pray that I may be admitted a citizen of the United States of America, and that my name be changed to

___No change___

...tioner, do swear (affirm) that I know the contents of this petition for naturalization subscribed by me, that the same are true to the best of my own ...as to matters therein stated to be alleged upon information and belief, and that as to those matters I believe them to be true, and that this petition is ...with my full, true name: SO HELP ME GOD.

Adolfo Giusti
(Full, true, and correct signature of petitioner without abbreviation)

By ~~Grace Maguire~~

OATH OF ALLEGIANCE

I hereby declare, on oath, that I absolutely and entirely renounce and abjure all allegiance and fidelity to any foreign prince, potentate, state, or sovereignty of whom or which I have heretofore been a subject or citizen; that I will support and defend the Constitution and laws of the United States of America against all enemies, foreign and domestic; and that I take this obligation freely, without any mental reservation or purpose of evasion; SO HELP ME GOD. In acknowledgment whereof I have hereunto affixed my signature.

X _____

Sworn to in open court, this 16th day of April A.D. 19__

By _____
Deputy Clerk

NOTE.—In renunciation of title or order of nobility, add the following to the oath of allegiance before the words "SO HELP ME GOD": "I further renounce the title of _____ (give the title or titles) which I have heretofore held." or "I further renounce the order of nobility _____ (give the order of nobility) to which I have heretofore belonged."

Petition granted: List No. ~~one~~ of List No. ~~1662~~ and Certificate No. _____

Petition denied: List No. _____

Petition continued from _____ to _____

1/19/45 List #447

The following witnesses, each being severally, duly, and respectively sworn, depose and say:

My name is Mr. Joe L. Mallia , my occupation is County Commissioner

reside at 613 Avenue E (Number and street) Galveston (City or town) Texas (State) , and

My name is Mrs. Alice Dinklage , my occupation is Waitress

reside at 812 Avenue L (Number and street) Galveston (City or town) Texas (State)

I am a citizen of the United States of America; I have personally known and have been acquainted in the United States with ADOLFO GIUSTI

, the petitioner named in the petition for naturalization of which this affidavit is a part, since September 1 1939 (Month) (Day) (Year)

my personal knowledge the petitioner has resided, immediately preceding the date of filing this petition, in the United States continuously since the date last mentioned,

at Galveston (City or town) in the State of Texas continuously since September 1,1939 (Month) (Day) (Year) and I have personal

knowledge that the petitioner is and during all such periods has been a person of good moral character, attached to the principles of the Constitution of the United States, and well disposed to the good order and happiness of the United States, and in my opinion the petitioner is in every way qualified to be admitted a citizen of the United States. I do swear (affirm) that the statements of fact I have made in this affidavit of this petition for naturalization subscribed by me are true to the best of my knowledge and belief: SO HELP ME GOD.

Joe L. Mallia (Signature of witness)   Mrs Alice Dinklage (Signature of witness)

Subscribed and sworn to before me by the above-named petitioner and witnesses in the respective forms of oath shown in said petition and affidavit in the office of

Clerk of said Court at Galveston Texas this 9th day of September

Anno Domini 1944 I hereby certify that Certificate of Arrival No. 17-11479 from the Immigration and Naturalization Service, showing the lawful entry

for permanent residence of the petitioner above named, together with Declaration of Intention No. 7976 of such petitioner, has been by me filed with,

attached to, and made a part of this petition on this date.

H. H. Treaccar

By Grace Maglitto   Clerk.   [SEAL]

Deputy Clerk.

OATH OF ALLEGIANCE

I hereby declare, on oath, that I absolutely and entirely renounce and abjure all allegiance and fidelity to any foreign prince, potentate, state, or sovereignty of whom or which I have heretofore been a subject or citizen; that I will support and defend the Constitution and laws of the United States of America against all enemies, foreign and domestic; that I will bear true faith and allegiance to the same; and that I take this obligation freely without any mental reservation or purpose of evasion: SO HELP ME GOD. In acknowledgment whereof I have hereunto affixed my signature.

x Adolfo Giusti (Signature of petitioner)

Sworn to in open court, this 16th day of April , A. D. 1946

H. H. Treaccar   Clerk.

By Anita Reyder

Deputy Clerk.

NOTE.—In renunciation of title or order of nobility, add the following to the oath of allegiance before it is signed: "I further renounce the title of (give title or titles) which I have heretofore held." or "I further renounce the order of nobility (give the order of nobility) to which I have heretofore belonged."

Petition granted: Line No. one of List No. 468 and Certificate No. 6122579 issued.

Petition denied: List No. _____

Petition continued from 11/22/44 to _____ Reason Investigation

1/19/45 List #447

☆ U. S. GOVERNMENT PRINTING OFFICE : 1942 16-19120-1

TRIPLICATE
(To be given to declarant)

UNITED STATES OF AMERICA

DECLARATION OF INTENTION
(Invalid for all purposes seven years after the date hereof)

District of
Massachusetts
} ss:

In the United States District Court
of Mass at Boston

I, Paulo Michel Mangiofico

now residing at 95 Maverick St E Boston Suffolk Co Mass
(Number and street) (City or town) (County) (State)

occupation Paver, aged 36 years, do declare on oath that my personal description is:

Sex male, color white, complexion dark, color of eyes brown,
color of hair black, height 5 feet 7 inches; weight 180 pounds; visible distinctive marks none

race Italian So; nationality Italian

I was born in Canigattini Italy on Oct 18 1899
(City or town) (Country) (Month) (Day) (Year)

I am married. The name of my wife or husband is Sabastina

we were married on Jan 18 1922, at Boston Mass; she or he was

born at Canigattini Italy, on Jan 27 1904, entered the United States
(City or town) (State or country) (Month) (Day) (Year)

at New York 1920, for permanent residence therein, and now
(City or town) (State) (Month) (Day) (Year)

resides at E Boston. I have 2 children, and the name, date and place of birth
(City or town) (State or country)

and place of residence of each of said children are as follows: Bridget Jan 2 1925 Boston E
E Boston Sebastina Sept 7 1928 E Boston E Boston

I have not heretofore made a declaration of intention: Number, on
(Date)

at
(City or town)

my last foreign residence was Canigattini Italy
(City or town) (Name of court)

I emigrated to the United States of America from Palermo Italy
(City or town) (Country)

my lawful entry for permanent residence in the United States was at New York New York
(City) (State)

under the name of Mangiafico, Michele, on Oct 4 1920
(Month) (Day) (Year)

on the vessel Canada
(If other than by vessel, state manner of arrival)

I will, before being admitted to citizenship, renounce forever all allegiance and fidelity to any foreign prince, potentate, state, or sovereignty, and particularly, by name, to the prince, potentate, state, or sovereignty of which I may be at the time of admission a citizen or subject; I am not a polygamist nor a believer in the practice of polygamy; and it is my intention in good faith to become a citizen of the United States of America and to reside permanently therein; and certify that the photograph affixed to the duplicate and triplicate hereof is a likeness of me: So HELP ME GOD.

Mangiafico Paolo Michele
Original signature of declarant without abbreviation, also alias, if used)

Subscribed and sworn to before me in the office of the Clerk of said Court
at Boston Mass this 31st day of Oct

anno Domini 19 36 Certification No 1-189068 from the Commissioner of Immigration and Naturalization showing the lawful entry of the declarant for permanent residence on the date stated above, has been received by me. The photograph affixed to the duplicate and triplicate hereof is a likeness of the declarant.

James S Allen

[SEAL] Clerk of the U S District Court

By John F. Davis, Deputy Clerk

Form 2201—L—A
U. S. DEPARTMENT OF LABOR
IMMIGRATION AND NATURALIZATION SERVICE

No 81106

SALOON, CABIN, AND STEERAGE ALIENS MUST BE COMPLE[TE]

Form 500 is
Department of Commerce and Labor
IMMIGRATION SERVICE

LIST OR MANIFEST OF ALIEN PA

Required by the regulations of the Secretary of Commerce and Labor of the United States, under Act

S. S. EUROP[A] _sailing from_ **NAPOLI**

No. on List.	NAME IN FULL.		Age.			*Calling or Occupation.	Able to—		Nationality. (Country of which citizen or subject.)	Race or People.	Last Permanent Res
	Family Name.	Given Name.	Yrs. Mos.	Sex.	Married or Single.		Read.	Write.			Country.	City
1	Carmина	Gennaro	33				yes				Россия	
2	Prerti	Valentine	35	m	m		no					
3	Cutine	Grazia	11	f	s		yes					
4			20	f	s							
5	Schield	Martin	33	m	m		yes				NON-IMMIGRAN
6	Curti	Antonio	16	m	s		no					
7	Zizzi	Antonio	23	m	m		no					
8	Luciano	Austin	18	m								

2596 **REGISTRATION CARD** No. 77 Reg.

1	Name in full	Nicola Vielardi	28
		(Given name) (Family name)	Age in yrs

2 Home address 5 School Norwalk Conn
(No.) (Street) (City) (State)

3 Date of birth Feb. 22 1888
(Month) (Day) (Year)

4 Are you (1) a natural-born citizen, (2) a naturalized citizen, (3) an alien, (4) or have you declared your intention (specify which)? Alien

5 Where were you born? Donati Catanzaro Italy
(Town) (State) (Nation)

6 If not a citizen, of what country are you a citizen or subject? Italy

7 What is your present trade, occupation, or office? Laborer 30

8 By whom employed? Norwalk Fire & Rubber
Where employed? Norwalk Conn

9 Have you a father, mother, wife, child under 12, or a sister or brother under 12, solely dependent on you for support (specify which)? Wife and 2 Children

10 Married or single (which)? Married Race (specify which)? Caucasian

11 What military service have you had? Rank Private ; branch Infantry
years 2 ; Nation or State Italy

12 Do you claim exemption from draft (specify grounds)?

I affirm that I have verified above answers and that they are true.

(Signature or mark)

6-1-17. A. **REGISTRAR'S REPORT**

1 Tall, medium, or short (specify which)? Medium Slender, medium, or stout (which)? Medium

2 Color of eyes? Grey Color of hair? Brown Bald?

3 Has person lost arm, leg, hand, foot, or both eyes, or is he otherwise disabled (specify)?

I certify that my answers are true, that the person registered has read his own answers, that I have witnessed his signature, and that all of his answers of which I have knowledge are true, except as follows:

Lawrence J Paolino
(Signature of registrar)

Precinct 1

City or County Norwalk

State Conn

June 5 1917
(Date of registration)

387

U.S. Department of Homeland Security
U.S. Citizenship and Immigration Services

Certificate of Nonexistence of Record

HQORM-70/42.4 - C

11/14/2006

I, Mike Quinn, certify to the following:

1. That I am the Chief in the Records Services Branch, Office of Records, Headquarters, Citizenship and Immigration Services, United States Department of Homeland Security, and by virtue of the authority contained in Section 475(b)(1) of the Homeland Security Act of 2002, Section 290(d) of the Immigration and Nationality Act and 8 CFR 103.7(d)(4), I am authorized to certify the nonexistence of an official Service record.

2. That Citizenship and Immigration Services maintains centralized records relating to immigrant aliens who entered the United States on or after June 30, 1924, to nonimmigrant aliens who entered on or after June 30, 1948, and a centralized index of all persons naturalized on or after September 27, 1906.

3. That I, or an agency employee acting at my direction, performed a search for records relating to the subject identified below. Specifically this office searched Deportable Alien Control System (DACS), Computer Linked Application Information Management System (CLAIMS), the Central Index System (CIS), and the Master Index.

4. That after a diligent search was performed in these database systems, no record was found to exist indicating that the subject listed below obtained naturalization as a citizen of the United States.

File No:
Subject: Salvatore   Ciardullo
Also known As (AKA):
Born on: 1/5/1914
Country of Birth: Italy

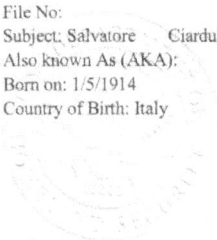

MIKE QUINN
Chief
Records Services Branch

ICN# RSB   Searched by LJ

388

APOSTILLE

(Convention de la Haye du 5 octobre 1961)

1. Country: United States of America

   This public document

2. has been signed by   DONNA PINKNEY

3. acting in the capacity of   Local Registrar, Division of Vital Statistics

4. bears the seal/stamp of   Ohio Department of Health

CERTIFIED

5. at Columbus, Ohio

6. March 7, 2007

7. by the Secretary of State of Ohio.

8. No. 270605

9. Seal/Stamp: 10. Signature:

Jennifer Brunner
Secretary of State of Ohio

This certification certifies only the authenticity of the
signature of the official who signed the document, the
capacity in which that official acted, and where appropriate,
the identity of the seal or stamp which the document bears.
This certification does not imply that the contents of the
document(s) are correct, nor that they have the approval of
this office.

www.ingramcontent.com/pod-product-compliance
Lightning Source LLC
Chambersburg PA
CBHW081143020426
42333CB00021B/2642